The Future of Memory

Children of the Dictatorship in Argentina Speak

Andrés Jaroslavsky

Translation by Niki Johnson

LATIN AMERICA BUREAU
LONDON

The Future of Memory: Children of the Dictatorship in Argentina Speak
was first published by
Latin America Bureau
1 Amwell Street
London EC1R 1UL
in 2004

Latin America Bureau is an independent research and publishing organisation. It works to broaden public understanding of issues of human rights and social and economic justice in Latin America and the Caribbean.

Translation by Niki Johnson,
with additional translation by Marcela López Levy
Editing: Marcela López Levy
Cover Design: Diseño Atlántico
Interior design and setting: Kate Kirkwood
Printed by J.W. Arrowsmith, Bristol

A CIP catalogue record for this book is available from the British Library.

ISBN 1 899365 55 9

Contents

Acknowledgements

This book would not have been possible without the collaboration of Susana L. Barco, Carolina Kaufmann, Fernando Hevia, Patrick Crozier, Martín Ezpeleta (Jr) and the unconditional support of Verónica Ongaro.

Although not all their accounts were included, I would like to express my thanks to each of the interviewees for the trust they showed in me. My aim in this book was to look through the window of their eyes and into the landscape of their memories, to learn about a part of the history of our country. To learn and to get to know each other. Once again, thank you to:

Andreani, Ernesto
Avila, Luis Roberto
Balustra, Pablo Martín
Barrios, Cecilia
Bellingeri, Daniel
Bertolessi, Marcel
Binder, Paula
Bonasso, Federico
Bravo, Nazareno J.
Camargo, Alba
Castelli, Verónica
Ceballos, Miguel
Centurión, Josefina
Concha, Ana
Coria, María Julia
Coronel, María
de Pedro, Eduardo
del Valle, Santiago
del Valle, Pablo
Di Toffino, Agustín
Dillon, Victoria

Di Vito, Pablo
Ezpeleta, Martín
Fernández, Gerardo
Ferreyra, Juana
Fessia, Emiliano C.
Flores Lescano, Eduardo
Fresneda, Juan Martín
Fresneda, Ramiro
Ghigliazza, Carolina
Gigena, Eugenia
Giglio, Josefina
Giuliani, Luciano
González, Josefina
Lavalle, María
López, Ernesto
Loto, María José
Meza Niella, Walter
Mónaco Felipe, Paula
Moreno, Matías F.
Nachman, Eduardo
Olivencia, Victoria

Paoletti, Ana
Pérez, Mariana E.
Quieto, Lucila
Quintana, Diana R.
Reynaga, Diego
Sachi, Andrea
Schapira, Daniel
Slepoy Benitez, Natalia
Sosa, Rodrigo
Soulier, Sebastián
Tello, Mariana Eva
Toranzo, Mario
Vega, Martín
Vicario, Jimena
Vicente, Viviana
Viecho, Alejandra
Viecho, Susana
Villanueva, Débora F.
Zamudio, Dafne
Zurita, Gonzalo

*To the memory of the victims of state terrorism,
including my father, Máximo Jaroslavsky, a cardiologist, who was
abducted in Tucumán, Argentina, on the night of 19 November
1975 while visiting his patients...*

'A constant and rhythmic noise, crossed by an occasional shouted command, rose from the Zeltnergasse. It was dawn, the armour-plated vanguard of the Third Reich was entering Prague. On the 19th, the authorities received a denunciation; on that same day, at dusk, Jaromir Hladík was arrested. They took him to an aseptic white barracks on the opposite bank of the Moldau. He could not disprove a single one of the charges brought by the Gestapo: his maternal surname was Jaroslavski...'

Jorge Luis Borges – *The secret miracle*, Ficciones
(English translation, Grove Press 1969)

THE MARXIST MONSTER...

'We are witnessing the most important chapter in Argentine history. At this moment in time, when the Marxist monster is hurling itself on the world, the world is weak, defenceless. For this reason we must react decisively. This is everyone's struggle, it is about being a Nation or not, and we should take seriously the fact that for 500 years before Christ there has existed an international Communist-Marxist movement which has been hanging over the world. The monster of a disciplined, ordered Marxism is hurling itself on a fragmented Western world, which is suffering the consequences of its own disorganisation.'

Lieutenant General (Retired) Cristino Nicolaides

'Military intelligence is a contradiction in terms.'

Groucho Marx

Introduction

I returned to Tucumán one summer morning. Some years previously I had left the province, while I still had a few exams to take before graduating from the Conservatory.

In 1970, there in Tucumán, the Jewish genes of my father mingled with the Arab genes of my mother, and first I was born and two years later my brother. Then they bought a house where I had my first dog - I found it one night hiding in the garden, terrified by the Christmas fireworks.

In February 1975 Operation Independence was set in motion and the prelude to the dictatorship began. My father, Máximo Jaroslavsky, worked as a cardiologist. Towards the end of November, the Armed Forces decided that he had lived long enough and one night, while he was visiting patients, he and all his dreams disappeared. The accusations made against him - which could not only not be appealed against, but were unknown - also involved his car, a fearsome Citroën Ami 8...

At that time the leadership of the Operation was changing hands: General Adel Vilas was handing over the reins to an officer from Entre Ríos, who, after the coup, would head the provincial government. His name was Antonio Domingo Bussi.

Meanwhile, at home, the anguish caused by that inexplicable absence began to distort everything and my memory from when I was five is of entering a dark tunnel. In March of the following year, while I was starting the first year of primary school, there were thousands more cases like that of my father. A cloud of denial and fear invaded my home and my father disappeared into silence. Nothing and no one mentioned him again, except the surname that he left us and that was so conspicuous, especially in the school run by Salesian priests where they sent us later on.

Years later, defeated by its own stupidity, the military dictatorship collapsed. Alfonsín's government took the first three juntas to trial and soon afterwards decreed impunity as a condition sine qua non for the country to live under a democracy. Thanks to this bargain, in 1987 Bussi returned to Tucumán.

Then came Menem's 'everything goes', the pardons he issued dealt the death blow to justice and Bussi became another stain on an Argentina that was already looking like the *Exxon-Valdes* oil spill. In 1993, when the military leader was heading inexorably for office as governor, I interrupted my studies in the Conservatory and settled in the province of Córdoba.

I rented a house, took piano pupils, and one day began to trace the tracks left by my father; a search to turn that 37-year-old doctor whom they had transformed into photographic paper, back into a person. At least in my memories. I visited Chaco to find out about his childhood, his friends, his neighbourhood, I traced his years as a student in La Plata and the activism that had brought him to Tucumán in the mid 1960s. I crossed the ocean to find his family (my family) scattered in exile and in this way I gradually collected memories to kill off the ghost and get to know the person. Perhaps also to give him back the death that had been denied him.

I still had not graduated as a music teacher, so at the beginning of 1997 I decided to return to Tucumán. I graduated and in 1998 secured a post in a remote neighbourhood. In Córdoba I had worked as a supply teacher, firmly avoiding primary schools. Tucumán, by contrast, offered no alternative. When I started out in my new job I found that the teaching hours assigned to me contained a dramatic surprise: nine of them were to be in the nursery class.

Fate put me in a classroom full of crazy little people, all of them five years old, the age I was when the military decided to eradicate my father from this world, when I started at primary school at the beginning of the military dictatorship, when the Armed Forces used to give us lessons in morality at the same time as they tortured and murdered; and, if that were not enough, the same governor was in office.

Bussi was finishing off his destruction of the province, while his secret foreign bank accounts were coming to light, the *honoris causa* of banana dictatorships. Hemmed in, he presented his son Ricardito as candidate for the governorship. The electoral advertising of his party, Fuerza Republicana (Republican Force) flooded Tucumán and, as in so many other places, Bussi's party flyers began to appear as stickers on the notebooks of some of my pupils. One happily showed me his t-shirt printed with the surname of the governor.

That group of little people gave me a resounding lesson on the consequences of forgetfulness. I could see in that classroom that being five years old was not synonymous with anguish and I could also see these little beings – who could scarcely write their own names – carrying publicity for a serial murderer.

I now had a clearer understanding of the fact that if you do not actively work against impunity, you become one of those responsible for it; or at least you become an agent who transmits it.

When I began to read in 1976, the dictatorship banned *The Little Prince* by Saint-Exupéry, that story in which a fox teaches that what is essential is invisible to our eyes, thus inviting us to scrutinise reality afresh. An attentive gaze would show that the country was sinking as the foreign debt grew. It could also make out those subtle threads linking those sectors that sponsored the dictatorship and the benefits they obtained. A careful look could uncover the sequence of events leading from the auctioning of the country to the murder of the opposition at the hands of the Armed Forces, to the impunity that today guarantees them power, true power, invisible power, the power that survives all governments.

Once the darkness of the dictatorship was past, the majority of Argentinian society felt a hard blow: they came face to face with common graves, the testimony of survivors, torture. That huge swathe of citizenry that, faced with the suspicion of the horrors committed by the military had opted for ignorance, had to confront the legacy of a regime they had actively or passively accepted.

The shame gave way rapidly to slogans put forward by the accomplices of terror, particularly the church: 'don't look to the past, but to the future', 'forget old grudges' and so on. In short, to escape forwards.

As a counterpoint to impunity, the phrase 'the people who forget their history are condemned to repeat it' was also heard frequently. The question is whether it is the most appropriate quote, if it says enough. It is attributed to a number of thinkers, and it speaks to a process that took place in a particular period and, if its consequences are not remembered, could happen again. I feel that in the case of Argentina the words of philosopher Herbert Marcuse give memory a more adequate value: 'to forget past suffering means to forgive the powers that caused that suffering – without overcoming those powers.' In his words memory has a more active and wide-reaching remit. It not only warns us of a possible danger, but tells us that memory holds the key to our present.

The economic programme put in place by the dictatorship on the back of crime and terror does not need the same violence to continue today. It continues because the fragmentation of society, the lack of education, misery and desperation clear its path. The architects of the economic plan of the dictatorship enjoy total impunity and are still reaping its benefits. The dictatorship persecuted and eliminated thousands of Argentinians, denying them the right to due process because their extermination was a fundamental part of imposing a new system.

Bringing those responsible to justice is crucial to reach a serious degree of democracy; but Argentina continues to be trapped in the system the dictatorship imposed. The country has not managed to reverse the damage done, by for example the illegal external debt (taken on by an illegal government), and that debt is being paid with child malnutrition, illiteracy and exploitation.

Memory is then fundamental, well beyond its commemorative aspects, to understand the economic and political order inherited in Argentina.

Perhaps by searching in our history for the reasons why in our country impunity reigns, and identifying the sectors that encourage that impunity for their own benefit, we might be able to construct a reply. Perhaps the first step towards creating a democracy with substance, with memory and justice, is to discover what reality conceals. This book comes out of the humble desire to collaborate in that project: to a country without impunity.

Andrés Jaroslavsky

The dictatorship fan club

From the origins of the Argentine nation, the Army and the Church have had a very close relationship. The army defines itself as a Catholic army and the Church had (and still has) an important degree of intervention in the affairs of state. The rise to power of the military with the coup of 1976 presented the Church with a much-awaited opportunity: the reaffirmation of the project of Argentina as a 'Catholic Nation', a nation governed by Christian morality. We must remember that it was not until 1987 that a divorce law was passed in Argentina and that the protests of the Church against that law were deafening, especially when compared with the icy silence it maintained in the face of the crimes committed by the dictatorship. While some priests opposed the 1976 coup (and many of them paid with their lives for doing so) the Church, as an institution, played a fundamental role in supporting the dictatorship and its influence was placed at the service of the regime.

'Would Christ not wish the Armed Forces some day to go beyond their function? The Army is expiating the impurity of our country (…) the military have been purified in a River Jordan of blood to lead the whole country…'

Monsignor Bonamín, 23 September 1975

'…There is a unique and encouraging coincidence between what General Videla says about winning peace and the Holy Father's desire that Argentina may live in and win peace…'

Monsignor Pío Laghi (Papal Nuncio), 17 June 1976

'If the process initiated six months ago in our country fails, its successor will be Marxism.'

Monsignor Guillermo Bolatti, 8 October 1976

'…Providence has placed at the disposal of the Army the duty to govern, from the presidency, down to intervening a trade union...'

Monsignor Bonamín, 10 October 1976

RAMIRO AND MARTIN FRESNEDA

Ramiro was born in 1973 and his brother Martín, known as *el Ñato*, in 1975. Their father's name was Tomás José Fresneda and their mother's María de las Mercedes Argañaraz.

The family lived in Mar del Plata. Fresneda was a lawyer, specialising in labour law, who had participated in drafting the bill to reform the Law on Work Contracts. He was also a trade union lawyer and defended political prisoners. He was twice arrested by the Federal Police, on both occasions for having presented a writ of habeas corpus. During one of these arrests, the police issued him with a warning: 'Dr Fresneda,' they said, 'why don't you practise civil law instead?'

July 1977, La Noche de las Corbatas*

RAMIRO: I was four and half. What happened remained engraved on my memory. It was about 8 pm, my mum was making supper, my brother was playing with some toys on the floor, when these men came in. What I remember most clearly is the fight my mum put up, hanging on to the stove, anything she could grab. It was all so hurried and violent. I remember clear as day: one of them grabbed my brother and another grabbed hold of me. We lived on the second floor, in a small flat, there was no lift, so we went down the stairs. They put us in a car; I remember clearly that I was on the back seat, and there were a lot of guns around. From there they took us to my dad's office.

That night a friend of Fresneda's, 'Pichi' Bougeri, was having a barbecue. Before going to the barbecue, Tomás stopped off at home; when he found the flat had been raided he called his office, but they had cut the phone line. When he tried to get in touch with his partner at the law firm, Juan Carlos Bozzi, and Bougeri, he met with the same answer: both of them had gone to his office. His office was located on the top floor of his mother's house. Fresneda knew that it was him that they were looking for, so he went to the office and gave himself up.

---

* Lit. The Night of the Ties.

I'll never forget it. They put both of us on a bed, I was paralysed with fear. I remember my dad's face. Mum was shouting, Dad was calmer. Some of the men were in plainclothes, others were in uniform. I remember that I just stayed put on the bed like this [pressing his lips together and opening his eyes wide]. I was holding on tight to Ñato, my brother. We were left in the dark. The lights of the cars reflected on the ceiling as they moved off. I was completely paralysed, I couldn't even speak.

Bougeri and Fresneda's mother – who was very ill – were also left behind in the flat. The taskforce left with Bozzi, Tomás Fresneda and his wife. This kidnapping was one of a series that included Dr Arestín, Dr Centeno, Dr Alais, Dr Candeloro and his wife Marta. The kidnappers called the operation *The Night of the Ties*.

Months later, Candeloro's wife and Bozzi were freed.

The shipwreck

The cops took my parents away, and then some second cousins of mine took Ñato. I went somewhere else. I remember that at night I used to cry because I wanted to be with Ñato. From one day to the next I was left without my parents, without Ñato, without anything. I used to see him once in a while. Then my grandmother found out and came to get us. My granny tells me that when I was asked who had taken them away, I'd reply: the police. When I came to live in Córdoba, I couldn't walk past the police station, I couldn't bear the sight of a policeman, I used to freeze up. I thought they were going to come and get me.

The bravery of Granny Otilia

The whole thing was crazy. I'll never figure out how the old lady didn't end up in a mental asylum, never went to a psychologist, never took any pills. To cut a long story short – they killed her brother, then her husband dies, then one of her sons dies, followed immediately by her daughter, and then her other son is taken prisoner. She takes my brother and me home with her and also takes in Yamila and Ernesto. Ernesto's father is killed in Villa María and his mother gives herself up. I remember feeling that the air was heavy, dense, grey in that house.

So there we were, four orphans living with Otilia. She didn't have a penny, she used to knit to keep us. She'd leave us alone all morning to go out and sell sweaters.

7

JUAN MARTIN (ÑATO): I can remember my mum saying to me 'Juan Martín, tie your shoelaces, tie your shoelaces!' I fell over and broke my nose, that's why they call me Ñato. I also have another memory of bathing with my dad.

I was a naughty child, I always used to hit my brother. My brother was very withdrawn, he used to cry a lot because he could remember. I was a disaster and he was all quiet.

To Catamarca

Mirtha is the sister of Mercedes, Ramiro and Martín's mother. In 1976, while she was living in Córdoba, a group of soldiers went to look for her at work. She and her husband grabbed what they could, got into their Renault 4 with their three children and fled. The next day the army cordoned off the neighbourhood in a fruitless attempt to capture her. Mirtha and her family finally settled in Catamarca.

At the beginning of 1979, Otilia took Ramiro and Martín on holiday there. Ramiro made up his mind to stay there, and although Martín didn't want to leave his grandmother, the family explained to him that it would be best for him to stay too.

ÑATO: Until then I hadn't understood really why they kept shifting us from one place to the next. They didn't explain much to us, you've got to remember that they didn't know what was going on either. A three- or four-year-old kid doesn't understand. If they say 'your mummy's not coming' you cry for a while and then carry on playing with your toy car.

Catamarca – the countryside, the forest, all the kids, it was as close to happiness as anything. There was a proper family there: my aunt, my uncle, with their children…At some point we became part of it, but we never really understood what we were doing there. That's where we began to learn how a family functions. We began to play the role of children. A family isn't about living with your cousins and grandmother. A family is a daddy, a mummy, a couple with children.

I used to go mad wondering what the hell I'd do if they turned up again – as if I'd be the one making the decisions [he laughs]. If they appeared one day and knocked on the door and said 'I'm your father…' What on earth would I say?! I used to think seriously about this whenever I was told off. I was always the one getting into trouble, needing attention, every day. They used to send me to my room the whole time, that's when I felt alone, unprotected. 'Because I haven't got a mummy and I haven't got a daddy, and what's more that woman

– who isn't my mummy – tells me off…' [imitating a child crying].

At school

ÑATO: It was amazing! I think I wasted more brain cells lying than I use now when I have an exam. They hadn't told us 'they are disappeared'. At one point we were told 'they've been abducted'.

'My dad's a lawyer, he's in Mar del Plata and he'll be coming to fetch us soon…' But we never really understood the magnitude of the situation, because it was much simpler to feel part of that family. I found it so difficult! It was awful. We became so much a part of it that at one point I wasn't sure that I wanted my parents to 'turn up' because I felt that I loved my uncle and aunt more than them.

Next door was rented by a Japanese family. I used to say, 'If my folks turn up we'll move in here because I'm not going back to Mar del Plata.'

Christmas time, truth time

RAMIRO: I was a young kid, six or seven. I was next to the Christmas tree, crying silently. I was saying 'I'm not going to ask for any presents because I want all my energy to go into asking for my parents back.' My aunt came up and said, 'What's the matter, Ramiro?' and I told her. She started crying and said, 'Look, Ramiro, they've killed your parents, and they did it for this and that reason.' I started crying again, but it was like a huge relief, I gave up hoping they'd come back. Instead I began a long mourning process.

'…on the occasion of the upcoming Christmas festivities and to express our most fervent and cordial wishes for a happy Christmas…in support of your Excellency and of those who accompany you in the harsh and exacting task of serving the fatherland even at the cost of their own lives, this Permanent Committee sends your Excellency its most humble greetings and the promise of daily prayers and homilies to the Lord…'

Christmas letter from the Argentine Episcopal Conference to Videla, December 1976

ÑATO: The thing with Ramiro was very strange, but afterwards, when we talked about it with others we found out that it's what generally happens. It was like we used to talk about our parents, but the way we talked was as if his father wasn't the same person as my father, and as if my father wasn't also his father. Each one worked out his version on his own.

The neighbourhood

ÑATO: They all knew something strange had happened but nobody really knew what was going on. They weren't sure whether we were adopted, but some comments went around the neighbourhood. There were rumours that the military had something to do with it.

I remember once we were playing football and a kid said to me 'you shut your mouth, because you're adopted.' It was as if I'd been hit over the head with a stick. I threw the boy who said it to the floor and hit him over and over…They had to drag me off him.

At one point we thought we were the only ones who were children of *desaparecidos*.* We didn't know any other children of desaparecidos. We thought of it like a mental handicap, a strange disease…

RAMIRO: I was about 12 and I was going out with a girl in the neighbourhood, a pretty dark-haired girl. We had a thing going, and one day her father finds me making out with this young lady in the empty lot near the entrance to the house. There we were snogging away. He tried to hit me, I ran off and his daughter took the blows. Then one day he comes by the house, stops me and says: 'I'm not going to let the son of guerrillas go out with my daughter. Your parents were subversives!'

Malvinas

ÑATO: I was at primary school at the height of the dictatorship, so we had to go to all the parades. There were parades everywhere. I'd march along with the others, I wanted to be like the others, but there was something that prevented me from feeling part of it.

I have one terrible memory: seven in the morning, all lined up, bloody freezing, frost on the ground, raising the flag, in our white smocks†, singing the Malvinas hymn 'Undertheblan-ket-of-foooog…'. We used to sing with such dumb patriotism…but it was amazing, you really felt wrapped in the Argentine flag and almost on the way to war.

1983

ÑATO: With the return to democracy my uncle and aunt were activists in the PI.§ I remember that afterwards everyone celebrated Alende

---

* Trans. disappeared.
† School children in Argentina wear white smocks over their own clothes in lieu of a uniform.
§ Partido Intransigente.

coming third. There was a party, a huge crowd of people, everyone talking politics…Only an exorcism could have got Alende out of my house. I think we were all at the table eating. They didn't want Alfonsín to win, they wanted Alende to win, but they celebrated anyway. We all ran out to the square and blocked off the street.

RAMIRO: We went to the square to celebrate. So full of emotion, because in the face of the fear, the silence and the darkness, there is a tension that keeps one alert. That's what I saw in my family. But when democracy came, it was like letting out your breath and night falling, because that's when you began to see who was missing. Those who wouldn't be coming back…

More…

RAMIRO: I was out in the patio in the paddling pool with my aunt. She always showed us great respect, was very protective of us. I was in the first or second year of secondary school. Ñato couldn't remember my parents and would sometimes call my uncle and aunt Daddy and Mummy. If we were going to feel more secure emotionally calling them Daddy and Mummy, even though we knew they weren't our parents, that was fine.

My aunt asked me why I didn't call her Mummy and I said 'I can't, it doesn't feel right.' I got upset, but she was more upset. And while we were on the subject of children, and crying, she let the cat out of the bag: 'and what's more there's one missing who we don't even have,' and I was like 'What?!…'

That's when she told me that my mum had been pregnant. That's when I learnt that they used to take the babies away from pregnant women as war booty.

ÑATO: I was told a lot of things, but it was like I had a filter. I know that they told me these things, but it's as if they were on hold, then at a given moment a little window would open to let the memory through and I would rationalise it. Really, it wasn't until I was twenty that I became fully conscious of the fact: 'I've got a sister. I've got a sister out there somewhere.'

It made me so angry because it was something I wasn't going to be able to get over. With those who've died it's different – whether or not I ever actually saw their remains, I was going to get over it. Disappearance is complex, but in one way or another you come to understand it, to find justifications. Some justify it from a political point of view, others from a religious standpoint…Each person finds the crutches that suit their particular disability, but having a sister and never knowing her...

Secondary school

ÑATO: At secondary school they used to ask things like 'You never saw them again?'

'No, stupid, they're disappeared,' I used to answer.

'What, they never came back?'

RAMIRO: Catamarca is a tough idiosyncratic kind of a place; very conservative, very religious, very structured. Here there are seven desaparecidos. Appearances and disappearances were the stuff of witchcraft. Our Civic Education teacher took the whole third year to the cinema to see *La Noche de los Lápices.**

All the classes were there. A whole load of us, about two hundred, and my school mates were pissing themselves laughing, thinking it was all made up. 'Look at that sexy girl', and other crap of the kind...So I put my hand up and shouted: 'This really happened, man! This happened here in Argentina. It's no fantasy, it's nothing to laugh about.' My voice broke with anger. 'What you've seen here happened to my parents!'

Ñato's déjà vu

ÑATO: I was a party animal at school. I used to spend my whole time thinking up ways to have fun. Our student union was not into politics at all...! All it ever did was organise parties. I put myself up for election and became president. Life was one long party. We were playing basketball, just fooling around. The radio was on and I say to Jorge, 'Listen! Listen!...' It was a terrible shock, we were 15, 16. María Soledad Morales[†] had been killed. I knew her by sight, we went to the Colegio del Carmen's beauty queen contest, she was there taking tickets.

A march was called and that's when I began to get involved. I began to think about the question of justice, began to relate it to my dad. It started to be an issue when the cops laid into us; the military dictatorship and repression at the marches. The cops began to appear all around and began to advance in rows of four. "Pow! Pow! Pow!"

---

* Lit. the Night of the Pencils. The title of a widely-seen testimonial film about secondary students disappeared by the dictatorship (see Glossary).

† In 1990 a young woman was found dead and disfigured. Judicial investigations come to nothing and staff and students from her school begin silent marches that are soon mass events, as it is suspected that members of the provincial political elite are involved.

Everybody on the floor, people running and the pigs taking aim and firing. Then suddenly one of the demonstrators falls down and Jorge says 'they shot him'. Rubber bullets? You must be joking! We went to have a look and he had a bullet hole through him. He pulled through. I felt that there was something familiar about all this.

Back to Córdoba

When they had finished secondary school, Martín and Ramiro settled in Córdoba, where they began to study law. The two brothers returned to their grandmother Otilia's house, and the house was transformed. On a number of occasions they returned to Mar del Plata to try to reconstruct their history.

RAMIRO: It's not easy going back to a house where the last memory you have is of the military taking you away. In the dark, with just a candle, alone…Please! [He sighs heavily].

I went in and images began to flood my mind, I began to recognise the house…The issue of memory is very complex because there are times when you don't know where the fantasy begins and reality ends.

In Mar del Plata there is a survivor, a woman called Marta Candeloro. She shared a cell with my mum. They killed this woman's husband and told her: 'Here, wash the lawyers' clothes.' Clothes covered in my dad's blood, the blood of all of them.

They told her: 'We're keeping you alive so that those outside know what's waiting for them.'

'I went down about 20 or 30 steps, I could hear large iron doors closing, I knew that the place was underground; it was a large place, because the voices echoed and aeroplanes were taxiing overhead or very close by. The noise was deafening (…) One of the men said to me, 'So, you're a psychologist, are you? A whore, like all psychologists. Here you'll learn what's good for you,' and he began to hit me in the stomach…my hell had begun. I was in the illegal detention centre known as the Cave.'

Marta Candeloro – File No. 7305, Conadep

The Cave was an old abandoned radar station, located on the Mar del Plata Airforce Base. Here Marta shared a cell with Mercedes, the mother of Ramiro and Martín, until she was released.

The day that Ramiro went to see Marta Candeloro is engraved on his memory. He knocks on the table three times and re-enacts the exchange:

'Yes, who is it?'
'Ramiro.'

'Ramiro who?'

'Ramiro Fresneda.'

She almost died of shock. She didn't even cry out, it was like a spasm. On top of everything I look a lot like my father. I couldn't speak (…) Anyway, after a glass of wine, I began to pluck up the courage.

'Look, I'd like to know what it was like.'

'That night of fear and terror that I shared with Mercedes was given the name 'the Night of the Ties' by the repressors because almost all the prisoners taken were lawyers (…) There was a lot of noise and music turned up high; at times the groans and shouts of the torture victims were louder than the music (…) When the torturers left, I had the feeling that they left behind a trail of dead bodies…Dr Centeno was moaning incessantly. (…) I don't know if it was exactly the next day, but several hours had passed. The interrogators returned, they said, 'Bring Centeno'. They tortured him again while he was in that state. We thought [with Mercedes, her cell mate] that he wouldn't hold up. And we were right. They killed him. They dragged his body along and must have left it lying against our door. We heard a thud against the wood.'

Marta Candeloro – File No. 7305, Conadep

Can you believe that this woman lives three hundred metres away from the Cave? Do you realise what I'm saying? It's crazy. You leave her house, see the lighthouse and there's the Cave.

She's the one who told me: 'Your mum wasn't tortured, she was well fed. They were looking after the baby. They looked after her in order to take the baby away.' She told me that my mum believed that they weren't going to kill her…

Fresneda and Fresneda

Martín still lives with his grandmother Otilia. He gets up early, has unsweet-ened *mate** for breakfast and starts studying. He plans to get his degree by the end of the year and then work in criminal and penal law and human rights. Every Thursday afternoon he goes to a folk dance class and calls himself an 'old peñero'.†

Ramiro, like Martín, plays the guitar and is into folk dancing. He's renting a flat, has got his law degree, and is a trade union lawyer, like his father.

Ramiro and Martín continue to search for the brother or sister that the dictatorship stole from them.

---

* Ubiquitous green tea drunk in Argentina.

† Belonging to a 'peña', a folk music group.

2

Cynicism

After the coup of 24 March 1976 a military junta made up of the Commanders in Chief of the Army, Lieutenant General Jorge Rafael Videla, of the Navy, Admiral Emilio Eduardo Massera, and of the Airforce, Brigadier General Orlando Ramón Agosti, took power. Videla was named de facto president.

'No Argentinian can accept minority groups with totalitarian doctrines attempting to impose their will on the country by force or through fear; the Armed Forces, in defence of national sovereignty, would never permit it.'

Brigadier General Orlando Ramón Agosti
La Prensa – 11 August 1976

'I declare that at this moment there exists complete respect for human rights for all Argentinians and well-meaning foreigners who are present in our country, and if there are any who do not believe this to be the case it is because they are not Argentinians.'

Lieutenant General Jorge Rafael Videla
La Prensa – 13 August 1976

'Man is political by nature, that nature cannot be killed off nor detained by decree,' Videla declared to journalists on his return from his tour of Buenos Aires. 'What is suspended is political activity.'

La Gaceta – 15 December 1976

'Save me, God, from those people who join the masses behind a single idea, and who do not know how to express their differences in a constructive manner.'

Major General Albano E. Harguindeguy
La Razón – 30 July 1979

ANA PAOLETTI

Ana was born in La Rioja in 1968. She is the fourth of the six children of Lylian Clementina Santochi and Alipio Eduardo Paoletti, better known as 'Tito' Paoletti.

> My father was editor of *El Independiente* (The Independent), a newspaper in La Rioja. He'd moved there because he had family connections and he founded the newspaper with some friends of his. He was 23 years old when he arrived, he was pretty precocious.
>
> My life was very quiet and normal, like any child's. The only activity as such that I can remember is my mum's activities in church voluntary groups and at the weekend we'd go to poor neighbourhoods to make cakes with the children there. Then we'd go round selling them with people from the church. I also remember that on some days we used to go and help make cement blocks to build a house for someone.

In 1970 the owners of *El Independiente* donated their shares (together with the machinery, building and everything in it) to organise the country's first journalistic and graphic cooperative. The paper's editorial board was elected in an assembly on the basis of 'one worker, one vote.'

The coup

> At the time of the coup I was seven years old and living in La Rioja. I remember that night, my father was in Buenos Aires and I had fallen asleep with my mother. I have a memory of being in a light and strange sleep, in fact it felt so strange because my mother had been listening to the radio all night long. It was playing military marches. I know that the next day we didn't go to school. My mother was nervous.

VIDELA'S REFERENCE TO THE FUNCTION OF JOURNALISM
'The president of the nation yesterday met with newspaper editors and producers from private radio stations in the Federal Capital, and at the meeting stressed the important function that journalism serves [...] He stated that he was sure that the media "would accurately reflect the vocation of the

military government to restore and assure the continuity of the fundamental principles that underpin our way of life." '

Clarín – 3 April 1976

Too independent

So the coup happens, they raid the newspaper, arrest my uncle, arrest everyone at the newspaper – my honorary uncles – and my dad's told not to come back because the situation is tricky. That night they take control of the newspaper and falsify my father's resignation.

TWO PUBLICATIONS SANCTIONED

Two provincial newspapers have been closed down for being considered 'tendentious' or 'seditious'. The La Pampa paper *La Arena* (The Sand) and the La Rioja paper *El Independiente* have been closed by the provinces' respective military authorities. According to the military authorities in La Pampa, the closure of La Arena, which is published in Santa Rosa, capital of La Pampa province, was carried out because 'in its 2 April 1976 edition, in an article entitled "Mundo 76", it questions the clear action taken by military and security forces, disseminating in an insidious and underhand manner an imprecise account of the procedures followed.'

El Independiente, a morning paper from the city of La Rioja, was closed by the military, due to the 'tendentious character of its articles', as was confirmed by the office for the media and communications of the local government. The paper, closed for 24 hours, will reappear today.

Clarín – 4 April 1976

My father didn't come back to La Rioja. We were living with my maternal grandparents in a large house. A few days later my mother decided to travel to Buenos Aires with my two younger sisters, me and an uncle of ours. Elsa and Sara were three and four years old.

My other brothers and sisters stayed with our grandparents. [In Buenos Aires] we stayed with aunts and uncles, but my mum sent me back to her father's house in La Rioja after a short time.

La Rioja

I remember that one day my aunt came round all happy to tell us the news that my dad was in Mexico. My grandmother wept with emotion and I didn't understand anything.

'How can you be happy that Daddy's in Mexico?' I asked.

My dad wasn't in Mexico, the idea was to let up the pressure on those who were in prison. They were beating the shit out of them. At the time my uncle was in prison.

To Córdoba

My grandmother fell ill and they took her to hospital in Córdoba. The four of us who were living with her were farmed out to uncles, aunts, and godparents. That's how we lived for a while.

Then my aunt decided to move us from La Rioja because my mum told her that she was going to Córdoba. One day she takes us out in the car and says, 'We're going to have a picnic.' It was during the winter holidays, we had the clothes we were wearing and a picnic basket. La Rioja was controlled territory, there were soldiers every-where. They'd stop you and ask where you were going. I didn't know that I was going to see my mum and sisters.

On the road to Buenos Aires, July 1976

We arrived in Córdoba and my mum was reunited with her parents. That same night we set off for Buenos Aires in two groups - one made up of the boys and an uncle, my mum's cousin, and the other, us girls with my mum. We had to be as inconspicuous as possible. We were so clear on this issue that when we arrived at the terminal, and found the army mounting an operation there, one of my sisters said: 'Mummy, Mummy, the army!'

So we reach Buenos Aires, go to the house of a friend of my parents', who lived in Castelar, and when we open the door, there's my dad. The friend, who was a doctor, had rented a house in his name in Moreno for us to live in. That's where we became the Fernández family and my father worked as a tools' salesman.

After the winter holidays we began to go to a school run by the congregation that used to work with Angelelli in La Rioja. The head-mistress was the only one who knew who we were. Every day we'd go to San Miguel from Moreno with the following instructions: 'Never take the same route, take the bus and if you see anything out of the ordinary, get off at the next stop, turn round and come straight home…'

News from La Rioja

In 1968, the same year that Ana was born, a new bishop had been appointed to La Rioja diocese. His name was Enrique Angelelli. The following were some of the words he said on taking over the bishopric: 'I do not come to be served, but to serve; to serve everyone, without distinction, whether by social class, or by ideas or beliefs; like Jesus, I want to serve our brothers, the poor.'

My childhood was surrounded by priests and cassocks. Angelelli used to come and eat at our house. I used to go to his church. My father was a Marxist atheist and Angelelli used to say to him 'Tito, you're really a Christian, you just don't realise it,' and my father would reply 'And you, Pelado,* you're a Marxist only you don't know it.' They spent the whole time arguing about what the other one was.

'…During one of the interrogations, Captain Marcó and Captain Goenaga told me that the Bishop of La Rioja, Enrique Angelelli, the psychiatrist Raúl Fuentes and Alipio Paoletti were going to be killed…before the month was out, Angelelli died in circumstances that are still being investigated, Fuentes has been disappeared since the end of 1976 and an intensive search was made for Alipio Paoletti (…) In August of the same year, due to the physical state I had been left in after the torture sessions, I was transferred to the Presidente Plaza Hospital. One night while I was there, the body of Angelelli was brought in to be autopsied; my guards, all members of the Provincial Police, made comments in reference to the Bishop's death along the lines of: He had it coming, that commie priest son of a…'

Testimony of Plutarco Antonio Scheller, File No. 4952 – Conadep

The house had a fireplace; it was winter, the month of August. That day it was raining, and it was a very cold house. We were in front of the fireplace listening to the radio and the announcer says 'Angelelli has had an accident.' I remember that my mum started crying and said, 'They killed him! They killed him!…' It made a great impression on me.

'On 18 July 1976, after being kidnapped by men who identified themselves as members of the Federal Police, the priests P. Gabriel Longueville and Carlos de Dios Murias were murdered in cold blood, in the town of Chamical (La Rioja) where they had their parishes. The morning after this crime, hooded men went to look for the parish priest at Sanogasta, but he had left on the recommendation of the Bishop, Monsignor Enrique Angelelli. When the layperson who answered the door told them that the priest was not there, they riddled him with bullets. On 4 August, 17 days after the murder of those priests, Monsignor Enrique Angelelli, Bishop of the Diocese of La Rioja, died, allegedly in a car 'accident'. Evidence quickly mounted pointing to the fact that it was really a murder case. The Bishop's body was left lying on the ground for six hours, the van disappeared and the only wound on Monsignor Angelelli's body was that the nape of his neck was smashed, as if it had been beaten in.

---

* Affectionate nickname, lit. 'baldy'.

The file the Bishop was carrying with him was never found.'

Memoria Debida, D'Andrea Mhor

Upping sticks

My father was active producing clandestine newspapers, by then they already had information about the camps. In fact, when my dad decided that we should leave the country it was because they had begun to raid all printing presses, and activists who worked with him began to disappear (…) This friend of ours who was a gynaecologist worked in Posadas Hospital. In the hospital rumours began to circulate that he 'collaborated with the terrorists' and my dad decided to leave the house we were living in so as not to get him into trouble. So we upped sticks and split up. My mum lived with us and met up with my dad from time to time. They were trying to get hold of papers for us, passports for everyone.

Buenos Aires – Brazil – Madrid

After several months they managed to get hold of the papers. It was more difficult for my dad to leave as there was warrant out for his arrest. He got some false papers and, under the name Ceferino Fernández, left for Brazil, via Santo Tomé. He crossed the river on a raft and spent some days in Rio de Janeiro, in a nunnery. Then he went to Madrid, got set up there and we left to join him.

We went as 'tourists', winter holidays again. My family paid for it. My grandmother was there with a box of pizzas that a friend of hers, a neighbour, had made. It was as if a lot of people were wishing that we'd make it.

I remember my dad and some friends waiting for us at Barajas airport [in Madrid], arriving at the flat my dad had rented and he put on records of Viglietti and Carlos Puebla songs (…) It was a complete change in the way we lived. Everything was allowed. When my sister arrived she whispered to my dad, 'Dad, while we're here…what name are we going to use?'

'Here you're going to be called Sara Paoletti Santochi, because in Spain they use the mother's surname too.'

For a long time she'd go round saying: 'My name's Sara Paoletti Santochi, and Fernández too.'

On the house

The day we arrived we went to the corner shop to buy drinks and stuff.

When the shopkeeper heard my dad's voice, he says, 'Are you Latin American?'

'I'm Argentinian and in exile,' my dad says.

The man got all worked up, hugged him and said, 'I'm Spanish, my family had to go into exile in Argentina and I want to thank you for all that you did for us. Today your purchases are on the house, but I never want you to go short. Here you have limitless credit.'

Don Santiago gave us credit and sweets. Real honest solidarity. The day we left Spain to come back Don Santiago cried. He cried!

The 1978 World Cup

We took part in the demonstrations organised in Madrid by Argentinians. It was strange because we didn't support Argentina. I wasn't much interested in football, but I remember my dad sitting in front of the TV because he'd swear away, but at the same time he had a real sense of national identity. He had mixed feelings. My dad loved football. In his head he was always in Argentina, listening to tango, to folk music. To me it seemed like a contradiction that he should be watching football and want Holland to win. I'd go to the bakery, and the man there would say, 'Hey, great, you won the World Cup!'

'Yeah, but my dad's not happy about it.'

A message

My dad was extremely active during the whole period we were in exile. He took down the testimonies of everyone who arrived from Argentina. He prepared almost all the testimonies of the Argentine Human Rights Committee (CADHU), which later provided the basis for the trials of the junta members. My dad's professional work was always linked to activism. I remember that during those years he was travelling constantly to Brussels and Paris to denounce the abuses being committed.

'...if I could speak to the government I would say that we should stand our ground and pay no attention to the foreign claims about disappearances...'

Army vicar Monsignor Bonamín, Declarations, 20 November 1977

I remember that the first Thursday of each month we'd protest outside the Argentine Centre. What struck me most was the Molfino case. It caused a lot of tension there. A woman who had been kidnapped in Lima had been found dead, and her children were disappeared. Protests were held there outside the embassy.

Back again

We were all sure of the fact that we were going to go back. I remember that it was June or July when we read in a newspaper that Argentina had set a date for the elections. I arrived back on 10 December 1983, my dad had gone back earlier.

Saturdays and Sundays at home were family days. We were there all together, having family meals, going shopping...

We were unpacking the shopping with my mum, and my dad says to me, 'Ana, tomorrow I'm going...'

'Yeah, don't tell me, you're going to Belgium. Will you be back before we leave?'

'No, Anita, I'm going to Argentina.'

And I began to shake with fear because for me Argentina was linked to terror.

It was also a process of mourning. The day we left Spain almost a hundred people came to see us off. All my friends were there, all my brothers' and sisters' friends, our neighbourhood friends. There were more! Three hundred, I'd say. Really...We were also the first ones to return, so the community of exiles was all there to say goodbye, because we were 'the test' and a small part of each of them was returning with us.

Like the Nazis, like in Vietnam

As soon as my dad got back to Argentina he started collaborating with the *Madres de Plaza de Mayo* (see Glossary) newspaper, gathering information and denunciations about the concentration camps and about those who had run them. He started writing articles that later on were published in a book called *Como los nazis, como en Vietnam* (Like the Nazis, like in Vietnam). My dad wrote that book.

I remember, it was 22 August 1986, I arrived home that night and he said to me, 'Look, I finished the book.'

He also made all of us collaborate in one way or another, whenever he needed help, papers, archive files. By then he was very ill, he wasn't working and it was like his last...it was his personal fight.

'...Bussi took the initiative: "This is one of the detainees," he said and then he introduced me as a common criminal. Laghi asked me if I was all right, if they were looking after me...Bussi, clearly emboldened, ...began to urge Laghi to ask me – I had been held and tortured for 5 months less than 60 metres from there – "if it was true about the cattle prod", about "the violation of human rights". Laghi moved forward away from the group, although not sufficiently, and asked me my name and whether my parents knew of my arrest and where I was being held. Bussi and Arrechea caught him up as I identified myself, told him how long I'd been held and the fact that my parents didn't know my whereabouts. In response, Monsignor Laghi hugged me, gave me a copy of the Bible and urged me to have 'faith and hope'. And we both left immediately: he with Bussi and the rest of the delegation, towards the helicopter, and I with my guards' back into the detention centre.

Testimony of Juan Martín to CADHU, 10 December 1981.'

Como los nazis, como en Vietnam, Alipio Paoletti, 1986

He used to get up at seven in the morning and begin to write. He'd finish at 7 pm. He was really annoying, because he would be constantly asking for help, for you to pass him *mate*, to read to him, to count the number of letters, anything…The prologue of the book is marvellous and not just because he wrote it.

'In its second edition, the Madres de Plaza de Mayo pay homage to Alipio Eduardo Paoletti, who died in Buenos Aires on 1 December 1986, at the age of fifty. He was an excellent journalist and a stalwart human rights activist. (…) His upright behaviour and the strong ethical basis of his beliefs were characteristic of his activist personality…'

Como los nazis, como en Vietnam, back cover, 1987.

My father died on the first of December 1986. I think the Ley de Punto Final (Full Stop Law, see Glossary) was passed on the 16th, and in the book he says that there can't be cut-off points or due obedience laws, that society has been split into two sides: those who are in favour of forgetting and those who are against it. That's the bottom line. In my view it was like giving up on everything that had been achieved with the trials of the junta members.

'If the Argentine people accept the distractions, the legal chicanery, and the limitless solidarity shown by the dominant classes for those guilty of genocide, if they do not focus their political activity on the issue of the *desaparecidos*, and if the popular parties and the trade unions with democratic boards do not include punishment for the murderers in their programmes, it will not be the dictatorship, nor the government, nor even the oligarchy that imposes the "cut off point" on them.'

Como los nazis, como en Vietnam, Alipio Paoletti, 1986.

He died before the Ley de Punto Final, but the law was already being discussed. All of that was talked about at home. He died of heart

23

failure, an illness that he'd been suffering from for a long time and that got a lot worse in that final year. He was ill and felt that his strength was running out, his batteries were low and I think that made him mad.

And I was still full of hope…I thought that they wouldn't dare to vote it through. It seemed like a complete aberration to me! I just couldn't get my head round the possibility - not with that level of awareness and participation of people.

'The issue of genocide divides society into two clear blocs: on the one side are those who demand justice; on the other, the oppressors and those who, consciously or not, serve their power.'

Como los nazis, como en Vietnam, Alipio Paoletti, 1986.

Holy Week

During Easter week [1987] I felt something akin to fear. My dad had recently died. We were at home because it was Maundy Thursday, a national holiday, and I felt that there was a climate of instability, I was scared. We turned on the TV and went to the Plaza de Mayo. We were afraid but we went. We spent all those days in the Plaza, we'd come and go.

I was in the Plaza. There was a lot of anger, a lot of indignation and that's when I felt that this country was all over the place. That's when I felt that we had lost, that the streets were no longer ours.

I felt that Alfonsín hadn't dared to speak out, because he said 'they are the Malvinas heroes.' I didn't cheer Alfonsín, I didn't feel that he deserved any admiration. We left, we left the square. I felt that Alfonsín wasn't taking advantage of what the people were offering him.

In memoriam

Ana has a partner and a two-year-old son called Joaquín. Until his birth she helped with the design of the newspaper of the Madres de Plaza de Mayo. Every day, after lunch, she takes Joaquín to nursery and then goes to work. For eight years Ana has been working at the newspaper *Página/12* and plans to continue studying 'when the boy is a bit older.'

A short while ago something happened that moved me to the core, something that made me realise that for my dad his journalism and activism were one and the same thing. Nora Veiras is a *Página/12* journalist who's writing a book on the trial in Spain. I was in the office looking for something or other, when she says, 'Ana, come here.' She tells me that the other day, while she was interviewing Castressana, who has filed the case with Judge Garzón, they realised that when they started to look into the possibility of making the case, they began by looking for materials and the first thing he got hold of was the book *Como los nazis, como en Vietnam*. That's what they used for the preliminary hearing with Garzón.

Hearing that made me cry. My dad's activism and work was always anonymous, he always took a back seat, in the sense that he wasn't the type to seek the spotlight, but he was always a hard worker, he never gave up. He spent those six and a half years in exile gathering testimonies. And bloody awful testimonies at that, because sometimes he came face to face with a torturer, with people linked to the repression. Peregrino Fernández, for example. Taking these awful testimonies about how they had tortured friends of his, how they had tortured his brother, and he never gave up, he stuck with his work, aware of its value. His life had meaning. In spite of all the time that has passed, he's still stirring things up. I find that amazing.

'From my own personal viewpoint, my greatest hope is that the result of all this work may serve as a humble contribution to the just struggle for the 30,000 people arrested and disappeared, and to the judgement and punishment of those guilty of these crimes, whose names and surnames – perhaps for the first time – appear in this book, linked to the concentration camps where they committed their atrocities.'

Como los nazis, como en Vietnam, Alipio Paoletti, 1986.

3

Thou shalt not kill

Double standards of morality became a commonplace of the dictatorship period.

AROUND THE WORLD PUBLIC OPINION IS CONCERNED BY THE IMMINENT DEATH OF THE YOUNG KAREN QUINLAN
'Until now, the doctors attending the young woman have opposed her parents' request that she be allowed to die. She has been kept alive with the use of an artificial respiration machine since falling into a coma on 15 April 1975.'

Clarín – 2 April 1976

KAREN, A CASE OF CONSCIENCE
'The people of our country are, on the whole, a sensitive lot. And that human sensitivity finds no greater expression than in the respect for life. The repercussions around a case like that of Karen Quinlan should therefore come as no surprise, despite the fact that it is taking place 15,000 kilometres from the River Plate. This became clear to the editorial staff of *Clarín* when we asked for considered opinions on learning of the ruling of the supreme court of New Jersey. That the legal system has authorised the parents of the young woman to end the state of 'living death' that she has been in from 14 April 1975 to date, is something that involves not only the law, but also medicine and, in our opinion, religion. It is a case of conscience. (…) For once, let us invert the order and begin with the religious dimension. In our Judaeo-Christian culture we are commanded not to kill, a command that holds the same force as it does in Eastern religions. And in this respect the doctrine of the Catholic Church, which has an unquestionable influence on Argentinian law, states its position categorically in the fifth commandment.'

Clarín – 3 April 1976

'If need be, as many people as necessary will die in Argentina to achieve the country's security.'

Lieutenant General Jorge R. Videla
Clarín – 24 October 1976

'The subversive criminals will be pursued and if any are left and give themselves up they will be tried, and if not, we shall kill them.'

General Domingo A. Bussi
La Opinión – 3 January 1976

'First we will eliminate the subversives, then their accomplices, then their sympathizers and finally the indifferent and the undecided.'

General Ibérico Saint-Jean
International Herald Tribune – 26 May 1977

'We will only negotiate with bullets because we have arrived at the following conclusion: no more words, only defeat and annihilation…'

Major Agustín Feced
La Prensa – 16 August 1977

At the same time…

OTHER MUTILATED BODIES FOUND IN URUGUAY
'Montevideo, 19 (UP) – The number of bodies found floating in the waters of the Atlantic and of the River Plate has risen to ten, sources close to the Naval Command reported tonight. A new body, of the male sex, was found by the authorities, who say that it bears the same signs of mutilation as the others. The corpse was found ten kilometres to the west of the port of Colonia, 170 kilometres northeast of Montevideo and 30 kilometres from Buenos Aires. The discovery of these bodies had become one of the greatest mysteries in the criminal history of the country. The series of discoveries began on 21 April, when three human bodies turned up in the department of Rocha, 250 kilometres from Montevideo. Since then more bodies have steadily appeared, totalling up till now eight males and two females.'

La Prensa – 20 May 1976

'Having taken power, our duty now is to govern, and our inspiration, in government, is to seek to create for the Argentinian man the necessary conditions for him to develop fully as a person, with dignity and in freedom. In our opinion, we consider that the essential condition necessary for this to be achieved is a democratic way of life, conceived according to our historic traditions and our Christian world view.'

Videla
La Prensa – 20 May 1976

More cynicism

NEWS REPORTING ON SUBVERSION

'The press secretary made it known that from last Thursday "the press is banned from reporting or commenting on, or referring to anything relating to subversive actions, the appearance of bodies or the deaths of subversive elements and/or of members of the Armed or security forces as a result of those actions, unless the information comes from a reliable official source. This includes kidnappings or disappearances." For this reason, we are not publishing any information of this nature.'

La Prensa – 24 April 1976

'Far be it from our intention and spirit to think of having a docile and non-objective press.'

Videla
La Prensa – 13 May 1976

WALTER MEZA NIELLA

Fortunata Ibarra was born in Santiago del Estero. When she finished primary school she moved to Buenos Aires looking for work. There she met her future husband, Néstor Antonio Meza Niella. The couple set up home in Vicente López and in February 1963 the fifth of their six children was born: Walter.

My dad started out in a textile factory, but gradually did well for himself. He had a couple of businesses, an ice-cream parlour, he was self-employed for a while, and in the end had a small estate agent's. He'd been active in the Peronist Party since 1946. My dad's grandparents are from Corrientes. My grandfather was an old landowner, and founder of the Colorado Party.* He was in the Liberal Autonomist Party of Corrientes, and my dad turned Peronist on him. This really annoyed my grandfather because my dad became Peronist when the 'Farmworkers' Statute' was reformed.

My grandfather, for instance, had his labourers working 12 or 13 hours under the hot sun and paid them with food from his own shop.

And his son became a Peronist…A real thorn in his side…

A kick up the backside

My dad had a real temper. I remember once, when I was a boy – a cocky, middle class boy – I was playing with some friends in a square in Florida† and some kids came along collecting cardboard from the rubbish. My friends start calling them 'worthless darkies', 'black slum kids' and I stupidly follow suit. They go after us and we run away. I reach home and try to open the door but it's locked. I ring the bell in desperation – they were about to reach me – and my dad opens the door. He comes out and asks me, 'What's going on?' At that point the kids get there and they tell him, 'Look, mister, this is what your son's like. We were there working and he called us black ghetto kids…'

---

* Provincial right-wing party.
† A Buenos Aires suburb.

29

My dad looks at me and says, 'Go inside'. At that point I wasn't sure if I wouldn't rather stay outside and let the others beat me…

He gave me a real hiding, a lesson to remember, because he also said, 'Here I am struggling against all those sons of bitches and you do this to me! How could you do this to me?'

At the time all I wanted was to get away, but I learnt my lesson.

Lesson number two

In 1973 he sent me on a Juventud Peronista (Peronist Youth, see Glossary) summer camp, organised by the grassroots 'Combative Peronism' group.

The day before I left, he got all my clothes ready, bought me chocolates, a whole load of things and said, 'I've bought you all these things so you can socialise them.'

I was ten years old, just a kid, and I honestly had no idea what he meant. I just looked at him as if to say, What on earth do you mean by that?

'These things are for you to share,' he said, 'because you're going to be with other children, that's what the camp's about. You're not just going on a summer holiday, you're going to share with other children who don't have the money to buy the things that I buy you.'

And that's when I learnt the meaning of the word 'socialise'.

It's coming

I remember my sister burning a load of books. There was a climate of tension, emergency measures were in place. You followed the rules, went home by certain times…Everyone was nervous.

My first personal experience of the repression was the murder of my cousin, an activist with the *Partido Socialista de los Trabajadores* (Socialist Workers' Party). The Triple A (see Glossary) murdered him in 1974. They kidnapped him in Pacheco and shot him. He was young, just 23. My dad was the one who went to identify the body. That was one of the few times that I saw him downcast, upset…

'…But far more serious than the outrageous justification given by the government, is the undeniable fact that the Triple A disappeared from the scene after the coup on 24 March 1976. From that moment on, your Honour, the most careful search to find some kind of information relating to that organisation proved fruitless. Why? The answer is obvious – because it became part of the state apparatus. Because tolerant complicity gave way to direct action, and the members of the Triple A were enlisted into the permanent forces of repression in the guise of the feared *patotas* (gangs). If this were not so, there would be no explanation for the anonymous arrest operations carried out in the early hours of the morning by bands of men in disguise.'

Extract from the case for the Prosecution, State attorney Julio Strassera,
Juicio a las juntas.*

The day of the coup I was going to play football in the morning with some friends from first year at secondary school. I was living in the province of Buenos Aires, in Florida, with my family. I remember that they wouldn't let us cross [Avenue] General Paz into the capital. On the other side there was a playing ground big enough to play football. Not only did they not let us cross, but the police stopped, searched and tormented us, even though we were only kids. I didn't fully understand the extent of the terror that was awaiting us.

January 1978

We moved to Caseros, elsewhere in the province. I wasn't there when they kidnapped my dad. At the time he was working on the land that my grandfather had left him. My dad left home on 24 January 1978 for the countryside, to Corrientes. At midnight on 25 January our house was raided.

There was a homely atmosphere in the house, my mum was making pizza and we were watching the Cup final – we're all football crazy. It was also an excuse for a family get-together. My sister and her husband and children had come round, and my other sister with her children too. They all stayed the night. The game was over, we were going to bed when we heard noises. The dogs started barking and as I went to look out of a window we heard a shot. That put us all on the alert. 'What the hell's going on?' We turned the lights on, another shot was fired and over a megaphone a voice said, 'all the people in the white house with stones are to come out with their hands up.' They were talking to us.

I was 14

I was one of the first to come out. We came out with our hands up, I couldn't see a thing, what I felt was the blow from the butt of a gun to my head and I was thrown to the ground. I was fourteen. I didn't lose consciousness, but they hit me so hard that it had after effects.

---

* Lit. Trial of the Juntas. Extracts taken from: *Memoria Debida* D'Andrea Mohr (see Bibliography).

They began asking, 'Where's your old man? Where's your old man?'

My dad wasn't there, we weren't lying. I was looking at the ground and at one point they grab me and go into the house using me and my sister as human shields. One man grabs me by the hair holding an automatic FAL rifle, I remember clearly because I saw it right next to me.

They started to search the house, throwing everything around, turning it all upside down. That's when one of them said something that I'll never forget: 'Aha! Look at the old man! I had an idea that he was a real Peronist, but he's got books by Karl Marx here.'

They took all those books and other things too. That's when we spent ten days locked up in Campo de Mayo,* in the 'little camp'. They took us all there, there were so many of us that they didn't have enough hoods to go round and they nicked a football shirt of mine to blindfold one of my brothers. They put us in an Encotel van they had parked there, I saw the van because I looked up before they blind-folded us.

The horror

Unfortunately I can remember everything because I don't like living with these things inside my head. I remember the hood, the dogs…I remember being alone in a kind of storehouse with bars, with the hood over my head the whole time. The guards used to take me to the loo. I cried, I was so afraid, I had no idea what was going on. Once they moved me to where my family was. That's where we recognised the voice of a friend of my dad's who was captured before us and who, poor thing, talked under torture.

I also went through that…They tortured my mum and me together. That was hard…

Ten days later they let us go, dumped us in a dead end street. We went home overcome by fear. It was really difficult getting home, the constant fear, not knowing what to do and the pain of knowing almost for certain of the loss of my dad. There was no way of getting in touch. He returned to Buenos Aires, got in touch with one of my sisters who hadn't been captured, found out that we'd got out, and then we lost all trace of him.

Walter suffered from a brain aneurysm as a result of the blow to his head. Through testimonies of friends of his father's he learnt that his father had managed to escape to Brazil, had returned a few days later

---

* Clandestine detention camp during the dictatorship.

and was captured at a meeting in Boulogne in the province of Buenos Aires.

Military service

My mum and I were left, with my brother, who had had polio when he was young and they beat him pretty badly, and a younger sister. I didn't finish school for a very specific and simple reason – because I had to go out to work, be the breadwinner. Amongst other things, we've gone hungry at times. I got my first job in a mechanical workshop, making bolts for a metal shutter factory and I'm still in the same line of work. When I had to do military service my mum was left alone to work. She worked doing whatever turned up...

I was drafted in 1981 and I started my obligatory military service in February 1982. When I was drafted I thought 'I can't believe I'm in these bastards' hands again, I can't escape them. Sons of bitches!' And there's nothing to it but to put up with it.

That day we were in the barracks, all the troops inside, kitted out in fatigues. We woke up and lorries started arriving, I was a new recruit, I was 18. They took my friend off with the Engineers' Battalion, to Parque Patricios, from there to Río Gallegos and from there to the Malvinas.

Children of 18

Walter remembers that in 1978, during his capture, he was taken to a hospital. Four years later, as a result of Galtieri's irresponsible military escapade, he returned to the same place, this time accompanying a friend, who was also a victim of the dictatorship.

From Campo de Mayo they took me to a hospital. When they put me on a stretcher they loosened my hood a bit and I saw the front of the building...When I was doing military service in 1982 they decommissioned me after the Malvinas war. A friend of mine came back from the Malvinas and was a mess psychologically. He was in the Campo de Mayo Military Hospital. When I went to visit him, I thought, 'I know this façade, I was here,' and I recognised the Military Hospital where they'd taken me.

My friend was sent to fight at Goose Green, where some of the fiercest fighting took place. They sent him to fight with a 9 millimetre and a Pan machine gun. He told me that the second time he loaded it, it stopped working and he had to cover his retreat with the 9 millimetre, with the Gurkhas* advancing. This friend of mine ended up committing suicide because he was so unwell. He came back totally screwed and there was no way of helping him to get over it. For example, when he was okay, he'd split, catch any bus that happened to be passing and just go. So you'd lose track of him for a week or two, everyone looking for him until he reappeared. I spent several nights with him, cooked for him, tried to comfort him, but it was a desperate situation because I could see that he was going. He'd tune out, sitting staring at a point in space remembering everything, and you couldn't get him to talk. Nothing, nothing, nothing…at times he was like a mummy. And he killed himself, aged 23, his family destroyed by it.

'If I hadn't done anything I'd still be in the Casa Rosada.[†] I was the Americans' prize pupil, they gave me VIP treatment…'

Galtieri (on the anniversary of the Malvinas)
Clarín – 2 April 1983

The end of the dictatorship

By that point I was involved in activism, but it wasn't exactly fun. On the one hand there was happiness, it was one of the first times that I could cry with other people around. It was in one of the Marches of Resistance, at the end of 1982. That day the end of the dictatorship was obvious, we were sure that they were on their way out. But at the same time, even though they were going to go there was a great feeling of sadness and a lot of anger, because many of us were aware of the fact that they were retreating without a scratch. They were leaving unscathed and sadly history has confirmed that fact.

'The document concerning the struggle against subversion is just. (…) It is a disinterested contribution by the Armed Forces so that Argentinians can close this period of our history (…) The document was produced with love…'

Videla
Clarín – 30 April 1982

A lot of my friends were crying, it was midday and the Plaza was full of people. I think there was an expression of social repudiation, but it wasn't strong enough to get justice for all that they did…it wasn't enough, let's hope that one day it'll be strong enough, that's what I'm counting on.

---

* A British regiment.
† Argentinian presidential palace.

I always say that in this country three generations of Argentinians have been killed. Two generations have been murdered, disappeared, imprisoned, exiled under the pretext of combating anti-patriotic Marxist subversion – very nationalistic, Western and Christian of them – and the other generation, my generation, was murdered in the Malvinas.

'When we act as the political power, we continue to be Catholic, when Catholic priests act as the spiritual power, they continue to be citizens. It would be a sin of pride to expect either one or the other to be infallible in their judgements and their decisions. However, like everyone we do our work out of love, which is the foundation of our religion, so we have no problems and relations are ideal, as Christian relationships should be.'

Massera, interview in the magazine Familia Cristiana
Cited in *Clarín* – 13 March 1977

Missing Dad

Fortunata, Walter's mother, works as a maid. Walter still lives with her and a sister. He's a machinist, he loves watching and playing football and he also likes reading about politics. Every day at 7 am he has *mate* with 'my old lady', as he affectionately calls Fortunata, and they go out to work to carry on earning their daily bread.

There were several moments when I really missed him. One very important moment in my life was when my partner left me. I really needed him then, I thought, 'I can't dump all this shit on my old lady.'

I would have liked my old man to be there to see me through it, to talk to, have his shoulder to lean on. It was a bad moment. I needed him because I felt completely alone.

He was an undemonstrative type of man, brought up the old fashioned way, he used to place great store by discipline, studies, all that. He took me to see my first local derby, both of us great Boca fans. We were great companions, perhaps because I was one of the youngest.

4

The arrogance of firepower

'National reorganisation is not simply a slogan or a mere motto. It is no more and no less than the recovery of the essential values of the Fatherland and the strengthening of its institutions through law and order, morality and authenticity.'

Videla – Armed Forces' annual dinner
La Prensa – 8 July 1976

'It is undeniable,' he explained, 'that we have the inescapable historical responsibility to rethink our Fatherland, to redefine this nation of Argentina, so that with the balanced participation of all its protagonists, we can hand down to our children the Argentina that they deserve.'

General Ibérico Saint-Jean
La Prensa – 10 July 1976

Appeal

Message from the Commanders in Chief of the three Armed Forces to their subordinates in which Videla, Agosti and Massera referred to the role played by the military:

'Standing firm in our faith in God and in the lofty destiny of the Fatherland, I appeal to all members of the Argentinian Army and the National Gendarmerie to continue their march along the chosen path, as they have until now, without doubts or hesitation, conscious of the fact that we are writing exceptional pages in the annals of the Nation.'

La Gaceta – 31 December 1976

MARIA LAVALLE

María was born in 1976. She is the daughter of Mónica María Lemos and Gustavo Antonio Lavalle, both disappeared. However, María tells her story today with a certain amount of joy, as years after her parents were kidnapped she managed to recover the sister whom the dictatorship had robbed her of.

We were living in José C. Paz, a town in the province of Buenos Aires. My dad worked with my uncle, my mother's brother, making things with leather – handbags, wallets, that sort of thing…They kidnapped us the night of 20 July 1977, in the early hours of the morning. I was just over a year old and my mum was eight months' pregnant. They took us to the San Justo Criminal Investigation Department, which was also being used as a camp. I was there for a week and then they took me back. They first took me to my maternal grandmother's house, but there was no one there, so they knocked on a neighbour's door and told her that they had the granddaughter of such-and-such a person. They had the telephone number of my other grandparents written on a piece of paper – the neighbour they left me with told me so later. My other grandparents were called and came to fetch me.

The Lavalles and the Lemos

I always knew that my parents weren't around, that the military had taken them away. I always say that I was extremely lucky: my four grandparents and all my uncles and aunts – none of them ever refused to talk about my parents. The relationship between the two families had always been good. They always showed me photos of my parents, and told me what my dad or mum liked. Told me stories the whole time of what they were like when they were little. They were a very strong presence in my life.

'La Catalina'

I remember once when my maternal grandmother came with some papers to sign. All my grandparents were there and I was singing 'La Catalina', which is a children's song that all the girls used to sing. Catalina's husband goes to war and she waits for him to come back.

One day this guy comes from the war and tells her that he's been with her husband and that her husband had told him to marry her to save her. And the woman says no way, 'For seven years I have waited and I'll wait another seven,' she says. She rejects this supposed friend of her husband's and he says to her 'hush, hush Catalina...' it is, in fact, her husband. She's talking to her husband and doesn't recognise him. All the girls my age knew 'La Catalina'.

I remember that there I was singing 'For seven years I have waited...' and there were all my grandparents...they all started crying. What a commotion! The words of the song touched a nerve for them, as by then they knew full well that my parents weren't coming back.

Three graves

I went to the same school from nursery through until I was 17. It was run by nuns. At school everyone knew that my parents were desaparecidos, that my mum was pregnant when they took her away, everyone knew that I had a sister or brother that I was looking for. The nuns knew that, the headmistress, the teachers, the cleaners, my classmates, my classmates' mothers... it was like it was completely obvious, I didn't need to explain anything.

Once something I did caused a real upset at school. I was only little, maybe eight years old. We had to do an essay on something like 'The cow' and I wrote a story about some people who died, something like that. And I was always such a cheery little soul. The thing is that we had to do a drawing with the essay and, since I had written about people dying, I drew a picture of three graves. A picture of three graves! All colourful, with flowers and grass...like a really pretty picture. So at school, where everyone 'knew', the teacher sees my drawing and goes and talks to the nuns. She says, 'okay, send her to the child psychologist,' and the child psychologist calls my grandparents...My four grandparents and all my uncles go to see her – none of my uncles were married, they lived with my grandparents and didn't have any children. So the whole family goes to see the child psychologist, the headmistress and the teacher to see what's up with 'Marita', who'd drawn a picture of three graves.

Wake up, wake up

It was a Friday night, a real shock, just before my twelfth birthday. I was at my grandparents' house, asleep and suddenly I heard people moving about. They wake me up: 'María, come on, wake up, wake up.' So in my pyjamas, half asleep, I come out of my room, go to the dining room and see my grandmother, my other grandmother, my uncles…'What's going on?'

One of my uncles used to go to a bar called the Nastase, and he says, 'I'm going to the Nastase, I'll be right back!'

He leaves and comes back with a bottle of cider for us all to drink a toast. I had no idea what was going on, I kept saying, 'What's the matter with you all? Please let me go back to sleep.' When we're all there together ready with our glasses for the toast, they hug me and say, 'Look Mariquita – my grandmother calls me Mariquita – we've found your little sister.' And I go: 'You what?!'

JUAN M. RAMOS PADILLA – FEDERAL JUDGE

'…and considering:

First: The material facts: I find it fully proven in the record of court proceedings that on 2 September 1977, on the property located in Siciliano and Vemet Street in Lomas de Zamora in the Province of Buenos Aires, belonging to the Criminal Investigation Department of the Buenos Aires provincial police force, a child of female sex was born, daughter of Mónica María Lemos de Lavalle and Gustavo Antonio Lavalle, and later moved to the San Justo Criminal Investigation Department of the same police force, where a non-commissioned officer of the aforementioned police department took her into her possession, from the hands of as yet unidentified individuals, who had taken her from her mother's arms, while she was being illegally deprived of her freedom in the clandestine detention centre known as the Pozo de Bánfield. With the collaboration of her husband, the non-commissioned officer who received the newborn concealed her true identity and her origins from the law and from the child herself, and they knowingly registered her as their own daughter, although she was not, and retained her in this situation until this Court put an end to it on 28 October 1987.'

First ruling given by Judge Dr Juan Ramos Padilla in the case investigating the crimes committed to the detriment of the girl María José Lavalle Lemos – 19 January 1988.

Abuelas de Plaza de Mayo*

The way the Abuelas work is that they don't say anything until the genetic tests have been completed. This 'is' your sister, they say, not this 'could be' your sister (…) I didn't know whether the baby was a boy or a girl, but I'd always had the idea that it was a girl. I always used to be on the lookout for girls who resembled me.

---

* Lit. Grandmothers of Plaza de Mayo (see Glossary).

'…As I indicated at the start, I find that the facts described above are fully proven on the basis of the following evidence: a) the results of the blood tests summed up in pages 274/293 which confirm the probability that there exists a biological relationship between the girl María José and the families Lavalle-Actis and Lemos-Vallino, establishing a likelihood of grandparenthood of 0.9977 according to the genetic information obtained from the analysis of HLA A and B histocompatibility antigens, which indicates a probability of 99.77% that the child María José Rubén is the granddaughter of the grandparents analysed, and that when these results are combined with those obtained from the RH-HR test, that probability increases to 99.98% (…) This proves without room for doubt that the girl María José registered with the surname Rubén is in fact the daughter of Gustavo Antonio Lavalle and Mónica Marta Lemos de Lavalle, and granddaughter of Angel Alberto Lemos and Haydée Vallino, and of Francisco Lavalle and Elsa Herminia Actis.'

Extract from the ruling – Dr Juan Ramos Padilla (Federal Judge)

Like in the movies

The next day we got up all happy and excited. We all got into my uncle's car, he had a Taunus at the time. So off we went, my three grandparents, my uncles and I – my maternal grandfather had died by then, my sister never knew him. I remember we were on the first floor of the building, overlooking the street, in a room they had assigned to us. I was a bit nervous, I kept going to the balcony to look out. My sister had to come all the way from Mar del Plata, and it took a while for her to arrive. I couldn't believe it was really happening, I thought it wasn't possible, it was like something out of the movies. My aunt came over and asked me, 'Shall we go and get an ice-cream?'

We were coming around the corner when we saw an official court car draw up, and a girl get out. I couldn't see her face, she had her back to me. But I said to my aunt:

'That must be her, don't you think?'

It's like kids experience things differently.

'Yes! It's her, it's her! Yes, yes!'

'Yesyes', 'yesyes' was all I could say…

'd) From the statement in answer to the charges made by Teresa Isabel González in page 187/188 it is clear that she herself has confessed that in the year 1977 she was working at the San Justo Criminal Investigation Department, where on 2 September she received a newborn baby girl, and from that same statement it is also clear that the accused was aware of María José's origins, since she stated her desire to collaborate to find the child's true family, and because she indicated that the person who gave the baby to her told her she came from the Pozo de Bánfield. The accused declared that although there were pregnant women being held in the San Justo Criminal Investigation Department, they were always removed before giving birth, thus showing that she was fully aware of the tragic fate of the parents of María José, whom she brought up as her own child, retaining and hiding her for many years; the truth was not only hidden from the law, but also from the child whom she treated as her own, denying her her history, her right to know the truth and her true identity.'

Extract from the ruling – Dr Juan Ramos Padilla (Federal Judge)

My sister was in Mar del Plata, they took her to the juvenile court in Morón, which is where the case was being heard. The woman who had kidnapped my sister was arrested on a Friday, because they didn't want to wait, she was about to do a runner. But it was the weekend and they had to wait until Monday. My sister spent the weekend in a hotel with the social worker, the psychologist, the public prosecutor, the judge…

'Given these facts, Teresa Isabel González is fully proven to be the author and perpetrator of the crime by way of the norms laid down in articles 315 and 321 of the Penal Code. Indeed, the accused herself made the following declaration in her statement in answer to the charges: "…That she wishes to be absolutely sincere with the Court, and collaborate in every way she can since she knows and is aware of the fact that this is the best thing she can do for the sake of María José, whom she has raised from birth as if she were her child. She clarifies 'as if she were more than my child' because I tell my older daughter that she was born from my womb and this is not the case with María José. I wish to request the Court to consider the possibility of allowing the accused to tell María José the truth. That the events took place in the following way: In 1977 I was working in the San Justo Criminal Investigation Department, where 68 political prisoners were being held; on 2 September a person from the San Justo Criminal Investigation Department – don't ask me who, Your Honour, I can't remember – came and gave María José to me, who had just been born and had her umbilical cord badly tied. I had previously commented that I would like a brother for my daughter, and I think that's why they brought María José to me." This therefore constitutes a straightforward confession, since the statement was made to an acting Judge…The marital relationship that exists between Nelson Rubén and Teresa González relieves me of the necessity of making any comment regarding the extent of the former's knowledge with respect to María José Lavalle Lemos. Nor has the defence provided any evidence that could raise even the shadow of a doubt concerning the fact that he knew and collaborated to conceal the situation.'

Extract from the ruling – Dr Juan Ramos Padilla (Federal Judge)

The other María

Before going to the courthouse we had stopped at a shop where they sold toys and had bought two monkeys hugging. The judge comes and tells us that she's arrived, that we shouldn't all go in together because there were so many of us. So the first three to go in were my dad's sister, my maternal grandmother and me. They opened the door, she was sitting next to the social worker. Looking completely normal. We said hello to her, gave her the present – the little monkeys I had bought – and I kissed her. At that moment it was like they were introducing me to some other girl, it wasn't like, ohhh! Just another girl you're going to live with – when you're young you don't think about things so much. Also, she was called María José.

'Reading between the lines, it would appear that the Counsel for the Defence is maintaining that only María José Lavalle Lemos's parents, and no one else, is qualified to act as described in the text of the article he cites, since there is no one who can sign the documentation certifying a family tie with the girl until a definitive pronouncement has been made regarding her identity. The first proposal appears a fraction more subtle, but I shall have to dismiss it outright, since to claim that only the parents can act legitimately in a case like this is to deny the sad reality of life in Argentina during the period of the dictatorship, which styled itself as a Process of National Reorganisation. The situation of the *detenido-desaparecido* is, as I have stated, a reality which we judges cannot deny, nor can we subject this reality to a purely formal treatment, since our fundamental obligation is to guarantee the rights established in the Constitution and in this particular case, the right of due process…'

Extract from the ruling – Dr Juan Ramos Padilla (Federal Judge)

The same mole

Inside the court building we started talking. My grandmother and my aunt were a bit left out. We didn't pay any attention to anyone else. I told her that I'd gone to buy an ice-cream and that I'd seen her arrive, blah blah blah, I'd eaten a lemon ice-cream and from there we got on to ice-cream flavours, TV, cartoons…So while we were there, talking about this and that, I can't remember exactly how we got on to the subject: 'I've got a lot of moles,'

'Oh, me too!'.

'Oh, look, look, we've both got the same mole here on our arm.' We went around everywhere going, 'We've got the same mole…' Everyone was very excited.

She was very lucky with the people who intervened in the case, she was really attached to the social worker – a lovely person – and the judge was great. So much so that we still see him today, my sister goes to have lunch with him.

'Fifth: General considerations and details of the sentence: Never before in the task of administering justice has this Judge felt so great a need to share some reflections on the recent and sad history that we have been through and the consequences of the still open wounds that plague our country. The crime of stealing children is penalised in our legislation with a prison term of between three and ten years, and I must therefore assess with great care the aggravating and extenuating circumstances that exist when I decide on the length of the sentence to be given to the accused couple.

My first reflection in this respect is a criticism of the legislator who established the aforementioned penalty for someone who appropriates a person and a penalty of nine to twenty years – to give one example – for someone who uses a weapon to steal a motor vehicle (Legal Decree 6582/58). This may have to do not only with a distortion in our scale of values, which leads to property being regarded as more valuable than a human being, but also with the fact that the legislator obviously could not imagine that such atrocious and aberrant acts as those that I must judge today would ever be committed in our country.

Extract from the ruling – Dr Juan Ramos Padilla (Federal Judge)

Going home

And so we went home. Once again, all in the Taunus. We arrived at my grandmother's house along with everyone else: the social worker, the judge, the psychologist from Abuelas and a psychologist friend of the family. We ordered takeaway pizzas because we were all starving. My grandmother takes her on a tour of the flat: 'This is my room, this is your and María's room', and so on. In my room there were two beds, I used to sleep in the bed by the window. That was my bed. My grandmother says to her: 'Which bed do you want?' I look at her, "What do you mean 'which bed do you want?' I'm sorry but…"

The bed by the window was mine, the other one…And María José says, 'thiiiis one' [putting on a child's voice]. Of course, the one by the window. I begin to protest, but my grandparents, uncles and the judge all look at me. 'Shhh! Is that okay with you María?', and I just went, 'Mmmmm…'.

Very strong

By now it was very late, so 'it's off to bed, girls'. We went to bed, I wasn't sleepy, I didn't want to go to sleep. María José goes to bed in the bed by the window, I go to bed in the other one, they switch off the light and we're off to sleep. I could hear their voices, everyone so happy, I wanted to get up and then I heard my sister crying. She cried and cried. And I wondered, 'What should I do?' I got up and went over to her bed. 'What's the matter María José, don't cry,' I said. But she just cried harder. I didn't know what the hell to do and I went to the dining room and told them that my sister was crying. The social worker went to talk to her and she calmed down. Then they all left – at some point they all had to go – and I went to bed. My sister cried all night long. She cried and cried and cried…

'In the case we are currently dealing with, there are items of proof to confirm that the defenceless child born in captivity was for many years treated almost as if she were an object. Indeed, the psychologist Roberto Saunier has declared in page 220 after interviewing González, that this woman had for years been expecting what finally happened in this case to happen, and had known that the child whom she says she called her daughter at some point would have to find out the truth. In her own words, she said, "…I could no longer go on like this and it's a relief that it's finally happened…" The psychologist added that when she referred to María José she would sometimes do so with expressions of tenderness and emotion, and at other times with indifference, for example, saying "…they handed me a package…".'

Extract from the ruling – Dr Juan Ramos Padilla (Federal Judge)

As if

The next day she got up as if nothing had happened. At lunch, I can't remember what I was doing, but my sister started playing cards with my grandmother. My grandmother is called Haydée. My sister was keeping score and she wrote G – M.J. So my grandmother said to her, 'Haydée is written with an H.'

· 'No, no. G is for grandmother,' she replied.

And the next day! She cried the whole night again and the next morning she gets up fine. She never spoke about what she was feeling, and that's when the psychologists began saying she should do some kind of therapy because she just adapted to her new life as if nothing had happened – a kind of over-adaptation.

Explaining things

What had happened was this: the judge told her that the couple she thought were her parents weren't her parents and that she had another family – this is what she says – so the first thing she imagines is 'I've got another family…another daddy, mummy.' You see? When they started talking about 'your uncle, your aunt, your grandfather, your grandmother, your sister…' there wasn't any daddy and mummy. So that first day she didn't understand what had happened. The next day the judge came and asked my grandmother for a photo of my father and mother.

He took the photos, sat my sister down – just the two of them – and said. 'Look, María José, your father and mother aren't here anymore, they are desaparecidos.'

My sister didn't know what that meant. The judge explained to her that the military had taken them away, that she had been born in the place where her mother had been held, that the woman she had thought was her mother had been working in that place, and had taken her. He showed her the photos and told her, this is your mummy and this is your daddy.

'The Rubén couple retained and hid María José Lavalle Lemos for more than ten years, while knowing her origins, and even depriving the child, whom they claim they treated as a daughter, of knowing her own history and depriving another family, her true family, of the right to have with them a member of their family group. I cannot see, therefore, wherein lies the lack of criminal intent motivating the defendants, referred to by Dr Verri. Dr Verri also contends that there is no case for equating the behaviour of the defendants to the action of detaining and concealing, since the latter only applies in cases where the minor has parents, a guardian or person responsible for him, and for that reason the action is not directed against anyone, and therefore cannot be categorised as such. And this judge wonders, "How can the child have parents or guardians when from the very moment of her birth the girl María José Lavalle Lemos was wrenched from her mother's arms, without those who would naturally become her guardians in the case of the forced disappearance of her parents being informed? Is the Counsel for the Defence perhaps attempting to deny the reality of life in Argentina during the years that these events took place? It would also appear that the Counsel for the Defence forgets that the principal victim in this case has been María José Lavalle Lemos, whose filiation was concealed from her, who was lied to for years and who was deprived of knowing her own history and true family, as well as her undeniable right to know the truth about her origins".'

Extract from the ruling – Dr Juan Ramos Padilla (Federal Judge)

'IX. In accordance with the provisions of articles 14 and 21 of Law 10,903 and also based on the legal precedent cited with respect to matters of guardianship, PERMANENT CUSTODY of MARIA JOSE LAVALLE LEMOS IS AWARDED to Haydée Vallino de Lemos, until she reaches legal age, or until her parents appear or something happens that requires that this situation be modified, with the express recommendation that the girl María José live with her older sister María, as advised in the request for guardianship and as requested by the closest relatives of the victim in this case. Notify and register the above. To be carried out and signed and executed by those present or the individual parts involved.'

Juan M. Ramos Padilla
Federal Judge

When we were little we used to spend hours talking mostly about things we had in common, looking for similarities as we'd done that first day. We used to watch TV, we liked the same programmes, the same cartoons. We got much closer as we got older, as teenagers. Today I'm still pissed off about the bed. I'm never going to love her, no way! She stole my bed.

Today María and her sister María José work in the office of the Abuelas de Plaza de Mayo, helping in the search for other children appropriated by the dictatorship.

5

The Argentinian Inquisition

THE COMMUNIST ANTI-CHRIST

'It is in that generalised barbarity that the Communist anti-Christ takes root, feeds and develops, devouring, in order to survive, the fainthearted, the corrupt, the weak in spirit and the soulless agents...'

Commodore Julio Salas, Director of the Armed Forces Officers' and Staff College
La Prensa – 24 June 1976

'In particular, Communism contains nothing that binds women to the family and the home, because by proclaiming the principle of their liberation, it separates them from the home and from caring for their children, and drags them out into the public sphere and into the world of collective production, to the same extent as men.'

*Manual de Conducción Interior. Boletín de Educación e Instrucción del Ejército
3. Hombre y la familia en el comunismo.*

'We are in principle living in a democratic state. Everyone can read what they consider appropriate. And what's more, if you wish to know, I, too, have read Marx and Lenin. You cannot claim that I am a Marxist or Leninist simply for having a book by Marx or Lenin. I would like to make that completely clear. So the students who are entering the universities need have no fear. One thing is reading to educate oneself, to learn about a doctrine or philosophy, another is applying procedures that are incompatible with the Argentine identity.'

General Jorge Antonio Maradona
La Nación – 14 February 1976

EXTREMIST LITERATURE TEXTS BURNT

'A communiqué reports that the Command of the Third Army Corps has burnt "pernicious materials that affect the intellect and our Christian way of life. This decision was taken in order that no part of these books, leaflets and journals may remain and to prevent this material from being used to deceive our youngsters about the true value of our national symbols, our family, our Church and, in short, our most traditional spiritual heritage, summed up in God, Fatherland and the Home."'

La Nación – 30 April 1976

PABLO BALUSTRA

The stigma

Early on the morning of 22 August 1972, during the military dictatorship of Alejandro Agustín Lanusse, 16 prisoners were shot at the Almirante Zar naval airbase. The base is located in Trelew, in the southern province of Chubut, which is why this event is known as the Trelew Massacre. On that same day, Pablo Martín Balustra, son of Pablo Alberto Balustra, was born in Córdoba.

I remember seeing him arrive from work and playing with him. We used to play football or fly a kite.

Balustra worked for the state water works and was a Montoneros activist (see Glossary). In the winter of 1975 he was arrested in the centre of the provincial capital.

I was at kindergarten, waiting to be picked up, and they didn't come... and didn't come... finally my grandmother came. By that time it was almost dark.

The big house

A few days after being kidnapped, Balustra was 'whitewashed', the term used to describe when a prisoner who had been illegally detained was placed at the disposal of the National Executive. Balustra was transferred to the prison where those awaiting trial were held in custody and then to Penitentiary Unit 1. Pablo remembers his visits as the days when he 'went to Daddy's big house...'

I remember queuing in Penitentiary Unit 1. Visiting hours were in the evening. I remember my impatience. We used to go in, they'd search us all, make us take off our trousers, everything. Then we'd get dressed again and go on in. I remember that we'd arrive and they'd shout 'Balustra!' I'd get all excited because I knew they were shouting for my dad. There was this long, long corridor. We'd pass through the iron gate and there at the end of the corridor was my dad, coming out of a small room, there he was.

Pablo is smiling now. He has a faraway look in his eyes. He comes back, takes a deep breath and carries on:

I also remember playing with a little friend that I made there, who also used to visit his father. They had given us these little wooden lorries. My father gave me one and this boy's father had given him one too. There we were in the prison block, running around pulling the lorries behind us on a string.

The goodbyes

In December 1975 President María Estela Martínez de Perón announced national, provinicial and municipal elections to be held in October of the following year. In spite of this announcement, a few days later General Videla, in a speech given in Tucumán on 24 December, gave the government an ultimatum of three months to 'fill the power vacuum and overcome the situation of anarchy and immorality.' The deadline given to Perón's widow, who suffered from chronic political shortsightedness, was 24 March 1976.

I still remember the last time I saw him. My uncle took me a few days before the coup. My dad could already see what was in store. It's like he prepared me psychologically. I remember that he hugged me very hard. Very, very hard. He went with me to the door, we started saying goodbye. He looked me in the eyes and told me to look after my mum and my sister, that I was going to be the man of the family now. We always used to wave to each other as I left. The gate slammed shut. I never used to turn away, I'd keep on looking at him as I walked away. He stayed by the gate. I walked slowly away shouting 'bye, Dad' and he answered 'bye, Pablito…'

COMMUNIQUÉ NO. 14
'The public is informed that the junta of Commanders in Chief has resolved that from this day forth the security forces, police forces, and national and provincial prison personnel have been brought under the jurisdiction of the military…'

Junta of Commanders in Chief of the Armed Forces – 24 March 1976

After the coup prison visits were stopped. The common prisoners played an important role in getting information to the outside world. The relatives of political prisoners used to stand watch outside the prison, but they only got hold of rumours. The prison walls became insurmountable.

Three months later, in June, during one of the run-of-the-mill beatings meted out to the prisoners, the prison guards invented the tunnel 'game'. The game consisted in making the prisoners run from one cell to another through a tunnel formed by two rows of guards. As they ran they were beaten to a pulp. Before the game started they were stripped naked and soaked, which not only added to the bitter winter cold, but also caused the prisoners to slip. This was the ideal situation for the guards, who would take advantage of a fall to 'disarm' the prisoner who had slipped. This brutal and basic strategy worked: in the midst of the blows raining down on Pablo Alberto Balustra, one guard's baton, among hundreds, hit him on the nape of the neck, leaving him irreversibly paralysed.

The image

Although it did not actually take place until April 1978, already there was a rumour circulating in the country concerning a possible inspection by the International Red Cross. Balustra was a living testimony to what was happening in Argentinian prisons. It was very difficult to disguise hemiplegia. They transferred a good number of the prisoners who were in Penitentiary Unit 1. Those who were 'fit to be seen' were sent to a maximum security prison to put on a presentable show. Balustra remained in PU1, prostrate, until 11 October 1976. His son vaguely remembers those days.

> I was at home one morning. Before they brought him in they took me to a neighbour's house and told me that he'd died of a heart attack. And I believed them...
>
> When I entered the living room I saw this dark shape. It's difficult to describe because at that age you're so small, so short that every-thing seems huge by comparison. I went past, I knew it was my dad. They delivered him in a closed coffin because they'd shot him. There were soldiers out front.

'Finally, thirteen of the legal prisoners in PU1, including myself, were also taken to La Ribera for a few hours and there Captain Barreiro threatened to kill us all if we said anything during the Red Cross's visit to the prison.'

Guillermo Puerta, File No. 4834 – Conadep

Truth and silence

> I was sleeping and I woke up to hear my uncle and my mother talking. It was about one or two in the morning. I got up slowly. She was saying '...that's why Pablo died, they shot him, you know...' Two days later I asked her about it. I was sitting on my bed and she told me everything. My world was shattered. For me, after that day, everything changed. That day marked the before and after. In the neighbourhood where I lived no one else had the same problem as me. I couldn't say that my dad had been shot. Everyone had a dad and I didn't. And not

only did I not have a dad, but I couldn't even say how he had died. So I carried on lying, saying he'd died of a heart attack.

THE AIMS OF THE *PROCESO* ARE SHARED BY THE PEOPLE
'The Argentinian people, brought up and educated in accordance with traditional Christian teachings and lovers of individual liberty, guided by the Armed Forces, will continue their struggle and triumph over the criminals who are attempting to change the Argentinian way of life, which is based on liberty, justice and respect for human rights.'

Declarations by Videla, *Los Principios* (Córdoba) – 22 October 1976

Secondary school

A teacher said it was a very special day and asked what had taken place on that date. I was the only one to answer: the Cordobazo.* A classmate asked me, 'how do you know?' So I told him that my dad had been there and another classmate, whose father was a policeman – I'll never forget him, his name was Cardozo – got up and started laughing in my face, saying my dad was an extremist.

That was when the film ET had just come out, so he put on the board ET = Ex-Tremist. And I started crying.

Where paths meet

At the age of 13 Pablo started going to the Cortázar workshop in Córdoba. Every Saturday at 2 pm the workshop brought together youngsters who had been victims of state terrorism. Painters, musicians, writers and psychologists participated in this initiative.

In 1994, ex-students of the Faculty of Architecture in La Plata organised a tribute to all the *desaparecidos* from the Faculty. A large number of young people got together for the event and the idea emerged to organise another meeting. The Cortázar workshop came in on the project and in April 1995 a camp was organised in San Miguel, Córdoba. Those who participated officially formed HIJOS, *Hijos por la Identidad y la Justicia contra el Olvido y el Silencio.*†

One night we were leaving an HIJOS meeting and someone – I think it was Seba – said to me: 'That boy's father was killed together with your dad. There's a list with his and your dad's names on it.'

---

* An uprising in 1969 in the city of Córdoba against the dictatorship of General Juan Carlos Onganía.
† Lit. Children for Indentity and Justice and Against Oblivion and Silence (see Glossary).

So I caught him up, he was walking ahead of me, and we started talking on the corner of Cañada and Laprida streets. I had seen the list whenever there were commemorative events or it was published in the press. And it turned out that he was called Miguel Ceballos. So he said to me: 'Yes, my dad was killed like this.' And I said to him, 'My dad too.' And we just stopped and stared at each other.

Pablo Balustra and Miguel Ceballos were executed early in the morning of 11 October 1976 together with other prisoners. Their sons, Pablo and Miguel, met 20 years later.

It was two years ago, we were drinking *mate* and Miguel said to me:

'Shit, isn't life full of crazy surprises! Here we are in 1997, only three years to go to the year 2000, living in a democracy and we have the same name and surname, the same blood, and we're discussing politics. See, Pablito, they haven't got the better of us...'

6

Slavery the American way

In the 1970s the United States was a great sponsor of dictatorships in Latin America. This not only reflected its security policy for the region, under which for years it had been training Latin American military personnel in the School of the Americas. It was also the era of the petrodollar, and US banks were anxious to offer easy credit facilities at low interest rates to encourage the countries in the periphery to buy imported goods.

The dictatorship took out huge loans and encouraged private firms to follow suit. Between 1975 and 1981 Latin America's foreign debt grew by an annual rate of 25 per cent.

So began the destruction of Argentinian national production and the country's condemnation to economic dependence by way of the foreign debt. From that point on it was not the Argentinians who would plan their future, but the International Monetary Fund.

At the beginning of the dictatorship Argentinian foreign debt stood at approximately 8,000 million dollars; by the end of the dictatorship the debt exceeded 45,000 million dollars.

The dictatorship would not have been possible without the backing of the establishment and in particular of the business class. The Minister for the Economy during the dictatorship was José Alfredo Martínez de Hoz, a grandson of the founder of the Argentinian Rural Association.

Towards the end of the dictatorship, in the 1980s, the military regime presented the private sector with a gift: international debts that had been incurred by private firms were converted into public debt. They were to be paid by the state, and therefore by the Argentinian people.

In 1976 every Argentinian owed $320 in foreign debt; by the end of 1983, when the military stepped down, each Argentinian owed $1,500.

MARTINEZ DE HOZ ENDS HIS SUCCESSFUL ECONOMIC TERM
'He obtained backing in the USA for his programme for recovery.'
La Prensa – 25 June 1976

WHAT IS NEEDED IS DARING
'We believe that in order to win,' he stressed, 'what is needed is daring and when one has the confidence and security that stems from knowing that one

is right, this helps give one faith and the necessary determination. Above all, when one can count on what many previous ministers for the economy did not enjoy – the total and unconditional support of the political forces in power, in this case the Armed Forces, who from the very beginning of our term in office up until the present have supported our economic programme. Only under these circumstances can an economic programme succeed.'

Martínez de Hoz
La Prensa – 2 July 1976

'The Argentine foreign debt is by no means excessive. It stands at more or less 8,500 million dollars (…) Foreign debt in itself is not a bad thing. What is damaging is a poor distribution of foreign debt payments over time.'

Martínez de Hoz
Gente magazine No. 597 – 30 December 1976

'It [the economic policy] was incompatible with any democratic system and could only be implemented with the backing of a de facto government.'

Guillermo Walter Klein – Secretary for Economic Planning and Coordination
(Alfredo Martínez de Hoz's right-hand man)
Clarín – 5 October 1980

Argentina never managed to deviate from the economic path set by the foreign debt, another disastrous legacy of the dictatorship. The weak democracies that followed the regime did not manage to stop the debt from snowballing, and so the nation found itself constantly obliged to take out new loans in order to pay the interest generated by the debt.

LUIS AVILA

Luis's father was the union representative for the employees of the Banco Español del Río de la Plata in Santiago de Estero. He was also very active politically in the PRT, the Revolutionary Workers' Party.

Bringing about change

He used to leave the bank and arrive home at siesta time, he'd eat something, rest for a couple of hours and then go out to sell insurance. Weekends were a delight for me because he used to take us to Fernández to talk to the peasant farmers. Around a hundred people used to go to the meetings. One of the few things I overheard was him trying to explain to them that they shouldn't let themselves be oppressed. That their fathers had been woodcutters, that their sons would be woodcutters and that they had to bring about a change, adopt a different attitude. The woodcutters in turn would answer, 'If you really want to bring about a change, we also want you to change your attitude towards us, because it's all well and good you coming here, telling us what to do, then getting in your car and driving back to the city, to your comfortable life. You have to show us that you say what you say because you really mean it.' So my dad would put us on the bus home and go up to the hills, sometimes he'd stay two or three days with them, sharing their lives…

THE CHRISTIAN AND INTEGRATED HUMANIST CONCEPT OF WORK
'The teaching of the work ethic is one of the most important contributions of Christianity to economic and social progress, in that it proclaims work to be a duty defined by divine law. (…) Teaching the poor: That poverty is not dishonourable, nor is working to earn one's living, as the example of the Son of God shows. (…) That true dignity and wealth consist in virtue. That the poor are better loved by God. (…) Conclusion: The aim of this doctrine is to bring about the reconciliation and friendly union of rich and poor, based on bonds of true brotherly love. If this doctrine prevails, all conflict will end.'
Internal guidelines manual. *Boletín de Educación e Instrucción del Ejército*
(BEIE, Army Education and Instruction Bulletin)

Birthday

On 24 March 1976 Luis Avila turned eleven, but that day there was no cake or candles...

I was sitting with my parents on their double bed – a habit I still have today – and I could see them thinking, both looking very serious. You could tell something was up. I asked them what was going on and they told me straight out that ugly times were beginning in the country, that the military had taken power and that from then on everything would be different.

St John's Day

I remember 24 June 1976, St John's Day. I live on St John Street in Santiago. They always used to light bonfires, but that year they didn't. I answered the door to the soldiers. They banged on the door: 'Does Don Avila live here?' and in they came. He got dressed, got a pair of sandals, a shirt...He said, 'Don't harm my children,' and left. He didn't resist because he knew it would be worse.

At that time there weren't any trials. They took him away on 24 June and gave him back on 24 March 1981 – quite remarkable, isn't it? He was released on my birthday and arrived in Santiago on the 25th. A great present...

Shortly after Luis's father was arrested, his mother was also detained, and spent four years in prison. They were never formally charged. Luis spent his whole adolescence living with uncles.

THERE ARE NO POLITICAL PRISONERS
'With reference to people detained for political motives, [Harguindeguy] explained that he orders the release of prisoners if there is no proof that they are subversive criminals. "I deny and refuse to accept," he insisted, addressing the journalist who had asked the question, "you telling me that there are political prisoners in Argentina".'

La Nación – 22 July 1978

My mum was found innocent and absolved of all charges, she got a clean sheet and a pardon. She's got this paper that says they made a mistake, that she's a good person. But she'd already paid a high price for being in the wrong place at the wrong time.

I've always been a homebody and a bit of a mummy's boy. I've got my business, I get up early, around seven. I travel round the country as a salesman – I run a small sweets distribution company. When I can I go to a football match. I'm unmarried. I think I've been through all of life's stages, but all the same I feel that there's a missing link…The lack of a proper adolescence, needing my parents at that time…

7

The sword and the cross

CARDINAL ARAMBURU OPENED ACCION CATOLICA'S ASSEMBLY
'The Church is not a force to be used to exert influence in the different temporal spheres, whether political or economic.'

La Gaceta – 19 June 1977

'For reasons of submission and jurisdiction, the Church does not confuse itself in the slightest with civil society, nor is it linked to any particular system...'

Declarations by the Bishop of San Luis, Juan Rodolfo Laise
La Nación – 4 April 1976

Bishop of San Luis appeals for collaboration with the authorities
'The Bishop of San Luis, Monsignor Rodolfo Laise, in a homily delivered during a mass held in the cathedral of this city, appealed to the population to collaborate, as always, in a responsible manner and for the sake of the common good, with the authorities who are assuming a difficult mission.'

La Prensa – 2 April 1976

CHURCH AND GOVERNMENT COINCIDE. DETERIORATION OF PUBLIC MORES. ETHICAL ROOTS OF THE *PROCESO*. A SHARED EFFORT.
'The Easter messages, of both the President and the Catholic hierarchy, share a common denominator in appealing for morality in our conduct.'

La Gaceta – 20 April 1976

'O almighty God! Creator of heaven and earth, Lord of the Armies, we are gathered here today to praise and thank you, on this new and glorious 38th anniversary of our National Gendarmerie. (…) We proclaim your name here today, we give thanks for this handful of veterans from the host of Güemes. For this group of valiant officers, NCOs and troops, in these last heroic years of the Fatherland, who created ramparts with their bodies and, with their spirits ablaze, with the barrels of their guns rooted out the subversive weeds from the Argentine jungle and countryside.

Father Menestrina – 38th anniversary of the Gendarmerie
La Prensa – 29 July 1976

MARTIN EZPELETA JR

Martín Ezpeleta Sr has a degree in Economics and was president of the Federation of University Students in Córdoba in 1961. His wife, Susana Cancela, is a psychiatrist. They were both imprisoned in 1971 for their political activism, he at Resistencia and she at Trelew prison in Patagonia. On 11 November 1974 the couple fled to Peru with their three daughters, when Susana was seven months' pregnant. There, in Peru, in the maelstrom, their first son was born: Martín. Shortly afterwards the whole family settled in Sweden.

Testimony of Martín Ezpeleta Sr

'When I left I was a lecturer in the Economics Department, teaching Rural Economy, but I had previously been a member of Obregón Cano's government.* My fourth child was on the way and the situation was very difficult: we could no longer sleep at home. (…) In the end we decided to go to Peru, where we had friends, including Francisco Delich, who was working in the United Nations Development Programme (UNDP) (…) During that period we also devoted a lot of our time to receiving and helping the many Argentinians who were leaving the country. Our house had become a type of refuge and 'informal consulate'. (…) That marked us out in the eyes of the Peruvian authorities as a militant family. (…) Maybe that's why we couldn't get a residence permit in Peru.

…That was when we got our flights out, thanks to the Latin American Refugee Fund, created by the Swedes. So on another 11 November, this time in 1976, I left for Sweden and in January 1977 Susana and the children followed me.

Por qué se fueron (The reason they left, Emecé, 1995)

My childhood involved a conflict between the rest of my family, who had all been born in Argentina, and myself, who had been born in Peru. I regarded myself as Peruvian.

Martín laughs about that situation that today seems so absurd to him and remembers that his sister always used to wind him up about it.

---

* Governor of the Province of Córdoba and member of Montoneros.

In Sweden there were a lot of Latin American immigrants: Bolivians, Chileans, Guatemalans…I was three years old, they had organised a barbecue for the Argentinians. They were talking about inviting the Uruguayans and my sister says to me: 'See, you can't come.' So apparently, I went up to the table and asked: 'And we Peruvians…can we come?'

Different children

There were the different communities. In primary school I started in a class in which there were only Latin American children. The teacher also taught the class in Spanish, we learnt Latin American history… the philosophy was to integrate us gradually. The first three years of primary school, classes were in Spanish and from then on they were integrated. The nursery school I went to had a section for Latin Americans, and another for Swedes, and we were constantly fighting, it was like ghettos in the Bronx.

That was my world, I learnt Swedish as my mother tongue. There was a time when I felt ashamed to be different. My father used to behave according to Argentinian social conventions – he used to greet his Swedish friends with a hug or a kiss, when in Sweden they barely shake hands. He spoke Swedish really badly and I realised that my friends couldn't understand him.

I remember that people couldn't understand that my parents had been in prison. Put yourself in a Swede's shoes: prison is for criminals. My parents had been in prison in 1971.

Lost in space

When I was sixteen, my world that had functioned so logically and which I felt so integrated into suddenly began to feel strange. I felt something was lacking, but I didn't know what. Things began to go badly for me at school. Everything felt meaningless. I dropped out of secondary school and in 1991 I came to Argentina on holiday. My dad was over the moon, my mum was more worried.

I went to the town my dad is from. I felt that things were so different there! I didn't understand the social codes. Everyone used to ask me 'how do you say this or that in Swedish.' I didn't understand that you only danced in pairs – in Sweden everyone dances together in a big group.

I went back to Sweden, finished secondary school and that's when my real problems began. I spent six months doing sweet FA, out partying every night. Getting drunk, but in a bad way.

A trip

I went to the first camp, with some 70 people, before HIJOS became HIJOS. That camp did my head in. The stories I heard, the truth is I had no idea. I knew it all in an abstract way, 'people were tortured, killed…,' but hearing it from the mouths of those who had suffered the experience…At one point I had to get up and leave because I felt that my head couldn't take any more of hearing one horror story after another.

When I arrived at the camp – and heard the stories that people there had to tell – I felt ashamed to tell my story. I was also ashamed to feel that my personal experience had been fucked up because, in general terms, for me exile has been a privilege. But today I understand what my personal conflict is about: the first generation of exiles live with the nostalgia for the land to which they can never return and in the second generation, the conflict revolves around the lack of a sense of belonging. Feeling like you don't come from anywhere. When I'm here in some sense I feel Swedish, I go to Sweden and I feel Argentinian. No man's land. Coming here from Sweden meant ending one exile and beginning another.

TESTIMONY OF MARTIN EZPELETA (SR)
'I should also add that, as part of our work to maintain permanent cultural ties with our country, a few years ago Susana and I founded a tango group, a school of tango…We already have some professional dancers who tour Sweden and Europe. And along the same lines, on Saturdays Susana and I present a radio programme dedicated to tango.'

Por qué se fueron – Emecé, 1995

I'm not one of them

Back there I already felt more Argentinian, of course. Besides, I felt that in Sweden I was living in a protective bubble in the middle of nowhere, where fifteen-year-old kids have existential crises because they've got everything sorted. And suddenly arriving here…there was so much to do. All the space that was created!

I started going through another crisis. I began to feel that there were two worlds, that I loved both very much, but that they were completely separate, and would always be so, and at some point I'd have to choose between them. I'd have to pick one of them.

I was living in a flat belonging to my aunt, with a balcony overlooking the centre of Córdoba, on Avenue Castro Barros.

I used to take my bedside table out on to the balcony and spend the entire night sitting there writing to try to make some sense of all this. On the one hand trying to get to the essence of Sweden, which distance made me see in a different light, and on the other trying to understand all that was happening to me.

Returning

I had to weigh up a whole load of things. It was the most philosophical moment of my life. It was also a time when I was losing all the close friendships, all the relationships that you've built up over twenty years. Very close, lifelong friendships. You gradually build those relationships, select the people to be close to. So far I haven't been able to do that in Argentina. I remember a letter from a friend, who wrote that she felt she'd lost me, that I'm not going back. What she said really got to the heart of my conflict.

I stayed here seven months and then went back, but with the idea that I'd come back to Argentina. I arrived in Sweden feeling that I'd changed drastically, feeling completely different. In Sweden I realised that I just picked up where I'd left off, doing the same things, going out on benders again…I wanted to die. Three weeks later I said, 'I'm going back.' My feeling was that there nothing would change, everything would always be the same.

TESTIMONY OF MARTIN EZPELETA (SR)
'I still continue with my work in Uppsala, because the struggle isn't over. I don't believe that ideologies have died, but I don't want to perceive reality through the lens of any ideology, because simple ideology is a poor way of looking at the world. I want to look at reality from a more profound perspective than those created by ideologies. I need to redefine my ideology. Because it's a very long struggle, this struggle on behalf of the oppressed – it's been going on for so many thousands of years that you can't be in a hurry. The experience of exile, on the other hand, has helped me to lose my impatience and has also made me lose my dependence on the present. I have learnt to develop a long historical patience. I am fully aware that very few of the things that I work and struggle to achieve will materialise during my lifetime, but that is not important.'

Por qué se fueron – Emecé, 1995

Five months later I returned to Argentina. The first year I was here I was like an anthropologist: 'look what the stones are like here, in Sweden they're different, squarer' [he says, smiling].

I used to compare everything: 'Look how much a packet of cigarettes costs, in Sweden they cost so much…', and the people too. The things you could talk to Swedish girls about and you couldn't to Argentinian girls, relationships with friends. The first year I wrote a diary, I was constantly making abstract reflections and at one point I realised that I was no longer doing it. The letters I wrote to my parents had changed, they no longer were about my place in the world. I started to tell them about things that were happening, how I was worried about my exams…

Here, there, everywhere

Two weeks after we left, the military went looking for my parents. We were saved because we left, we were lucky. I think it's been tough on my dad, he's had to stay in a country which he never felt was his own. But he's there and he'll be there forever.

TESTIMONY OF MARTIN EZPELETA (SR)
'With respect to our links with Argentina, Susana's links are exclusively friends and family-based. She's visited a number of times and had a good time, but she couldn't go back to living there, lose the closeness to our children and grand-children. I, on the other hand, never really left Argentina and sometimes I think that as time goes by I'm more and more rooted there. The work I do, con-sciousness-raising with popular organisations for the creation of the New Man, saves me from what might be a schizophrenic existence, living in Sweden and still dreaming about Argentina.

…My house is my homeland. I no longer have the dilemma of here or there. Wherever I am is here or there. I'm not going to choose between the house or the home. This is an old, long-running argument I have with Susana, and we came to the agreement that I would spend some time there and some time here with her, with my children and grandchildren. I need both things to live in harmony. But in order that this set-up doesn't just dissolve into senti-mentalism, there have to be life projects. That's why I'm working on this project to set up a chain of popular schools, from Río Cuarto, using the same methods and structure, changing what needs to be changed.'

Por qué se fueron – Emecé, 1995

Martín Jr finally settled in Argentina, shortly afterwards he got married and had a daughter called Federica. He's living in Córdoba and recently began working in the production team of a radio programme. He gets up at a quarter to five, has a quick breakfast and walks to the radio station. In the afternoon he studies, he is in his third year doing a degree in Social Communication at Córdoba University.

I think I'm going to write, I like to write about the economy. I realised that Argentina had gotten to me the day I cried when my team Talleres didn't get promoted to the first division. That was two years ago. I realised that something had happened, I was moved to tears…[he laughs].

Today I think about the future in terms of being here in Argentina, I no longer consider the possibility of working in Sweden. My plans are all linked to Argentina. The things I found strange before and that I looked at as if I were an anthropologist, an outsider 'look how these South Americans behave' are now part of my daily life.

Having a daughter was also fundamental, a way of putting down roots once and for all. She was born at the same time that Talleres didn't get promoted, two historical moments in my life.

My parents' little house

It was rented out, or lent to friends, but my dad always insisted on not selling. They often talked about whether to sell it or not, but he never wanted to because it could be of use to them if they ever went back or to any of us kids.

For me this house…from the outside it looks like its falling apart, but to me it's beautiful and it means so much to see my daughter growing up in it…I felt really strongly about it, the idea of coming and living here was exciting, really important. I felt that in some way our histories are repeating themselves, and I'm also happy for my parents; today they come here and it makes them very happy to see that I'm living here, in this house that meant so much to them. It symbolises a whole lot of things, it's the house they had to leave, where they'd set up home together, and which the way things turned out they had to leave. In some way they feel that my living here is like they've beaten their exile, that the bastards didn't get the better of them and that if they're not here at least their son is.

They always used to talk about this house. There's no way I'd leave this house, not even if I were a millionaire. Maybe I'd give it a facelift! But I'm not leaving.

8 ✳✳✳✳

Divine justice

'Martínez Zuviría went on to say that "we can perceive a mental and physical activity that consists of optimism and the desire to offer one's services in any effort and sacrifice that may contribute in some way to repairing the damage suffered by the Fatherland." He also explained that, "with respect to those responsible for this disaster, their contemporaries have already expressed their opinion; the judicial system for its part is applying itself to its task. And as far as divine justice – which is infallible – is concerned, it would also appear to be giving its verdict."

The Cavalry, like the whole Army, does not renounce God, nor the fatherland, nor its history, nor its dignity, and wishes to live in accordance with the principles bequeathed to it by its forebears in blood and in history. And this is also the wish of the Argentinian people, who are Catholic, patriotic and worthy, with the exception of those who are known to be corrupt.'

Retired General Gustavo Martínez Zuviría
Official ceremony on the Day of the Cavalry
La Gaceta – 25 April 1976

'At the time Martínez Zuviría was a lieutenant. By now he must be a Colonel of the Cavalry. One night, in El Campito [clandestine detention centre in Campo de Mayo, a military installation], they had begun killing a group of prisoners. Vosso was always in charge of these jobs. So Martínez Zuviría, who was one of the officers at the camp, went up to him and said: "With your permission, lieutenant colonel, sir!" La Parca (a nickname Vosso used) looked at him and handed him the gun with a new charge. That night this officer killed twelve people by shooting them in the head. When I asked him why he had done it, when it was not his job, if he was not obliged to do it, he answered, "I did it out of solidarity with my superior, that's all, corporal".'

Testimony of former Sergeant Victor Ibáñez in Almirón, *Campo Santo*, 1998

PABLO ERNESTO DI VITO

Pablo was born in Buenos Aires in 1973. His father, Gabriel Di Vito, was a mechanical engineer and worked as a draughtsman in a factory. Gabriel was kidnapped on 29 November 1974, when he was 28 years old. Pablo's mother, Martha Prieto, was a nurse and was kidnapped in July 1977; she was also 28.

July 17 1977

With my dad I never felt a sense of loss, but of absence…The only memory I have of my mum is of the kidnapping. I remember it like it was a film. We're on the bus, I'm looking out of the window. There are cars going by, then the bus stops, I turn around and these men get on. They come straight over to where my mum is sitting, grab her by the hair and lift her out of the seat. It all happened quick as a flash, like I was seeing it in a film. My mum starts shouting 'let me give my son a kiss'. The men pay no attention, they go to the back of the bus and grab hold of a woman who's sitting there. It must have left a strong impression on me, because it's the only memory I have. One of them grabbed me, heaved me over his shoulder like a sack of potatoes, took me away and that's all I can remember…

When I got home I said I'd been eating escalopes and crying. Crying a lot. My uncle knew what had happened.

José and Filomena

Pablo grew up with his paternal grandparents, José and Filomena, in Caseros.

It was an Italian household, a large household. They'd bought up the whole corner of a block and made three houses. On the corner lived my two uncles, one of my dad's sisters and her husband.

When my parents got married they lived for a time in the house downstairs while my other uncles and my grandparents lived upstairs. It was certainly a Di Vito corner.

When I was little I had a vague idea. You've got your friends, when you go to their house it's their mother who gives you your tea, do you see what I mean? Just that makes you aware that you're different. But you don't burst into tears over your tea either.

It's crazy, but I always remembered when they kidnapped my mother, but somehow, like you do when you're a kid, I didn't associate that memory with her absence. When children in the neighbourhood used to ask me where my parents were I'd say the same thing as I was told at home – that they were 'working in Europe'.

Later on the neighbourhood kids in their innocence used to ask, 'What, and they never come to see you?'

So I'd go home and ask the same question.

1983 – return to democracy

My uncles were all Radicals* and there was a festive atmosphere at home. I used to go around wearing the white cap and all (…) afterwards I ended up hating it. I was 10 years old. I used to listen to what my uncles were saying, that Alfonsín was going to be president, that the country was going to improve…

One day my grandmother told me. She finished bathing me, was drying me and began to tell me that the military had taken my parents away. I was 11 years old. My grandmother was crying. I remember that for a long time I half denied the true version of events. Once at secondary school they asked why I had no parents and I said they'd died in an accident, as if I were ashamed to tell the truth. These are fragmented memories of how I reacted to the truth of what had happened until I was older.

Silence

My family is kind of special. A few times my uncles sat down and talked about the subject without getting upset, but just once or twice. It's a rather painful subject. My grandmother can't talk about my dad without crying. Always. She can't get over thinking that his friends had led him on.

I remember when my uncles told me of what they knew about what had happened. I remember a talk I had with one of my uncles in which he told me everything they'd done after my dad disappeared, to try to find out what had happened to him. My dad disappeared towards the end of 1974 and until 1976 they used to pay a policeman to see if he could pass on any information. A huge amount of money they paid him. Once in Sierra Chica prison a Di Vito was being held, so my uncle went to see, but it wasn't him.

---

* Members or supporters of the Radical Party that won the elections on the return to democracy.

I had a fairly difficult adolescence, I was quite a rebel, I didn't get on with my uncles. And my grandparents were really old. My family remained marked by a strong feeling of fear. I was fifteen and I'd go out dancing, and it was a real issue…

In 1991, Pablo's grandfather José died, aged ninety.

I was left in the care of my grandmother. By the end we were getting on really well. But there was a time when things were very difficult. She used to light a candle in front of a photo of my dad, Italian style, I don't know (…) The thing is you always feel empty, like something's missing, it's not like one day you decide it's over. To understand it you have to understand the context: my dad was the youngest of five brothers in an Italian family that emigrated to Argentina after the war. He's the son that grew up in this country – the promised land – the son who made it to university (…) My grandparents' world was shot to pieces.

Getting things out

'"Walk down this street," the wind invited me, "you can come and go as you like, but you can't talk or touch anyone." Even before I looked I knew that there I'd find everything that, over time, I had lost forever.

…The first thing I saw was a couple, sitting on the edge of the pavement on a street corner. I went over to them and immediately recognised them – they were my parents. As young and beautiful as they were in the photos I have of them. My father had a guitar and was playing a simple melody, just a few chords. My mother was by his side, leaning against him. I was tempted to go over to her and kiss her cheek, say so many things to her, tell her that I remember that her birthday was also in October, the day before mine, tell her that I knew that she liked coffee, that she was very talkative, that she was energetic, and a dreamer, but that was all that I knew, and that among the other thousand questions I'd like to ask her, for example, what was her favourite song.'

El duende de la noche (excerpt) Pablo Di Vito, 1997

At one time I used to spend the whole day, every day writing. I started writing aged 7. Poems, stories, especially stories. I feel a need to write, it's like a fire running through my hands, my chest. It's a relief and a pleasure.

'…And as for him, the man, my father, what wouldn't I have liked to have said to him. I wanted to sing along with the melody he was playing, hug him, proudly show him that I was also a grown man like him now, almost as tall as him, and sit down and talk about so many things, man to man. And then hug him again and even shake his hand, but just so as to know what the touch of his fingers felt like, and touch his face to know what his half-grown beard felt like.'

El duende de la noche

Times

I returned home saying I'd eaten escalopes and had been with a blonde little girl – I worked out later what had happened: when they kidnapped my mother, they took her with two other women. Leila and Elena. Elena was travelling with her daughter Paula, who had blonde hair when she was little. They returned her on the same day as me.

I got hold of the phone number of one of Elena's relatives and asked for Paula's phone number in San Isidro where she lives. That was a year and a half ago. I called her and said:

'Hi, how are you? Look, I'm Pablo, my mum and your mum were kidnapped together. We were there when it happened.'

'Hold on a minute, I've got to sit down,' she said.

She'd only just found out a whole load of stuff shortly before I rang, only two months earlier. We talked a lot. She told me her life story, how her father is also disappeared, that she was having a hard time coming to terms with her whole history, she asked me to give her some time…

The day we meet will be amazing.

Thank you

Pablo's mother was kidnapped as she tried to flee to Brazil with false documents. Her final destination was to be Italy. At nine in the morning she had taken a Pluna bus at the terminal. A couple who were friends of hers had given her their own passports. Martha was using her friend Carola's passport for herself and the passport of one of her sons – Darío – for Pablo. After only a few blocks the bus was intercepted by a military patrol.

They had fixed the passports the day before at this woman's house. They put my mum's photo with all the information relating to this family. I was given all the details corresponding to her son Darío who was the same age as me.

A year ago I went to see them. I already knew them, they had visited on several occasions when I was young. It was a very happy meeting, I think it was a Sunday, they were all there. Darío was there, then Armando arrived, Carola's husband.

It was an emotional moment. She was my mother's friend. She told me that my mum used to drink a litre of coffee a day. They told me about the passport, they were very moved. They really stood by my parents.

Then Armando, at some point, it was like he was trying to justify not having been there, not having been an activist. So I said to him,

'The truth is I didn't come here to criticise you for anything, I came to say thank you...' It wasn't that they had only fixed the passports and nothing else. They'd hidden my mum and that wasn't easy in 1977.

Today Pablo lives in a small flat in Buenos Aires and is studying to be a litera-ture teacher. On one wall of the flat he has a portrait of his mother, who he resembles strongly. On the table one can see his father's union card.

Modernity

MORE THAN 3,000 DETAINED IN A GENERAL RAID IN THE CITY
'The provincial police headquarters yesterday released a communiqué in which it reported on the outcome of a general raid that took place last weekend in our city. More than 3,000 people were brought in for investigation, and it was established that 190 of them had arrest warrants in their name.

The official document reads as follows: The provincial police headquarters informs the public that to combat crime and all acts that threaten public decency and values, and for the good of the community, a general raid was carried out on the 19th and 20th of this month, in which more than 3,000 people were arrested. The raid revealed elements who, with intent to commit crimes, frequent nocturnal haunts, public shows, bars, tearooms and generally any other place in order to act to the detriment of the unity and good of society. A total of 190 persons detained had arrest warrants out on them. Regrettably, this police action has caused inconvenience to unquestionably honest citizens, but this fact is not the result of an indiscriminate intention against those who have nothing to do with illicit behaviour; on the contrary, *it is the price that a modern society like ours must pay* (...)'

La Voz del Interior (Córdoba) – 24 November 1976

Unseemly subversives...

ON THE HOME FRONT
'Several people arrested for not erasing subversive graffiti. The command of military sub-district No. 15 yesterday released a communiqué in which it reports that two days ago several people were arrested and are being charged with 'collaborating with subversion by omission'. The military communiqué, signed by Colonel Alberto Pedro Barda, reads as follows: The command of military sub-district No. 15 informs the public that in compliance with the orders detailed in communiqué 31, publicised on repeated occasions by this command, members of the Armed Forces and police initiated yesterday control checks on the cleaning up of those façades of commercial and public establishments and of private homes that have graffiti of a subversive or unseemly nature and of other types. As a result of the control the following people have been detained for infringement of communiqué No. 13

[There follows a lengthy list].

Likewise, this sub-district command thanks the extensive and generous collaboration shown by the majority of the population, in cleaning the fronts of their houses, where irresponsible individuals have invaded private property with illegitimate intentions. Finally, this command clarifies that these control operations will continue uninterrupted until we have a clean city.'

La Voz del Interior (Córdoba) – 27 November 1976

AGUSTIN DI TOFFINO

Article 4 of the EPEC (Córdoba Provincial Energy Company) collective agreement establishes the right of sons of workers who die to be taken on by the company. This was how Tomás Di Toffino started working shortly after his father died, when he was fourteen. In EPEC he met Dalinda Olmos – known as Negrita – who he married in 1964. When their fourth son was born they chose to give him the same name as a workmate and friend, Agustín Tosco.* Tosco had recently died in clandestinity and Tomás was the deputy secretary of the union. Agustín Di Toffino was born in August 1976, and three months later the dictatorship took his father away from him forever.

> I always avoided the question. 'No, he's away travelling', sometimes 'he died…' depending on who was asking. I had a certain advantage: my mum always told me the truth. What I do remember is when I used to ask my mum,
> 'Why did Dad die?' I remember, crystal clear, my mum saying,
> 'Your father died so that all the children can have a glass of milk to drink.'
> I remember that it made me feel very proud.

'The Army will take selective action against state industries and companies, in coordination with the state institutions operating in that sphere, to promote and neutralise situations of labour conflict provoked or that could be exploited by the forces of subversion, in order to prevent the agitation and insurrection of the masses and to contribute to consolidating the efficient functioning of the country's productive system.'

Point 2 of the Secret decree 504/77, Continuation of the
Offensive against Subversion

Tomás Di Toffino was a member of the trade union *Luz y Fuerza* and was kidnapped on 30 November 1976, although the Army plan that ended in his kidnapping was put into motion some time earlier. Worried by the imminent strike that the union was organising in 1976, the military decided to make it illegal, or as they termed it, 'make it Montonero'. This would provide them with the excuse to claim it was an act of subversion. To this end, numerous

---

* Well-known union organiser in Córdoba, centrally involved in the Cordobazo of 1969.

flyers calling on the workers to strike were printed in the La Perla concentration camp and signed by the military as 'Montoneros'. Patricio Calloway, a member of the Peronist Youth who had been kidnapped in September 1976 and was being held at that camp, was chosen as a key actor in this military farce. The 22 year old appeared shot dead 'killed in an armed confrontation', outside the EPEC, with the flyers in his possession.

'When the *Luz y Fuerza* workers began their strike action – yet another example of their consistent resistance to the military dictatorship – under the leadership of, among others, Tomás Di Toffino, an unusual thing happened in La Perla: one night Patricio was taken away alone, which seemed strange to us, since the "transfers" generally took place by day and in large groups.

Later we found out that they had killed Patricio outside the EPEC. The media said there had been a shoot-out between the forces of law and order and a Montonero militant who was calling on the workers to strike. To complete the sham the military put the flyers that they had previously printed in La Perla in Patricio's hands.

In this way the strike was made illegal, and they attempted to spread fear among the workers and this macabre manoeuvre ended with the kidnapping, shortly afterwards, of Tomás Di Toffino.

It was an inexorable circle: Patricio was murdered to justify the repression in Luz y Fuerza. The flyers were made up in La Perla. Di Toffino was kidnapped and taken to La Perla. Everything began and ended in La Perla.'

Graciela Geuna, File No. 764 – Conadep

Photos

It's always the oldest child in a family who has the most photos. The older children have albums full of them. The youngest never have photos taken of them [Agustín hypothesises with a smile].

I have only two photos, and not one with my dad. He's not in the photo, but he took it and I always used to ask, 'Why isn't he in it…?'

…And I started to think that he didn't have any photos taken with me because he didn't think he was going to die…

'When Tomás arrived at La Perla, as they couldn't prove that he was affiliated to any particular political organisation, they put him down on the daily register as "Undercover lefty". Tomás was transferred on Monday 20 or 21 February, the day that General Luciano Benjamín Menéndez [governor of Córdoba during the dictatorship] came to inspect the transfer. We were told that in the case of Tomás, General Menéndez would oversee the execution in order to "set an example" and "fortify troop morale", etc.'

Graciela Geuna, File No. 764 – Conadep

Holy Week

It was April 1987, and we had an 'American' party at my house. The girls brought sandwiches and the boys drinks. We were dancing and the television began to announce a 'military uprising', a 'Rico coup'.

We were young and we started saying 'the military bastards are back'. I remember that one classmate started crying desperately.

'The military killed my father,' she said.

I had no idea, none of us had any idea. And she cried,

'Call my grandmother (…) The military came into our house.'

And so to console her I also told them my story. The party ended there.

To appease the uneasy hearts of the military, who were not satisfied with the *Ley de Punto Final*, the Alfonsín administration obediently passed the *Ley de Obediencia Debida* (see Glossary). Menéndez, who had been accused in approximately 800 cases, was released without charge by the Supreme Court of Justice on 23 June 1988. The few cases left pending ultimately came to nothing, thanks to the pardon issued by President Menem. In 1989, General Luciano Benjamín Menéndez was invited by Sixto Ceballos, the secretary-general of the union, to participate in an event on the Luz y Fuerza premises. The room where he was received is named after Agustín Tosco.

The thing with the name Agustín is incredible. When we were little the people coming back from exile, or coming out of prison and those who had survived, all met up and all their children were called Agustín. All the children who were born after Tosco's death. You constantly find that in Luz y Fuerza. I'm not even original!

When there are marches or talks or debates you find people coming over to greet you, all emotional, to tell you anecdotes (…) During the Cordobazo, for example, I don't know, but my dad seems to have had five doubles – he was everywhere at once!

Menéndez lives five blocks from home. I remember I passed him on the street once, when I was very young, I think it was in 1983, when everything was coming to light. Everyone talked about him, but I didn't know him, I had never seen his face.

I think I even used to walk past his house on purpose to catch a glimpse of him. On my way to the club, I could have taken another route, but I used to go past his house, and I used to do it to have a look at him.

Until the day I came face to face with him. I remember I looked into his eyes. He has a shifty look. He was wearing blue trousers, a blue tie and a light blue shirt. He was on the pavement chatting to a neighbour and had an Army guard with him. He looked at me…I was 10 years old.

I think I wanted to see the man who'd murdered my father – and another 2,000 people – see him close up, see that he was real, see that the impunity is real, tangible, it isn't something abstract, it is palpable.

'…Did La Perla exist? Yes, it was a detention centre, not a clandestine prison… the subversives were held there mostly to protect them from their peers…'

General Luciano Benjamín Menéndez
Gente magazine – 15 March 1984

Agustín Di Toffino is doing a degree in Social Communication at Córdoba University. His brother Tomás, the second of four sons, started working at the EPEC company in 1990, thanks to the same clause that had provided his father with a job there when he was just fourteen. Tomás Jr is currently the union undersecretary.

The day my brother became undersecretary four years ago was really emotional. My two grandfathers, Tomasino Di Toffino and Francisco Olmos were founding members of the company, when it was still English. Other children of desaparecidos are also active in the union together with my brother: Gustavo Vives, whose father was a union representative and raised money for the prisoners. They kidnapped him at work (…) Mariana Cafaratti, the daughter of Alberto Cafaratti, who was also held at La Perla and was disappeared…

That day we went with my mum and the whole family to attend the inauguration of the new union leadership in the Agustín Tosco hall. The hall was full to bursting. Sometimes, at the table after eating they start recalling anecdotes. Do you remember when we did this? Do you remember when we went on holiday with Dad? Do you remember when we went to such-and-such a place? (…) And from what they tell me, my dad was a very likeable man, full of fun. I never knew him but still I sit there and take pleasure in the conversation, ask them what he was like (…) In that respect my brothers have been great with me.

"'Dito" or "el Bonyi" as he [Tomás di Toffino] was affectionately known, was always calm and peaceful, even on the day they took him away. He was worldly wise and always knew the right thing to say or had a cheery comment to make. Like the good leader he was, he knew how to talk intelligently. You got a very clear idea of his long history as a worker, his wisdom, his role as the workers' friend, a fan of barbecues, wine and chatting with his comrades. He never lost control of himself, nor of the situation we were in.

He never lost his cheerful attitude towards life. He used to remember his wife and sons with great affection and was proud of the work done by his workmates and the union.

Through him we got to know Tosco, for whom he had great respect. In La Perla they had all the photos taken by the rural police at Tosco's funeral. Di Toffino appears in a lot of them. (…) In mid-February Di Toffino was taken to the offices. They took him away with Joana Avendano de Gómez and María Graciela González de Jensen. That day General Menéndez came to La Perla for an inspection. The three left in a lorry. We all said "bye-bye Bonyi".'

Testimony of Teresa Celia Meschiati, Actor No. 4279

D'Andrea Mohr – *Memoria Debida*, 1999

10

Subversion in the education system (Getting to know our enemy)

The dictatorship placed special emphasis on education. Not on improving it, but as an object of control. In 1977 the Ministry of Culture and Education published an 80-page document titled *Subversión en el ámbito educativo (Conozcamos a nuestro enemigo)* [Subversion in the education system (Getting to know our enemy)], signed by Juan José Catalán, Minister at the time.

In the introduction, the document warned that 'the weakness of a single generation of Argentinians would suffice to ensure that the common destiny linking them, passed down from their elders, is transformed into an unhappy failure', and describes schoolteachers as 'guardians of our ideological sovereignty'. In this way the schoolroom became another imaginary battlefield of the dictatorship.

The document, the distribution of which was compulsory, contained four chapters. The first chapter detailed the 'methods' used by the forces of subversion to achieve Marxist 'infiltration'. It contains some revealing concepts. 'To achieve the subversion of individuals, through the stages previously described, Marxism uses the following procedures: (...) Destruction of the traditional concept of the family, (through divorce, cohabitation, etc.), replacing it with another that serves the political needs of the party. (...) Separation of the person from their religion. To achieve this objective, an atheist scientific action is carried out, the religious organisation is infiltrated, it is discredited and diverted on to an undesirable course. In this way, the individual, on account of his revolutionary spirit, is gradually distanced from his religion,' (pp. 20–21).

It is perhaps in Chapter III that one can see most clearly the mental imbalance of the dictatorship. It is worth remembering that the military regime banned 'modern mathematics' and also *The Little Prince*, by Saint Exupéry, because of their subversive nature.

'CHAPTER III: SPECIFIC STRATEGIES PURSUED BY THE FORCES OF SUBVERSION IN THE EDUCATION SYSTEM
3) Pre-school and primary levels
   a Subversive actions take place through ideologically captive teachers who influence the minds of their young pupils by encouraging the development of rebellious ideas or conduct, which prepare them for

the actions that will be applied at higher levels.

b Communication takes place in a direct manner, through informal conversations and through the reading and commentary of tendentious stories, used for that purpose. In this respect there has been a notorious Marxist offensive in the area of children's literature. (…)

c The ideological assault intensifies as the children get older during their final years in primary school, and is designed to modify the traditional scale of values (family, religion, nationality, tradition, etc.) (…)

d Up until now there have been no organisations carrying out training or agitation.'

(pp. 48, 49)

For its part, the text explained that there were two types of teachers who collaborated with the unpatriotic, Marxist, Leninist, atheist, etc. forces of subversion. In the first place, those who took advantage of the limitless freedom enjoyed under the dictatorship to introduce messages of Soviet origin. The second type of Marxist collaborator, no less dangerous, was the lazy teacher. The teacher who, 'attracted by the easy option', did not carefully check school texts, and thus allowed through the subliminal messages sent from Moscow.

When the Soviet Union invaded Afghanistan, the government of US President Jimmy Carter decreed a cereal boycott against the USSR. At the time Argentina was one of the principal providers of grain to the Soviet bloc, for which reason it decided not to comply with the measure.

In August 1979 a grateful Soviet military delegation arrived in Buenos Aires. The lieutenant general heading the delegation, Ivan Jacovich Braiko, received the gold medal from the General Staff of the Army. The mission was fêted in the state rooms of the Libertador building and the medal was presented by General Videla.

The fight against Marxism that the Armed Forces used to support their actions was no more than an excuse to justify hunting down the opposition.

SANTIAGO DEL VALLE

Santiago was born in Buenos Aires in 1975 and has an older sister. His mother was called Marta Pites and his father Miguel Andrés del Valle. Miguel was a schoolteacher, Marta was studying sociology and working at a photographic shop. When they were kidnapped Miguel was 27 and Marta 24.

When they took my parents away in May 1976, I was 8 months old. Over the years I found out that it had happened at my maternal grandmother's house, she's the one who brought me up till she died three years ago.

I know that they had raided a house owned by my other grand-mother in Flores. We used to live next door. In fact, they raided both houses at 2 pm.

When I started at primary school I already knew that they had been murdered, and I also knew that there were desaparecidos. I used to like fantasising that they were disappeared, that maybe there had been a mistake, that it wasn't their bodies.

Military justice

On 31 March 1976 General Cesário Angel Cardozo became Chief of the Federal Police. On 18 June the same year he died when a bomb exploded under his bed. The press immediately printed the story that the bomb had been placed by a young woman, Ana María González, a Montonero militant and co-student of Cardozo's daughter. Scores of people were murdered in revenge for the attack, among them Santiago's parents, who had been kidnapped four months earlier.

A YOUNG WOMAN KILLED GENERAL CARDOZO

La Nación – 19 June 1976

MURDER OF CHIEF OF POLICE GENERAL CARDOZO SOLVED
'The murder was committed by a young woman of 18 who is now on the run...'

La Prensa – 19 June 1976

When they killed Cardozo, the dead bodies of my parents appeared together with those of other people, and a banner spray-painted with the words 'we belonged to the ERP,* we were murdered for killing General Cardozo.'

Every night

My sister, my grandmother and I used to sleep together in a double bed and I remember that every night my sister would ask,

'What happened to mummy and daddy?' Every night.

At first my grandmother told us that they had died in a car accident. That story didn't last long, just until I was five. I remember that my sister used to ask every day, every day…I've been told – I don't remember myself – that my sister used to ask:

'What happened to my parents?' and I'd say:

'Yes, yes, what happened?'

When we were in bed one night she gave us the general details; she used the word 'war' – which I later questioned – and told us that the military had killed them. And my sister stopped asking.

The accident story had been perfect – an accident could have happened to anyone, but my sister used to ask every day. A psychologist would have had a field day.

'What kind of war is this in which there are no documents relating to the different operations carried out, in which there are no battle lines, no records of one's own or of the enemy's losses, no casualty lists; in which no prisoners are taken in battle and in which no one has any idea of what units have taken part? (…) Either there was no war, as I see it, and what we have here is a case of common criminal behaviour, or there was one and what we have are war criminals.'

Attorney Julio Strassera – *Juicio a las Juntas*

Not mum, just looks like her

I started calling my aunt, my mum's sister, 'mum' when I burnt my leg. That didn't last long – another one for the psychologist. I was six. We were doing up the kitchen and cooking sausages on a camper stove in the living room. I fell, knocked over the stove with my back and burnt my leg. I was kept in the Burns Hospital for a month and a half. My aunt stayed with me every night. When I was 18 I began to

---

* *Ejercito Revolucionario del Pueblo*, the People's Revolutionary Army (see Glossary entry for the *Partido Revolucionario de los Trabajadores*).

call my grandmother 'vieja',* like I'd call her Gran or 'la vieja', but never 'mi vieja'.

All soldiers…

We moved to Morón. We were baptised there with Farinello. My grandmother sent us to a private, parish school…priests. My sister started in the second year and I started in first. I was five or six and I remember that one day a kid – I can't remember the argument we were having – called me 'a shitty orphan'. Everyone knew. We fought and I started bawling my eyes out and it caused a huge commotion at the school. The kid's parents came to the school, not because of the fight, but because of what he'd said to me. The kid's father was in the army. His argument was that I'd called his father a son of a bitch, which was partially true – when I was little I used to say that all soldiers were sons of bitches – and he got mad at me because his father was in the army.

Being original

I remember that my grandmother and aunt used to take us to all the marches, even those dodgy ones at the height of the dictatorship. In my first year, after the return to democracy, we were asked who wanted to take part in the students' union. I put my name down with a friend from my class, we were just young kids. We were campaigning for a student travel pass. I remember that I used to get out of school at midday and one day I got home at six in the evening because we'd gone to a sit-down protest. We'd blocked the avenue to protest about the travel pass, nothing had happened, but my grandmother had a complete fit.

'I don't want to go through the same thing again (…) I can't take it again…'

I remember that I told her that ever since they took my parents away she had taken me to every fucking march there was 'and now I'm thirteen, THIRTEEN! What do you mean you won't let me?!'

I remember saying to her in that exchange, more to be deliberately morbid than anything else, 'If they ever come for me, I want it to be for something *I* did, not for what my parents did.'

Because there was that idea that we were all 'marked'.

After the march, when my grandmother told me that she didn't want me going to the students' union any more, I remember seeing

---

* 'Viejo' and 'vieja' are often used to refer to parents in Argentina.

two kids, Daniel and 'el Pollo', they were both important figures in the students' movement. I remember that at the time, for kids in the first year, sixth formers seemed...so grown up and sorted! I remember that I didn't go to a couple of meetings and Daniel came up to me in the school yard and asked what had happened. I told him the whole saga: that I wasn't going because of my grandmother, that my parents, and all the rest – my grandmother's strongest argument – and he told me that his father was disappeared. If Daniel was a leader, after that I began to dream.

The day of La Noche de los Lápices

I carried on going to the union, but in secret. I went 'underground' when I was 13. I remember clearly that my grandmother knew. At first I hid it from her, but then I said, 'Ok, that's enough. I'm 13, too old to have her on my case!'

I remember the first march that I went to as an 'activist'. We went with the students' union. It was 1989. The march was huge, just huge. We left school, where we'd been painting a banner. We met up with kids from another school in Flores and went to the train station. Obviously we didn't buy tickets. I remember seeing the older kids – the sixth formers – jumping over the turnstiles, as we ducked under them [laughing] 'Hey, how cool, he jumped over the turnstile!'

We got off in Caballito. I'm not part of the seventies generation, but from the eighties: I remember that march, I see the marches today and they make me want to cry. I was amazed by how many people there were. I remember being in the march and my aunt came along, one of my mother's sisters. She went to the demonstration knowing I'd be there, and looked for where my school was to come and say hello, she walked with me for a block, chatting. I just wanted her to leave!

When I was 14 I started going to my sister's school. Obviously the first thing I do is get involved in the students' union. My sister, who was in the year above me, also got involved. My grandmother accepted it, because my sister was going too. If my sister was there to keep an eye on me, then everything was under control. My sister ended up as union secretary, that is, she was president of one of the school shifts.

Hope

I lost all hope when I found the photos of their bodies in a drawer. I was 14, rummaging around on my own, looking for something or other and I found them all. I had already seen the photo, but had never paid much attention to it: the photo of my dad's body, unrecognisable, burnt, you can't see anything, it's practically a skeleton. There were several photos of my dad and my mum, who is more recognisable. They hadn't burnt her body. That's when I lost it completely. I think it was one of the worst moments of my life. I remember finding the photos and immediately realising what they were. Looking at them one after another, there were about ten photos in all. I felt faint, recoiled and started crying. I still can't say what I was looking for, it's like I was rooting around, not really looking for anything in particular. I was looking for something in my grandmother's chest of drawers.

Santiago sometimes visits the Recoleta cemetery, where his parents are buried. He repeated the third year in secondary school and dropped out in the fourth year. At 17 he started to work. A short time ago his grandmother died. Santiago remembers her as the woman he most loved, and will love the most, in the world.

At present he lives alone and works entering information on computer databases. Sometimes he goes to the football, and on Fridays and Saturdays he goes out dancing. This year he decided to finish secondary school so he can start studying to be a physics and maths teacher.

11

National symbols

TUCUMAN

'People who do not respect the symbols of the nation will be sanctioned.

Law 4605, passed and enacted by the provincial government, determined that those students who refuse to pay homage to the symbols of the Fatherland and our national heroes, or who refuse to sing the patriotic songs, will be expelled from educational establishments in Tucumán.

The measure will be in force for as long as the students continue to adopt such attitudes and they are banned from enrolling in the future so long as they maintain this attitude. Moreover, those employees of the provincial civil service who adopt in public the stance described above, will be sacked. This penalty will also apply to the workers and employees of national level institutions and offices based within the provincial territory.'

La Voz del Interior (Córdoba) – 26 November 1976

THE ARCHBISHOP OF SAN JUAN SENDS A MESSAGE OUT TO YOUNG PEOPLE

'The Archbishop of San Juan de Cuyo, Monsignor Dr Ildefonso María Sansierra, sent out a message to all young people. "The fatherland is in danger," he warned, "when the citizen loses his feeling for the symbols of the nation".'

La Gaceta (Tucumán) – 5 December 1976

Barracks school

CIRCULAR 60 OF THE NATIONAL BOARD OF MIDDLE AND SECONDARY SCHOOL EDUCATION – May 1976 – No 118
Bans

1) *Regarding personal appearance*:

(…) Long hair below the shirt collar in boys and worn loose in girls. (…) Beards in boys and excessive make-up in girls. (…) Clothes that do not comply with the guidelines given by the school authorities or by higher authorities. (…) Lack of respect and good manners.

(...) The offences detailed above are those that occur most commonly and the list obviously does not exclude others that could equally deserve sanctioning.

MINISTERIAL RESOLUTION NO. 1635/78
Buenos Aires, 3 November 1978
APPENDIX I: RULES ON THE TREATMENT AND USE OF THE
NATIONAL SYMBOLS
'The education system has been infiltrated and affected by the preaching and action of harmful ideological tendencies, whose goal is progressively to destroy the principles and values that sustain and define the Argentine identity (…) the lack of respect or reverence for the National Symbols in their different forms and degrees of importance, implies an attack on the very essence of the Argentine identity (…) The practice of teaching should consist of permanent patriotic preaching and training. The teacher must be the model of patriotism for the student body and demand from the latter at all times a like response (…).'

THE NATIONAL ANTHEM
Treatment and usage
'The National Anthem will only be sung at those events at which the National Flag is raised. (…) All those present will stand. The pupils will stand to attention. All those present will applaud when it is over, except the standard bearer and his escorts.'

Major General Albano E. Harguindeguy, Minister of the Interior and acting
Minister for Culture and Education, November 1978

MATIAS FACUNDO MORENO

Matías, known as 'el Gitano', was born in La Plata in 1975. He's the son of Susana Mable and Carlos Alberto Moreno.

I was born in La Plata, but went to live in Olavarría when I was a few months old, because that's where my dad was from. He'd gone to study in La Plata, where he met my mum. They got married and set up home together. I have a younger brother called Martín Alberto. When they took my dad away my mum was pregnant, so he never knew him.

My dad was a labour lawyer. He used to work as a lorry driver with my grandfather, then he won a local government scholarship to go and study and he got his degree in three and a half years. Once he'd graduated he returned to Olavarría to work as a lawyer.

He started being very active in labour unions with the mineworkers, basically at Amalita Fortabat's Loma Negra factory. He was the labour lawyer of AOMA, the Argentinian Mineworkers' Association. He also founded the Newspaper Sellers' Union – he'd worked as a newspaper seller – and the Caretakers' Union, because my grandmother, his mother, had been a caretaker.

He came from a very humble background, and had a clear vocation and political identity. My grandmother was a school caretaker and my grandfather used to deliver potatoes. So he grew up in the modest surroundings of a working-class family. As a student, when he came home for the holidays he'd help my grandfather with his deliveries.

Memories

I have two memories of my dad. One when he's chasing me. He used to get home late from work and call out 'Mati, Mati, Mati!' and he used to chase me and I'd hide behind a curtain. I could see him through the curtain, but he used to pretend he couldn't find me, go looking around the house and I'd imagine I had fooled him...

Another strong image I have is of sitting on his lap at the desk in his lawyer's office and seeing a stream of people coming in and out, dressed in overalls, their hands stained and calloused. A lot of workers, a steady stream of them. There was a mess of papers. The door was opposite me and people came in and out, in and out…they brought him papers and talked to him.

Cravings

'I call on God our Father for happiness to accompany the whole large military family in the two institutions during 1977 and for peace and love to reign in our Republic.'

Declarations by Videla
La Gaceta (Tucumán) – 31 December 1976

They took him from the house on 29 April 1976. We were renting a very small house. Downstairs he had his lawyer's office and upstairs was the bedsit.

My mother was pregnant with my brother. She was a teacher in a rural school in the area surrounding Olavarría. She asked my dad to let them know that she was feeling unwell and to take a medical certificate to the school to excuse her absence. She had difficult pregnancies.

My dad went in the car to the School Board offices. My mum always used to ask him to bring her a chocolate bar – I can't remember what it was called – a typical pregnancy craving. When he got back he parked his Falcon in the car park at a petrol station. Three cars cut him off, my dad was burly man, there was a struggle, a fight, they bundled him into an orange Renault 12 and took him away. The neighbours saw this happening and a passing cyclist was later tortured for the declarations he made: he saw everything, went to the police and three days later they took him away and beat the shit out of him.

My dad's case is one of the 30 being used in the appeal for the extradition of Suarez Mason. There was incontrovertible evidence that the person who had issued the order for my dad's capture and arrest was Guillermo Suarez Mason.

My mother heard nothing. Obviously, if she had heard something we wouldn't be here to tell the tale and I might be in the hands of other people. My dad had left at 7 pm. It was 1 am and he wasn't back. My mum set out to look for him in the neighbourhood, it was a rainy day and the first thing she sees as she crosses the street is the bar of chocolate in the drainpipe. She went to the corner shop, asked and they told her, 'Yes, he came to buy a bar of chocolate…' The car was parked in the petrol station.

The trigger

They took him away because he won a case against the Loma Negra company for lead poisoning. As a result of that victory the working day was reduced. They didn't take him to the police station or detention centre in Olavarría, for fear that the workers might come to find him. They took him to Tandil, a farmhouse lent to them by Méndez to use as a clandestine detention centre, where they killed him. They took him away a week after he came out of the courthouse having won the case, he'd already received threats…That case sparked it all off.

Three months before my dad was disappeared, they had arrested another lawyer in Olavarría, whom they'd released after a month. He always used to point to this as an example:

'When all's said and done, if they take me away, they'll ask me a few things and then let me go.' He was never fully aware of the magnitude of what was happening. The body was handed in at the police station and my mother went to identify it.

To La Plata

We returned to La Plata because my mum had lost her job, she's been thrown out of a lot of schools after what happened to my dad. The situation was really difficult, we couldn't stay in Olavarría any longer. We didn't have enough money to live somewhere else, so we went back to my grandmother's – my mum's mother. We lived there for a while until my mum could buy herself a flat. The three of us moved to this small flat on 16th Street.

Cause and effect

I also have a clear memory of the Malvinas/Falklands War. I was at school in City Bell. I used to ask my mum 'how is it going', and 'are we winning or losing?' and my mum used to try to answer me as politely as possible:

'Look, with this war, even if we win, we lose. It's a ridiculous war. They're sending kids to be killed.'

And I was like,

'No, we have to win, we have to win because the Malvinas…' And at one point she said to me:

'No, we've already lost the Malvinas, we lost them a long time ago.'

And I was completely downcast!

I remember that in 1983 I was at one of my cousin's playing

football on election day. I remember all the social upheaval at the time, the hope, everything that people had been bottling up inside …

Why does only your mother come?

In my first years at primary school there was the big deal of papers 'to be signed by your father, mother or guardian'. And at the parents' evenings:

'Why does just your mother come?'

I used to say that my dad had died in an accident. By the time I was ten or 11 I more or less knew what had happened to him. I think that in 1989 or 1990, during one of the national censuses they took – I remember clearly that we had to stay at home – my mum gave me all the papers from my dad's case, which was like 200 pages, and said,

'This is what happened to your father.'

I was 13 or 14. I was lying on the bed watching TV, I turned off the telly and remember that I first read the parts that weren't very interesting. Then I began to read the detailed eyewitness accounts.

Secondary school

I began my activism as a Peronist in the Secondary Students' Union (Unión de Estudiantes Secundarios, UES) before I found out that my dad was a Peronist, before I found out that he had very strongly held ideals, had been active in the left-wing Peronist movement and had been a leader in the Peronist Youth. When I found all that out I felt very close to my dad in terms of our beliefs. I began to read the books my dad had read, from John William Cook to Arturo Jauretche…

I was 13 when I started at secondary school in 1989 at Comprehensive School No.3 in La Plata. It was a school where there was a lot of political activity, it was very broadminded in that sense. There were politically committed teachers who used to tell us about when the military came into the classrooms to drag kids out by the hair; they used to take them out to threaten them, beat them up and leave them lying there to instil terror in the rest. Comprehensive No.3 had three desaparecidos from La Noche de los Lápices.

CHAPTER IV: BUILDING THE FUTURE

'…It is in the education system that clear and energetic action must be taken, to root out subversion, showing the students the false nature of the concepts and doctrines that were instilled in them to a greater or lesser degree over so many years. The alternative approach requires that we remain firm in our unending search for national identity and the relentless struggle to consolidate awareness of that identity.'

Subversion in the education system (Getting to know our enemy)
Ministry of Education and Culture – Buenos Aires 1977

The students' union is called after Horacio Ungaro, who was one of those kidnapped in La Noche de los Lápices. He was 15 when they took him. Panchito López Muntaner was 14 when they took him from his home. Every 16 September I return to give a talk. I have a good relationship with the board and the teachers. I'm very surprised by the fact that ten years ago this school was very politicised, there were seven lists of candidates presented for the student elections and today there's just one.

I am very moved talking to the families of the desaparecidos from La Noche de los Lápices. I see them frequently in commemorative acts and also on the street. I have a great respect for their stories. They weren't just taken away because they were demanding the student travel pass, they were all committed activists.

'The true and decisive struggle against subversion will take place in the hearts and minds of our students and youngsters. The Argentine Nation must awaken in its youth the hope for dignity, progress and the future.'

Juan José Catalán, Education Minister
La Razón – 1 April 1978

Hey, girl

When I was still a kid in secondary school it used to happen quite a lot:

'No, it's just that my parents…you're an activist and they're afraid…'

Then I'd go and persuade them that there was nothing to be afraid of and I'd really convince them! But I used to manage it not by getting all worked up or acting arrogantly or taking a hard line and confronting them. It was the fear instilled in them by the dictatorship. I never hid my background and was always active, both in human rights and other organisations. I was involved in a lot of grassroots activism.

I'd get to know a girl and sooner or later this issue would crop up. They'd say to her, 'No, look, he's a strange kid, he's involved in all this, you need to find someone who you've got things in common with…'

The girl would want to be with me and we'd have variations on this conversation.

91

'Okay, I'll go and talk to your folks.'

'No, no I don't want you getting mixed up in this.'

'It's ok, come on, I don't mind talking to anyone, it's not a problem.'

Then there'd be the first invitation to supper with her parents (…) I'm 24 now, but I always used to crap myself in those situations. [He laughs]. But I always had good relationships with my in-laws, even the most hard-hearted used to end up caring about me.

'Ok, why are you afraid? I'm active…' I used to tell them. After a glass of wine we'd end up the best of friends.

Argentinian schools

A short time ago I went to a secondary school to give a talk to all the classes. They asked a lot of very interesting questions and one boy, in all innocence, asked me:

'And why didn't you children go out and fight when they took your parents away?'

'Well, the thing is, we were very young.'

That kind of question, nothing nasty. The history books stop in 1976 and then skip to 1983. All the history textbooks, if they mention the dictatorship it is only very superficially. The 'de facto government', the 'Proceso', they say; they don't mention any 'dictatorship' or 'dictator' (…) Videla isn't called a former dictator; neither are Aramburu, Onganía or Lanusse. They're called former presidents…

The quince jelly pie

I was always had an idyllic relationship with my dad's family because my grandmother was from a very modest background but despite that, every week she used to send us a parcel with chocolates and things. My dad loved my grandmother.

My mum tells me the story of once when my grandmother sent a quince jelly pie in a parcel when my dad was a student and he invited my mum to Pereira Park to eat it. So they go to the park and have some *mates*. My mum leaves the cake on the ground next to a tree and when they decide to eat it they see that it's covered in ants. My dad was furious! It was a slight…

'How could you let the ants eat my mum's cake?'

And they didn't talk to each other for about two months.

He was dismayed:

'How could I have given the cake to this woman? My mum's quince jelly pie!'

I see him in other places

I used to go to the cemetery, with my mum or my grandmother. I don't go any more or I go very infrequently. It doesn't help or hurt me to go. I don't think my dad's there. That's where his body is, but I see my dad in other places.

He was loved and well known in the town of Olavarría. If you think that there were three lawyers, he was the fourth lawyer in Olavarría. The union leaders keep his memory alive. The union movement was very affected by my dad's death, the unionists themselves told me: 'el negro Moreno's dead, if they can take him, anything can happen'. After my dad's death a lot of those people stopped their activism. They realised what was really going on in the country: they had taken this man away and killed him.

Today Matías teaches at the Social Work Department, as an assistant lecturer, and he also works in the Provincial Council for Minors in La Plata.

When I finished secondary school I started out studying law. Quite apart from the fact that my dad was a lawyer, I've always been interested in labour law. Then I studied history for a year and then switched to sociology; I'm now in my third year. I'm still studying law, but on an optional basis, so I'm also in the third year of my law degree.

I get up around eight, have a few *mates* and head straight off to work, which is five blocks from where I live. I work till 4 pm and then I go to the university. On one day I teach a night class in Social Work. For a long time I played football, but I had to give it up because of an injury and because of a life decision that I took. I don't know whether I was a good player, but I did all right.

They call me Gitano both because of my looks and because of my outlook on life. My hair's short now, but I always wore it long. I live alone and have a girlfriend who comes round a lot. I used to play bass in a group called Talarga Rock'n Roll with my brother who plays the drums. We used to go to Mar del Plata and play on the waterfront, to make some money to pay for the holidays. I tried to do all the things I liked. That's another reason why they call me Gitano.

12 ✳✳✳✳

Bombardment in Tucumán

Tucumán is a small province in the north-west of Argentina. Historically it was devoted to sugar production, and its society is characterised by great social inequalities, extreme poverty and terrible working conditions.

In the 1960s and 1970s, revolutionary organisations were very active in Tucumán and it was also there that, in 1975, the army carried out Operation Independence, a dress rehearsal for the coming military dictatorship.

By the end of 1975 army reports claim that the active armed groups had been completely dismantled. However, the dictatorship was to exercise a brutal repression in the province and there was no let-up in the regime's propaganda.

11 June

'Mariano Grondona, a lawyer and columnist for various newspapers and magazines, came to Tucumán at the invitation of the Public Information Secretariat, which has organised a series of conferences. During his visit the well-known commentator stopped by to greet the governor, General Domingo Antonio Bussi (…)'

La Gaceta – 11 June 1977

12 June

MARIANO GRONDONA SPEAKS ON THE SUBJECT OF INTERNATIONAL POLITICS

'The countries that, like Argentina,' he added afterwards, 'have taken up arms to fight subversion and are now trying gradually and carefully to build a new democracy, are destined to be misunderstood at the international level until they can demonstrate in practice the beneficial nature of their proposal. It is inevitable,' he claimed. 'The thing is that we represent a new and original model, one that breaks with conventional thinking. How is it that a country can be fighting for human rights,' he asked, 'and in that battle leave aside conventional methods of combating crime? They do not understand. How is it that a country can abandon an apparently democratic path in order to build a true democracy? They do not understand this either. That is the price of originality,' he concluded.

THE GOVERNOR EXTOLLED TRUTH AND FREEDOM
'At the dinner in honour of journalism held in the town of Teniente Berdina, Governor General Antonio Domingo Bussi addressed the guests. On either side of the governor were Dr Mariano Grondona and the editor-in-chief of *La Gaceta*, Mr Eduardo García Hamilton. (…)

During the dessert course the governor addressed a few words to the guests. "We Argentinians are living the hour of truth, and in this state of mind we feel the need to speak sincerely. For this reason, following an inner instinct, it behoves me to express to you journalists our recognition of the support you have given, having received on occasion the rather harsh truth of your comments and opinions, which we have accepted and welcomed, because the truth, however harsh it be, is more important than a well-meaning lie, however well meaning it might be." He went on to say that truth and freedom are the "pillars of our hours and our lives" and that with them "we shall build the Argentina that we yearn for".'

La Gaceta – 12 June 1977

13 June

CORPUS CHRISTI PROCESSION
'Monsignor Conrero appealed to the example of the good Samaritan as a remedy for the evils that are afflicting society. (…) A large crowd attended the ceremonies of public worship to mark the Feast of Corpus Christi, which were moved from Thursday to Sunday and were staged in the Plaza Independencia. A stage was constructed on the pavement in front of the cathedral, (…) in front of which were positioned the standard bearers from the primary and secondary schools and the provincial authorities, presided over by the governor and commander of the Fifth Brigade, General Antonio D. Bussi, the presidents of the Supreme Court of Justice, doctor Horacio Poviña and of the Federal Appeals Court, Dr Eduardo L. Vallejos.'

La Gaceta – 13 June 1977

17 June

THE CHAMBER OF STATE BUILDING CONTRACTORS WELCOMES
His Excellency, the President of the Argentine Nation,
Lieutenant General JORGE RAFAEL VIDELA
During his Visit to Tucumán
[The list of companies takes up a whole page.]

La Gaceta – 17 June 1977

19 June – Independent Journalism

'The Head of State, Lieutenant General Jorge Rafael Videla, pressed the buttons on the electronic control panel that start up the modern printing presses of our newspaper, on the occasion of the special edition published yesterday, in the presence of the governor, General Bussi, the editor-in-chief, Eduardo García Hamilton, and the president of Papel del Tucumán SA, Felix Moscarelli.

AN HONOURABLE PRESENCE
'The visit by the president of the Nation, Lieutenant General Jorge Rafael Videla, to the printing rooms of La Gaceta constitutes an extremely important honour for us. For this reason, 19 June 1977 will remain as one of the memorable dates in the history of this newspaper.'

La Gaceta – 19 June 1977

DAFNE ZAMUDIO

Dafne was born in Chaco in 1970. She's the second of four siblings, the daughter of Carlos Alberto and María Cristina. Carlos was a private tutor and studied economics.

> When he was arrested they took us to the Investigation Department to see him. It was where he was being detained, in the Criminal Investigation Department. They showed us into a small room where we waited. It wasn't really a visit because we were not allowed to talk to him, just see him. He came in limping, he was all beaten up, haggard, in a bad way. It wasn't my dad...

A few days later Dafne's mother had some terrible news for her children...

> I remember she called us all into the room and told us that my dad had died. That he'd died, that's all...
> When people used to dig deeper I used to repeat what we'd been told: that he died of sorrow because he couldn't be with us. A year earlier he'd had to flee. He went into hiding, for a time around here, then he went to [the neighbouring province of] Misiones.

Margarita Belén

On the morning of 13 December 1976 a military squad arrived at the prison governor's office with a transfer order for a group of prisoners. The destination indicated on the transfer papers was a prison in Formosa, which is the first contradiction in the case, since the prison in Resistencia is one of the securest in the country. The group of prisoners, including Dafne's father, was handed over to the squad, as is clearly stated in the records and written confirmation of the transfer order. En route the prisoners were made to get out of the vehicle and were shot. Two days earlier, the authorities had flown over the area where the executions were to take place: Margarita Belén, a small town in Chaco alongside Highway 11. This information is contained in the flight logbooks of the Chaco Government House and Resistencia Airport. The official version explained what had happened by spinning a tale of a supposed ambush by subversives who tried to free the prisoners. In the clash only the prisoners being transferred died. The 'subversives' who had supposedly intercepted them suffered no losses or casualties; neither did the police or army personnel suffer a scratch.

They took their time giving us his body because they said that after the clash they had escaped. Then they told us that they'd captured him in Misiones, and that in Misiones he'd died in another clash (…) My mum knew that he'd died there, it was clearly all a farce. He could scarcely walk, how was he going to run away!

In March 1977 in his Open Letter to the Military Junta, journalist Rodolfo Walsh denounced the murder of prisoners in sham clashes: 'The denial of this Junta to publish the names of the prisoners amounts to a cover-up of the systematic execution of hostages in deserted places and in the early hours of the morning, under the excuse of invented clashes and imaginary escape attempts.' Rodolfo Walsh died resisting the group of men who tried to kidnap him the day he posted his letter.

The truth came out when my mum got involved in Familiares.* In fact, what happened was that they took him out of the Investigation Department, from the prison governor's office, and put him in a lorry because supposedly they were going to transfer him to Formosa. That's what they said. Halfway there they shot them.

MESSAGE FROM THE GOVERNOR OF CHACO
Democracy must be conquered
'The governor of this province, retired General Antonio Facundo Serrano claimed that "an authentic agrarian revolution has taken place in Chaco, without the need for organising sterile and destructive protest movements or sabotaging the roads. (…) Our objective is also to maintain a high level of security, burying all manifestations of terrorist crime and violence. No more violence, terrorism and murder. To achieve this goal the actions of the Armed Forces, security and police forces are being carefully coordinated and on the alert. We must prepare ourselves to conquer democracy and we need to train leaders".'

Tiempo de Córdoba – 4 June 1978

We were taken to an aunt's house because our house was surrounded by the police. They gave us two death certificates. They told my grandmother that the body was in Misiones, so she had to take the coffin and go and fetch it. Afterwards, when it all came out, they told

---

* Lit. Relatives, Familiares is one of the main human rights groups in Argentina. Their full name is: Relatives of the Disappeared and Detained for Political Reasons.

her that it had been a mistake. That's why we have two death certificates. The story goes that they were ambushed in an escape attempt and that there was a shoot out. They mounted this whole elaborate operation, way too elaborate for this region, where nothing was going on. From early in the morning the highway was blocked off. There are also tales of people who saw the bodies on the road – farm workers and people living in the area. The bodies strewn on the ground and the squaddies eating a barbecue (…) because after killing them they had a barbecue next to the bodies. It just happened to be the birthday of one of the soldiers (…) When they put together the Margarita case all the witnesses were tracked down.

'I was detained in an operation on 29 April 1976 together with my eight-month-old son in the city of Resistencia. The personnel who carried out the kidnapping were from the Chaco Criminal Investigation Department. I was immediately taken to that Department, a few metres from the Government House. (…) There I was stripped naked and they tortured me with an electric cattle prod and beatings during 48 hours in the presence of my son. (…) I was also raped and hit on the soles of my feet with a hammer for three hours. On the sixth day they took me to the recovery cell, where I was visited, interrogated and threatened by Colonel Larrateguy, Chief of the Chaco First Regiment. I remained in detention there together with several prisoners who were shot on 13 December in Margarita Belén.'

G. de V., File No. 3102 – Conadep

They weaved a whole fantastic tale about what had happened, I assume so as not to hurt us and so that we could live as normally as possible (…)

Once I collected a lot of his things: photos, jackets and ties, medals from when he played basketball, I can't remember what else. There was an empty cupboard and I put his photos there, like it was an altar. All that was missing was the lit candle…

Every year there are commemorative acts; every time you go to an act or a homage, it's like a new funeral, it's horrible. Just recently I began to see him as a person who also made mistakes, no as a god… which he was for me.

When my dad's friends decide to tell me more about him – and don't make out he was perfect – it makes me see him more as a real person.

Dafne has four more exams to pass before graduating as a nursery school teacher. She currently works in Resistencia where she lives with her partner.

13 ✳✳✳✳

✳
✳
✳
✳

Christian, Western… (and white)

'The Minister of the Interior, General Albano Harguindeguy, declared that it was necessary to attract immigrants of European origin, so long as we hope to remain one of the three countries with the highest proportions of white population in the world.'

Tribuna de la República magazine – October 1978

THREE JEWS

'The current crisis of humanity owes itself to three men. Towards the end of the nineteenth century Marx published three volumes of *Capital* and thus cast doubt on the absolute right to private property; towards the beginning of the twentieth century the inner intimacy of the human being was attacked by Freud, in his book *The Interpretation of Dreams*; and as if this were not enough to undermine society's system of positive values, in 1905 Einstein reveals his theory of relativity, in which he casts doubt on the static and dead structure of matter.'

Admiral Emilio Eduardo Massera
La Opinión – 25 November 1977

JIMENA VICARIO

Jimena was born in Rosario, in May 1976. From when she was little she knew that she was adopted. Susana, her adoptive mother, was unmarried and worked as a haematologist at the Pedro de Elizalde Hospital in Buenos Aires.

I remember the moment when I asked how she had adopted me. I was three years old. I remember that she told me that you could put your name down on a list at the court and when babies appeared the court would call the first person on the list and they got the baby.

Jimena's parents were called Juan Carlos Vicario and Estella Maris Galichio. Juan Carlos was kidnapped in Rosario on 5 February 1977. On that same day Estella Maris was with Jimena in the capital applying for their passports. Both were kidnapped while carrying out the application in the Central Department of the Federal Police. Jimena was 9 months old.

I thought they'd gone to the South Pole because I had a story about a penguin that had problems because he didn't like the cold and so he'd gone to the Caribbean.

I had this idea that they couldn't take me with them; yes, they'd left me, but they hadn't abandoned me. They loved me.

A blood matter

In 1984 two elderly women knocked at the door of Jimena's house. Both were members of the Abuelas de Plaza de Mayo. They had received a report and were following it up. Susana wasn't in at the time.

I had already noticed that over the previous few months lawyers started turning up every day. I remember that Susana was on duty at the hospital and one night she called me to ask me to tell her the number of a lawyer from her address book, which she'd left at home. She had an older brother who more or less was in charge of things since their father died. I saw that the brother was coming round a lot, they used to shut themselves away in her room to talk and I realised that something was up.

One evening she sat me down in my room and said,
'The thing is this, you know you're adopted (…) and that there is

a woman who says she's your grandmother. You're going to go to court with a judge, they're going to call you to give you a blood test…'

I wasn't bothered, since she was a haematologist, so I'd seen transfusions all my life. At that age one doesn't think too deeply. One just lives life as it comes.

I asked who the family was, so she showed me a photo that had been published in the national daily *Clarín*, along with an interview with my grandmother, a photo of me when I was a baby and a photo of my parents. The photos in the newspaper were very dark and I said,

'No, that can't be me,' because it didn't look like me.

What's more, it looked like a boy. I can still see it, it was a passport photo, a horrible thing. A mugshot, do you know what I mean?

Introduction to psychology

They sent me to the state psychologist to have the situation fully explained to me. It was a dark place. You opened the door and there were cement block offices with wooden panelling.

The psychologist was called María Luz.

'Okay, do you understand what is happening?'

'Yes, of course I understand!' I say. 'I was adopted and now a family has turned up who say they're my relatives.'

Susana had never told me that I was her biological daughter, so I didn't find the situation I was in problematic. I knew that I was adopted, so I always had the idea that I had a family somewhere (…) Because I wasn't brought by a stork! A family could turn up at any point, so I wasn't particularly surprised when they did. She was going to explain about the blood tests to me.

'There's a blood test that can show whether you belong to that family or not.'

And I say, 'Okay, but what happens if it turns out it's not my family?'

She told me that the results of the blood test would take about a month to come through. 'Meanwhile you're going to go and live with your grandmother who you're testing with. If the results don't match, they'll do the same test with another grandmother.'

The thing is when I got home I asked,

'How many grandmothers are there?' and Susana said,

'I really don't know how many, but there are a lot.'

Then she showed me a photo in the newspaper of a march by the Abuelas that had taken place recently, and where you could see all of them with their placards and handkerchiefs. There were lots with handkerchiefs! And I thought that I'd have to live with each of these grandmothers in turn and have blood taken to test with each of them!

Of course, I said, 'Oh my god!' and that's when my problems started – thanks to the psychologists I developed new psychological problems.

Positive

Shortly afterwards they came to the house to take my blood. I didn't understand why. Later I found out that Susana didn't want to take me to the hospital, so the judge had to come to the house. I remember that the woman who came was so afraid (…) Afterwards my grandmother told me that seeing me made a great impression on the woman. I could see her hand shaking, so I wouldn't let her take blood. In the end Susana took the blood. She gave the woman the needle and that was that.

The lawyer rang and when she'd hung up she told me 'the test came out positive'. That's when the trial started, the visits, the problems. They posted a uniformed cop outside the house and a plainclothes one as an escort. Apparently the judge was afraid that my biological family would kidnap me or that the family that had me would try to take me out of the country.

I used to talk about Snoopy, Barbie, the Frutillitas picture cards. When I went to school the mothers of the other children were afraid because I was accompanied by a policeman. Half the other children's mothers wouldn't send them to my birthday party and didn't invite me to theirs because if I went they'd have to have a policeman in their house. And it's understandable, the parents didn't want a policeman in their house. I could understand that at the time, so I didn't even go.

The judge's ashtray

I had to go see the judge three times a week. The first time I went, he said, pointing to his desk,

'Imagine that you're this ashtray.'

So there's me, seven years old, saying,

'No, sir, I'm not an ashtray, I'm a person.'

'Okay, but just imagine.'

'No, sir, because I'm a person.'

So after half an hour of arguing, I say to him,

'All right. I'll imagine I'm the ashtray!'

Because by that time I was sick of the discussion.

'Carry on.'

'Imagine the situation is the following.' Which I already knew.

'One person says that the ashtray is hers and another person says it's hers and that's a problem.'

'No, that's not a problem,' I tell him. 'The person who has the receipt for the ashtray gets the ashtray.'

'Well, it's not that simple…'

'Yes, it is that simple because it's just an ashtray. And if you like we can drop it, break it and no one gets the ashtray, or we buy another ashtray exactly like this one and so we have two and the problem's solved.'

Besides the ashtray was really ugly! One of those ashtrays that the courts buy wholesale and put in all the courthouses, a round, glass ashtray, like you get in a cheap restaurant…

Off to Gran's

One day the youth social worker introduces me to my grandmother. They say, 'we're going to see your grandmother'. I get on the train and we go to Morón. When we arrive, my grandmother is sitting outside. I was in my school uniform, because afterwards I'd go on to school. As we were approaching they told me,

'That's your grandmother.'

When we got there she looked at me with a happy birthday face, so I went past, said, 'Hello, how are you?' and went on in.

Later they let her come in. My grandmother came in, didn't let me say anything and began to take out photo after photo after photo:

'This is your mother, this is your uncle, this is your dog…' and on and on. All the photos were making me dizzy and when I got home my head hurt so much that I said, 'I'm not going to school.'

I couldn't get a word in edgeways because she talked so much. She showed me the photos one after another so quickly and so nervously – my poor grandmother – that she'd show me a photo with fifteen people in it, and how was I meant to recognise my father and mother?

'And this is your mother at school,' and she'd pass me a photo of my mother aged seven with her whole class…

Reconstruction

After that there followed more visits. My grandmother used to take me out with Susana. She wanted to take me out on her own, but she used to want to take me to art galleries. And of course, I told her I didn't want to go. I was ten years old…I used to invite her to Ital Park, where she didn't want to go in. She'd refuse to go in – she couldn't possibly go on the rides! It was a generation problem.

In my case there was no crime because Susana had a legal adoption, signed by a judge. My adoption is the first legal adoption to be annulled in this country, which set a precedent for the Civil Code of the Nation. That means I'm now an article in the Civil Code. I'm in the Civil Code! [She laughs, putting on a snooty expression].

On 9 August 1991 Court 10 of the Morón Judicial District, Buenos Aires, annulled Jimena's birth certificate and adoption.

The judge's ashtray – part II

One day the judge decides that I have to go and live in Rosario, so they drag me out and take me there. I wanted my grandmother to move to Buenos Aires. All of a sudden, from one day to the next, I was taken to live with a family I didn't know, in a city I didn't know, where I had no friends, where I didn't know a single street. I didn't know where there was a shop, had no memory of a square, couldn't remember anything at all about the place. I felt like a fish out of water, a guinea pig on display, with everyone coming to see me. It was awful, I didn't want to see anyone at all, I used to shut myself in my room, but they'd come anyway.

During the legal proceedings there was ample evidence to show that Susana was aware of Jimena's origins. One of the case's witnesses, a co-student on a course that Susana did, declared that on one occasion Susana had told her that Jimena was 'the daughter of subversives'.

After I left other things came out. A denunciation by a neighbour who said that during the first few years there had been a policeman following me and Susana to see how we were getting on (…) She's done some terrible things to me. She doesn't love me like a mother, as she says she does, but sees me as a kind of trophy. Once she told my grandmother, 'I'll cut my hands off rather than hand her over to you', that's where the nickname Venus de Milo comes from. My uncle started calling her that and it stuck.

The grandmother

As time went by I came to realise everything she'd done to find me, everything she'd done and still does for me. I help my grandmother in Abuelas in Rosario because she's on her own. When there's a denunciation we go and check the register, so that they don't do a runner. I don't know if I like the work, but I owe a lot to Abuelas.

Thanks to Abuelas I'm where I am today. I recovered my identity, which is a human being's most valuable possession, because without a history there can be no future.

'What is being said about children being stolen is a fairytale, a barbaric fantasy.'
General Luciano Benjamín Menéndez
Página/12 magazine – November 1999

Jimena graduated in advertising in Rosario and settled in Buenos Aires to continue her studies. She doesn't have a set time that she gets up and never goes to bed before 2 am. Her boyfriend still lives in Rosario.

At weekends my boyfriend comes and we take the dog out, eat, watch TV, take the dog out, go for a walk, etc. I don't go to Rosario because I haven't got anyone to leave the dog with.

In the name of the father and the son...

I met a boy once who had found everything out, had done the tests, etc. One day I went to Abuelas and he was there and we start talking. He lived in Mar del Plata. When he told me his name, I couldn't place him, so then he said,

'Actually, I'm called such-and-such,' a name I did recognise from the Abuelas' *Librito Rosa* .* So then we started talking about names. He didn't want to change his name.

'My real name is Andrés, but I've been Martín all my life.'

'Yes,' I said, 'but just think that the only thing your parents left you is your name because they never got to choose a school for you, or a university, they couldn't choose your clothes. They never got to choose anything at all for you. But they did want to call you Andrés. How can you like the name given to you by the people who stole you and lied to you? The only inheritance your parents left you is your name and surname.'

And we left it at that.

A few months ago, talking with one of the girls, she told me that Andrés had just been by to do the papers to change his name. And that really means something to me. We talked for an hour and no one made him do it, but the experiences you recount can move other people. He took a year to realise that and he might have taken 20, it doesn't matter.

---

* Lit. Pink Book, a record kept by the Abuelas of all known facts relating to children stolen by the dictatorship.

14

The name of the rose

The banning of texts (and frequently the public burning of books and magazines) formed part of the plan for the 're-education' of Argentina. Mere possession of books banned by the dictatorship implied a high security risk. This is just one example of the circulars that were sent to universities, 'advising' a 'restricted' use of these texts.

RESOLUTION NO. 100: 13 SEPTEMBER 1976
HAVING SEEN: The inventory of this Faculty's library; and
CONSIDERING: That the Faculty library contains works that represent ideologies that are alien to our national identity, incompatible with a valid socio-political and educational project for our country; that the use of such works by the students constitutes a true indoctrination, expressly prohibited by article 7 of Law 21276:

THE ACTING DEAN OF THE FACULTY OF EDUCATION RESOLVES:
Article 1 – The works belonging to the Faculty library listed in Appendix I of the present Resolution will be marked RESERVED.
Article 2 – The works belonging to the Faculty library marked RESERVED will only be made available to Faculty Lecturers and will only be available for consultation on the library premises.
Article 3 – The works marked RESERVED will remain permanently in the Faculty library and their use – in accordance with the guidelines issued in the current Resolution – will be the sole responsibility of the Library staff.
Article 4 – No exceptions will be made to articles 2 and 3 of the current Resolution.
Signed: JULIO ALBERTO CUSCUETA
Acting Dean
Faculty of Education
[Appendix I lists scores of books, with their respective library class marks, including, among others, the following titles].
Ciencia y Política en América Latina – A.O. Herrera
Psicoanálisis y Dialéctica Materialista – J. Bleger
La Cultura de la Pobreza – C. Valentine

Nuevos Aportes a la Teoría del Conflicto Social – L. Coser
Las Venas Abiertas de América Latina – E. Galeano
Imperialismo Hoy – J. O'Connor y otros
Quiere el Pueblo Votar? – E. Ortega
Historia Económica de la Ganadería Argentina – H.C.E. Giberti
La Dominación de América Latina – J. Matos Mar
El Autoritarismo en la Escuela – A.Alberti, G. Bini, L. Del Cornó, G. Giannastoni
La Educación como Práctica de la Libertad – P. Freire
El Problema Educacional en la Patagonia – A. Igobone
Etc.

ERNESTO ANDREANI

Ernesto was born in Buenos Aires, in 1974. People call him Tico. His parents, Esteban Silvestre Andreani and Sara del Carmen Fagnani, were members of the FOETRA union (state telephone company). Four days before Tico's third birthday his father was abducted.

> I remember once I had dropped a fork and I refused to pick it up, and he made me. To put me to sleep he used to take me out in the car, he'd take me out for a drive.

Mock executions

> We were staying at my grandmother's in Morón and one night when neither my dad nor my mum were in, the military came. I have fragmented memories of what happened. My grandmother told me that the soldiers came in, she was bathing me, they took me out of the bath, put me on the table, from where you could see out to the patio, and then pretended to execute my grandfather.

COMMUNIQUÉ NO. 7
'The government of the Nation reminds the population that the necessary intervention of the Armed Forces has taken place on behalf of the whole country and not against specific social sectors. In the process of reorganisation that is just beginning and which has as its goal the prompt recovery of the country and the well being of all its inhabitants, it is essential that we can count on the collaboration of everyone.'

Junta of Commanders in Chief of the Armed Forces – 24 March 1976

Esteban was kidnapped in April 1977. In May Sara managed to flee to Brazil where a few days later she gave birth to her second son.

> I left with my grandmother. On our papers she appeared as my mother and I appeared as my uncle. My uncle, my mother's brother, is only a year and a half older than me.
> My mum arrived the next day using false papers. My uncle stayed behind with my grandfather. Then my grandmother went back for

him and they fled too, because my whole family was being persecuted.

We stayed in Brazil till September. From there we went to Sweden, to a refugee camp called Ronneby. Then we went to Lindängen, in Malmö. They are like ghettoes. A whole load of cultures all mixed up together in one neighbourhood. In our school there was such a mixture of children that no one bothered to ask each other's background, because everyone was a refugee from one country or another.

Screwed up

My mum always told me clearly, there was no need to ask. When I was a kid I used to say, 'I prefer him to be dead, rather than in their hands, suffering so much…'

I had a problem: when I was little I was very aggressive. I used to get aggressive when I was told what to do, when people laid hands on me, things like that. When I came here I was already screwed up. I didn't realise it. At school I used to fight with the teachers, throw chairs, stools, everything. If they tried to correct me or grabbed my arm I'd go mad. What my psychologist says is that this is a reaction from when the soldiers came to our house. They came three or four times. When I'm cornered I panic and don't know what to do.

At that age

I was four or six years old and the psychologist I was seeing used to make me play and draw. I used to draw everything in black. Everything black, black, black. I remember him asking,

'Why don't you use another colour? Draw me the Argentinian flag, the Swedish flag…' and I'd draw the outline in black.

'Draw a picture of Argentina.' And I'd draw soldiers everywhere.

Three years ago I was called up to do military service, and I didn't want to. I went to get a certificate from him and he started showing me different photos: of me drawing, playing in the sand (…) he had everything on file and that made a great impression on me. I said,

'At that age I was already so screwed up, it was already clear that I was all screwed up…'

Talking to his little friends

When they use to ask me where I was from, I'd say 'From Argentina.'

'And why did you come here?'

'Because my father was disappeared.'

'Why was he disappeared?'

'Because he had different political views. It's not just my dad – there are 30,000 desaparecidos.'

'But, how can 30,000 people disappear? That's not possible.'

'I didn't think it's possible either, but that's what happened. I can't explain it any further. They aren't anywhere...no trace, no place, nothing...'

Go home

They go by on the street and shout at you, 'go back to your country, nigger'. You go into a shop and there are two of them watching you. It happens more when the Swedes get drunk and go looking for trouble.

The Swede who I feel has been the kindest to us is Bosse, who's my father now, my stepfather. My mum met him in 1980. If I'd met a woman with kids like we were at that time...there's no way I'd get involved. The guy put up with it all and was always there for us.

In Sweden going to school is obligatory, if you don't go the police come to find you. I had been getting into trouble and the school didn't want me back. So my mum said, 'Ok, he can go to Argentina'. That was the first time I came. I was really happy.

At that time I didn't speak Argentinian Spanish. My Spanish was all over the place because in Sweden there were Chileans, Uruguayans, Bolivians, Paraguayans, Peruvians (...) A real mix. You could come across a Chilean saying *che* and a Uruguayan saying *huevón*.*

Understanding

At 16 I left home, just took off, which calmed things down a bit. I didn't have to deal with the tense relationship with my mum. I moved out and didn't speak to her till I was 18. It was all fucked up.

Today I can understand my mum better, but at that time I couldn't understand anything. Instead of reacting like a mother should, she used to say, 'This kid is crazy. Take him away, because I can't take it any more.' She was also messed up, that's what I now realise.

Today me and my mum are...inseparable. I talked about it with my psychologist. She also sees a psychologist. We reached the conclusion that we were both not well. We were treating each other badly. Both of us were victims of what had happened. If she treated me badly I'd get into more trouble. But things didn't get better overnight.

---

* *Che* is a distinctive Argentinian expression, while *huevón* is very Chilean.

Rap with a Latin flavour

We're making music. I'm in a band. We play hip-hop, I rap. The group's been quite successful, we have a studio…

It all began when I was 20. I'd always liked music. We are three Latin Americans in the group: my uncle, a Chilean friend and me. We've done well, won competitions, attract audiences of ten or twelve thousand at festivals. We've made records, have our own studio and make our own productions. The group's called 'Latin Flava.'

The dad who made your dad

Tico lives in Sweden where he has started a family. He's still rapping and working in the recording studio.

I have a son and a daughter. The boy's 4 and the girl's 7 months old. In my room I have photos of my father. For my kids, 'grandad' is my stepfather, but when my son began asking about the photos on the wall I told him,

'That's your dad's dad'. To which he replied,

'But Bosse is dad's dad!'

'No, Bosse is dad, but the dad who made your dad is this man.'

And then he asks,

'Where is he…?' So I tell him the soldiers in the posters – in my mum's house there are pictures of *escraches** directed at '*el turco*' Julián – took him away, no one knows where. And he says,

'They're so bad.'

Sometimes, when he comes in he says,

'This is dad's dad and these are all baddies.'

'Then Julián tells them to take me to the machine, so this pair of gorillas take me to a room and start beating me because I refuse to get undressed. One tears my shirt off and they throw me down on a metal table and tie my hands and feet. I tell them I'm two months pregnant and Turco Julián says, 'If so-and-so could stand the machine when she was six months pregnant, you will too. And rape her,' he ordered. The torturers treated me with increasing cruelty for two reasons: because I came from a Jewish family and because I didn't cry, which exasperated them…'

Testimony of Mónica Brull de Guillén (blind), File No. 5452 – Conadep

---

* Public demonstration in repudiation of a repressor who remains at large, a form of protest developed by HIJOS.

15

Incredible as it may seem

In 1977 the Military Junta intensified its 'anti-subversive strategy'. The initiative included the distribution of a leaflet in all educational establishments, aimed at the parents of children of school age. The leaflet was titled *How to recognise Marxist infiltration in schools,* and the following are extracts from it.

'Marxist vocabulary used by pupils: (...) The first thing that can be detected is the use of a specific type of terminology, which, although it may appear unimportant, in fact plays a crucial role in the "ideological transformation" that concerns us here. Thus, words such as dialogue, bourgeoisie, proletariat, Latin America, exploitation, structural change, capitalism will frequently crop up.

'The subjects chosen for subversive indoctrination are usually History, Civic Education, Economy, Geography and Catechism Class in religious schools. It is also common in Spanish Language and Literature, subjects from which classical authors have been eliminated and replaced by "Latin American novelists" or "politically committed literature" in general.

'Another subtle method of indoctrination is to make students discuss newspaper or magazine cuttings on political, social or religious issues, which have nothing to do with school. It is easy to see how the conclusions drawn can be manipulated.

'Likewise, group work, which has replaced individual responsibility, can easily be used to depersonalise the youngster, accustom him to being lazy and thus facilitate his indoctrination by pupils who are pre-selected and trained to "pass on" ideas.'

MARIA JULIA CORIA

María Julia was born in Buenos Aires, in 1976. She is the only daughter of Roberto Julio Coria and María Esther Donza. On 19 February 1977, Roberto and María Esther travelled from the town of Bosques, where they lived, to visit their families in Adrogué. Both were abducted that same night. Roberto was 22 and María Esther 26. María Julia was two months and four days old…

My dad was an artisan, my mum a teacher, she taught in a religious school and was studying psychology. They had started out in the grassroots Peronist movement and ended up in Montoneros.

VIDELA'S MESSAGE AND EXHORTATION TO YOUNG PEOPLE
Current goals
'The armed forces are not in power simply to carry out an administrative restructuring, but to achieve fundamental goals. These goals will lead to a revitalisation of ethical values, the affirmation of a true national pride, the construction of a vigorous and just society, and the consolidation of a true plural democracy. What young Argentinian could refuse to join this joint endeavour? What young Argentinian could refuse to take up this challenge to his capacity for imagination? Obviously few or none at all, because this broad and generous proposition is directed towards what is most noble in the spirit of each youth.'

La Gaceta – 2 December 1976

On 19 February 1977 my mum went first to my paternal grandmother's house – my grandmother Blanca – with my father. They went to show them their granddaughter. Afterwards they went to my maternal grandmother's, which is where I now live. My dad returned to his father's house. My mum went to visit a friend, partly to take me to meet her, partly to return some books. When she leaves she says goodbye to my grandmother; my grandmother says, 'Why don't you stay the night?' and my mum answers that they can't, they have to get back to Bosques. My mum took me to her friend's and never returned.

My grandmother went to see her brother-in-law. At ten o'clock, as she arrives home on foot, she sees two figures, one holding a baby and my mum's handbag. My grandmother says,

'Children! You're going to stay the night after all!' and then realises it's not them...A man puts me in her arms and tells her,

'Your daughter will be back shortly.'

My dad, who this whole time was at his father's, realises the time it is and that my mum hasn't returned. He goes out to look for us on the bicycle and never returns. Shortly afterwards my grandmother and my aunt went to our house in Bosques, talked to the neighbours, who told them that some soldiers had taken my father into the house and he'd come out all beaten up.

The truth

I remember that one day at a parents' evening at school I saw my grandmother crying; I pretended not to notice and went out to the playground. I ran away. I don't know why.

That summer we went on holiday to the coast, my grandmother took me to the beach, to the cliffs and told me that she was going to tell me the truth because my teacher had told her that I was saying that my parents had abandoned me. She told me,

'They have been abducted.' The first thing I thought was,

'That's not how my Granny Esther talks, in the passive voice. This is something she's practised...'

I clearly remember the day of the elections in 1983. I accompanied my grandmother when she went to vote. She asked for permission to take me into the voting booth. I didn't understand why she was so happy. It must have been the hope that everything would be clarified...

Pick a dictatorship

I was 15 and we had to do an assignment on the dictatorships. We were told to work in groups and each choose a dictatorship from the many we've had. We chose the 1976 dictatorship, so I went to the Ecumenical Human Rights Movement (MEDH), and came away with five boxes full of photocopies. I think that was the first time it really made an impression on me, the first time I said 'What bastards!,' the first time I became aware of the desaparecidos as a social fact...

To live

I have the photos, but what really obsesses me is not knowing what their voices sounded like. My mum had a cousin who lived in the United States, whom she used to send 15-page letters telling her all about her boyfriends, everything. I even called up one of her boyfriends. I looked him up in the phone book and he was great because I'd always been told, 'Your mummy was so good' [in an ironic tone], whereas this bloke said, 'What a woman! What a woman!' So the goody goody image I'd got from my grandparents…

In one of her letters my mum gives a detailed analysis of Cámpora's rise to power, which also meant that the 'Estercita wasn't a militant' line was also shot to pieces…

My mum was four years older than my dad. I have letters of hers to her cousin in which my mum tells her about a camp she went to with him:

'That clown Robertito came along to carry our bags…' she didn't take much notice of him. Later on she had to do an assignment at college on Third World priests and she went to see this lefty she knew. My dad was by then fully involved.

I had two dead people whom I'd never seen alive. I needed them to live to be able to kill them off.

NEVER AGAIN (CONADEP REPORT)

Alsogaray vs Conadep

[*Journalist*]: But in the interview that sparked off this polemic you said that all the desaparecidos died in action.

[*Alsogaray*]: No, that is a simplification of what I said. What I said was that there are desaparecidos abroad probably training to come back here as part of the guerrilla when the moment is ripe (…)

Somos – 12 April 1985

It was in Corrientes Street, the book *Never Again* was on offer, and I thought,

'This is a sign, it costs 24 and here it's going for five pesos. I have to buy it.' I read the testimonies in one night. Until then I had seen the fact that they had handed me back to my house as a sign that I was 'a chosen one'. I was Moses.

And no (…) it's just one of the things they did within the method: they are killed, appropriated, returned and I'm returned too.

It was my entry into the world at large:

'It's not just your parents, it's lots of people.'

One day I was at home reading the magazine from Ghandi, the bookshop, which had an interview with a forensic anthropologist, they were talking about a body that had been found and it was signed Jorge I can't remember what. It was the first time that it occurred to me to look for their bodies. I looked him up in the phone book and called him. He was moving house and he told me to visit him at his office the following week.

I went to the office, said, I'm the daughter of so-and-so, and she said 'Come in, sit down.'

That week an article had come out about that boy Pablito and that's where I first found out what El Vesubio* was really like.

On 24 March 1998, the daily *Página/12* published an article reconstructing the calvary suffered by Pablo Miguez. He had been abducted together with his mother, was detained in El Vesubio and then transferred to Escuela de Mecánica de la Armada (ESMA).† Lila Pastoriza, a survivor of ESMA and the author of the article, spent a month with Pablito, who remains disappeared.

'In that long and fleeting month that we spent together, Pablo told me about El Vesubio, about the prisoners transferred from there, who were later declared "fallen in action" in official communiqués, about his mother, who he didn't say goodbye to ("she was in the kitchen"), about his hope that he'd be taken to where his father was, about his life in the outside world – school, swimming, his brothers, his grandmother, his cousins and horseracing, about his loves and his fears.'

No more was ever heard of him. Pablito was 14 years old.

The woman tapped into the computer: Roberto Julio Coria and Esther Donza, pressed Enter and reams of information came piling out, and the only thing I read was 'Vesubio'. The only word I read on the whole page. That's when a whole new story began, from that moment everything changed for me.

Social life

María Julia hopes that one day she will find her parents' remains. She lives with her maternal grandmother and is studying Sociology.

I really like a phrase used by the guy who's going to be my lecturer now, he says, 'Studying social life allows us to learn about certain determinants and on the basis of that knowledge you can construct your life as a project and not as a destiny.' I think that that's what attracts me about social questions.

---

* Illegal detention centre.
† Escuela de Mecánica de la Armada (trans. Navy School of Mechanics), an illegal detention centre in Buenos Aires.

16 ✳✳✳✳

✳
✳
✳
✳

Moral curriculum

NEW UNIVERSITY REGULATIONS

'With respect to the teaching staff, article 18 of the previous law, which established a selection process involving interviews and competitive examinations, has been eliminated, although the current regulations do not specify mechanisms covering the appointment of replacements. What is stressed is "suitability with respect to scientific and teaching ability, moral integrity and respect for the fundamental laws of the Nation".'

Clarín – 3 April 1976

BRUERA ANNOUNCED THE ELIMINATION OF A RANGE OF UNIVERSITY COURSES

'The Minister for Culture and Education, Ricardo Bruera, officially announced the elimination of a range of university courses and said that the total number of students that will be admitted to higher education establishments will be 69,479. Likewise, he said that new degree courses will be created in technological subjects. (...) According to the minister's declarations, the degree courses cancelled are: Psychology, Anthropology and Sociology, as well as several faculties and other minor degrees, such as Social Work, Librarianship, Drama, Film Studies, Audiovisual Studies, Information Science, Trade Union Leadership, Public Relations, Oceanography, Art and Folklore and Environmental Health.'

La Voz del Interior (Córdoba) – 28 November 1976

VERONICA CASTELLI

Verónica was born in Buenos Aires in 1974. Since she was born on 11 September, Teacher's Day, she claims she was a present for her mother, María Teresa Trotta. Her father, Roberto Castelli, was also a teacher. He had studied in a seminary for four years, was a philosophy and pedagogy teacher, and also worked as a private tutor. Both worked in Montoneros drawing up false documents.

> I remember eating sweets on the patio and my dad tearing a strip off me because I ate the paper. I remember a jumper my dad had with diamonds. I'm not an only child, but I don't know where my brother is.

Teresa and Roberto were kidnapped in separate operations on 28 February 1977. Teresa was seven months' pregnant. Verónica, who was two and a half, was with her father and witnessed his abduction.

> When they took my dad, we were on the street corner outside my grandmother's house. The Ford Falcons stopped in front of us, my dad goes to the shop and leaves me inside. He goes out with his hands up, they tie him up and start hitting him. Afterwards I ran out of the shop. I went over to where they were beating him up and a soldier picks me up and another who's in one of the cars says, 'No, leave the girl', and they took him away. For a long time I felt guilty, thinking 'He gave himself up so as not to put me in danger, or why didn't he escape over the rooftops?' The whole block was most likely surrounded and he wouldn't have been able to do anything, but those are the kind of irrational self-reproaches that you think.

'Sometimes physical repression is necessary, compulsory and as such, legitimate…'

Declarations by Monsignor Miguel Medina
Vicar-General of the Armed Forces – May 1982

My mum told me your mum…

I thought they'd gone on a trip, I was ashamed that they'd left me alone, had abandoned me. I was adopted by my dad's brother who was Superintendent of the Federal Police, a fascist. When I started at primary school he said first off that I was his daughter. I thought, 'I must have done something bad to make them leave.' I was really unlucky – even the teachers said, 'there must be a reason'. One day, when I was seven or so, the girl who sat next to me in school came and said,

'My mum told me your mum and dad are dead.'

Veronica and the sea

You know how they tell you that the people who die go to heaven? I used to say 'you can't go to heaven because the sky's got no floor'. So I decided that they went to live at the bottom of the sea and I watched all the Atlantis films to see if I could spot my parents. That was my own free adaptation of religion.

When I was little I used to speak to the sea to talk to my parents. We used to go on holiday south of Buenos Aires, we had a chalet and from my room you could see the sea. Every year I'd spend one night sitting there and telling them everything I'd done that year, the grades I'd got at school, when I'd been naughty…

Sadly, Verónica's fantasy regarding the whereabouts of her parents was not so far from the truth. While Agosti was declaring on 31 December 1976 that 'during those nine months the Air Force fulfilled its mission of being the loyal guardian of the skies of the Fatherland', its aeroplanes were used to throw anaesthetised people into the River Plate.

ANOTHER CORPSE IS FOUND ON THE URUGUAYAN COAST
'Today the number of mutilated bodies that have turned up in Uruguayan waters reached 12, in a new chapter in one of the greatest mysteries of the criminal history of the country.'

La Prensa – 7 June 1976

When the newspapers began to publish reports about corpses 'appearing' on the Uruguayan coast, the Armed Forces took the precaution of throwing the bodies out over the high seas.

'In 1977, as a lieutenant posted at the School of Mechanics, under the operational command of the First Army Brigade, while you were Commander in Chief and complying with orders issued directly by the Executive, while you were President, I took part in two air transfers, the first carrying 13 subversives on board a Skyvan belonging to the Naval Command and the other with 17 terrorists in an Electra from the Naval Air Force. They were told that they were being taken to a prison in the south and that they therefore needed to be vaccinated. They were given a first dose of anaesthesia, which would be boosted by a second larger dose during the flight. Finally, in both cases they were thrown naked into the waters of the Atlantic from the aeroplanes while in flight.'

Letter to Videla from the former member of the military Adolfo Scilingo
Verbitsky, El Vuelo – Planeta, 1995

An abrupt change

And then there followed a whole different period during which the 'there must be a good reason for it' was history; there was the return to democracy, everyone was talking about human rights. The whole Argentinian population had abruptly changed their way of thinking and once again I was a misfit because I was the daughter of a policeman. When I was little it was because I was the daughter of subversives, and once I was older it was because I was the daughter of a cop. They just couldn't let me live in peace.

Permission

My cousin is like my brother. I saw him with his head buried in his pillow, so I go and lie down beside him. He tells me that Carolina, his girlfriend, is pregnant, and 'we're going to have it. I have to tell dad today'. And I tell him that I had been to Abuelas, what had happened there and that I too was going to tell.

So he says to me,

'You go and tell him first, because with these two items of news he's going to have a heart attack and you're going to feel guilty.'

I went and he was watching telly. He turned it off and said, 'Did you want to speak to me?'

I felt like I had a two hundred kilo load weighing down on me, I was sweating, I thought I wouldn't be able to speak. I began,

'The-thing-is-I-want-to-look-for-my-bro-ther-be-cause-he's-my-bro-ther-and-you-can't-tell-me-not-to!" [Veronica puts on an adolescent's voice].

He looked at me and said that he understood. What's worse, I was bawling away 'Waaahhh!' and couldn't even talk. He told me that he'd never spoken to me about my father, that he'd tell me about him just that once and then he'd never mention him again. He said that I'd lost my father and he'd lost his brother. That he was very hurt, that he couldn't deal with the pain and that he had to forget it had ever happened, otherwise he wouldn't be able to carry on living. That he wasn't going to go Abuelas to have blood taken, but that if I wanted to do it that I should, but that I had to make sure that they didn't come bothering him.

One after another

When my paternal grandmother died I found this and it moved me so much! (…) She used to write letters to the Ministry of the Interior, one after another, I was so moved by her innocence. What a place to ask for information from! There's this short letter, that she obviously didn't get round to sending, asking please for information about her son, her daughter-in-law and the baby. In reply The Ministry of the Interior used to send her forms to fill out. They'd already received the completed form which said, 'With reference to the letter received on the…' followed by a date, 'Regarding the whereabouts of …' and so on (…) She had about fifteen of those letters and the one that she hadn't sent. I loved my grandmother's writing because her hand shook. It was so sweet. I was moved by the simplicity of the woman, you know what I mean?

'If my son is missing, where should I go and file a report? To the state…'

'We haven't made a confession to the Inter-American Human Rights Commission. We have merely laid bare the facts. Argentina only confesses to God.'

Albano Harguindeguy, Minister of the Interior
La Nación – 22 September 1979

17

Five centuries later, nothing has changed

'The Argentinian concept of national identity owes much to our conception of the world and of man, which is based on the Christian view of the world and of man, within which man as the protagonist of history must first accept that both his origin and his destiny lie in God; that is, starting out from God, he reaches God. Man is the protagonist of history precisely because he is the son of God, and since he is the son of God he is made in his image and likeness, and under these conditions man is free, and since he is free he is an honourable being, precisely because of his likeness to God.'

Lieutenant General Jorge Rafael Videla
La Gaceta – 15 December 1976

'Before each military attack, the captains of the conquest had to read to the Indians, without an interpreter, but in the presence of a public notary, an extensive and grandiloquent Notification urging them to convert to the holy Catholic faith: If you were not to do so, or with malicious intent delayed doing so, I certify that with the help of God I shall powerfully come against you and shall wage war on you in all places and manners that I am able, and I shall subject you to the yoke and obedience of the Church and His Majesty and I shall take your wives and children and I shall make slaves of them and as such I shall sell them, and I shall dispose of them as His Majesty decides, and I shall take your goods and I shall to do you all the evils and harm in my power...'

Vidart, *Ideología y Realidad de América*, Montevideo, 1968

MARIA CORONEL

María is the mother of a boy who recently turned four, she is studying psychology and has a younger sister called Lucía. The father of both of them, Juan Carlos Coronel, an attorney, died in September 1976 in Buenos Aires resisting the taskforce* who were trying to kidnap him. Their mother, María Cristina Bustos, was a lawyer and was abducted on 14 March 1977.

When Roberto Coronel, Juan Carlos's brother, found out that his sister-in-law had been kidnapped, he tried desperately to find her, and as a result was himself abducted on 21 March 1977. María and her sister grew up with their paternal grandparents, Gringa and Carlos in Ledesma, Jujuy.

I was born in Buenos Aires on 31 December 1974, but my birth certificate says I was born 31 March 1975, in Libertador General San Martín, Jujuy. When we were little my sister and I didn't have papers. My paternal grandmother registered us after my mother disappeared. My mother had told her that if anything happened to her, that she should register us giving false dates and places.

I remember that, when we were starting out at school, we had to say that my parents had died in an accident (…) Over time I've come to realise how stupid it was, because Ledesma is a small town, everyone knew. It was like everyone pretended to swallow the story about the accident.

Madres

The greatest contradiction for me was that, while we had to make up a story for school, every Thursday that we could, my grandmother would take us to the main square. There the old ladies would stand in front of the Town Hall, which is where the police station is, and shout, 'Murderers!'

I had no idea what it was all about. The only thing I remember – and that stuck with me – was that no one used to cross the square. No one would cross the square because we were there, they used to watch us from the corner. I found it really entertaining because there

---

* Name given to death squads made up of police and military personnel who carried out kidnappings.

were a lot of kids, other children of victims. I remember they'd show me photos of their parents. 'This is my dad and this is my mum', but they'd go with their grandmother. It seemed completely normal to me because that's how I'd grown up too.

'On this occasion I join in prayer with the millions of fellow countrymen to ask for peace, happiness and the well-being of all the families who inhabit our land and I call on God, Our Father, to protect us, so that the light of the Easter message may illuminate the path that all Argentinians have taken.'

Jorge Rafael Videla, *La Gaceta* – 13 April 1976

Basic notions

One day Lucía started crying because at her nursery school they'd asked her why she didn't have a mummy or daddy. We were four and five at the time. I felt that it was no good crying about it, and all I said was:

'Look, I don't know why we don't, but don't cry. Be quiet and don't let them see that you've been crying.'

I had the idea that we should keep quiet firmly instilled.

I only started to realise that something was wrong when I started going to nursery school myself, because my grandmother used to take me and everyone else went with their mummy and daddy.

I remember that one day – when I was six or seven – my grandmother called me into the kitchen, said she had something to tell me and that my father hadn't died of a heart attack but had been killed by the military (who 'the military' was, I had no idea). And that my mother was disappeared…

Let the little children come to me

I disagree with my grandmother over a lot of things, but I remember her fight with the priest who didn't want to give me communion in Ledesma because I was 'the daughter of subversives…'

His first excuse had been that I was too young for communion and then he came out with it. My grandmother went wild and banned us from going into the church in Ledesma ever again. I had never seen her like that, an image of a strong woman.

'…I remember that during my stay in prison (Gorriti Prison – Jujuy), the Bishop of Jujuy, Monsignor Medina celebrated mass and in his sermon he told us that he knew what was happening, but that it was all for the good of the Fatherland and that the military were acting correctly and that we should tell them everything we knew, for which purpose he offered to take confession from us…'

Testimony of Ernesto Reynaldo Saman, File No. 4841 – Conadep

Hope

I have no hope that my dad will ever come back, because there's a grave, but my mum on the other hand (...) I used to spend hours looking at women on the street, thinking, 'She looks like me, she looks like me...' or telling myself that she was suffering from amnesia. 'Something must have happened to her to prevent her from coming looking for me...' For years and years I had these thoughts!

When María was 16 her grandfather Carlos died. She and her sister went to live in Tucumán with Juana – her maternal grandmother – and two great-aunts.

Do you see?

Some of the other kids found it strange that my aunt used to take me to school, that there was no sign of my mum or dad. All I used to say was that I didn't have a mum or dad, and that's was that!

I remember a run-in I had at school, one 12 October, when I was about 17. It was the five hundredth anniversary of the Spanish conquest of America and they assigned me to escort the Flag of the Race. What a pain! When they told me, I said,

'No, I won't do it, I'm not going.' I caused such a fuss that I convinced the student who was meant to carry the Argentinian flag and his escort not to go either. So they took us to see the Head.

'I'll go, but only if you let me wear a black armband as a sign of mourning, because I haven't got a damn thing to celebrate. This goes against my principles. I don't want to be part of this.'

That day I felt as if my own personal history were being attacked because the Head was like 'don't make a fuss and get yourselves noticed'. He said:

'There are a lot of things that you don't know about the past, don't be stupid. I have great respect for your principles, but there's a generation that's no longer around because of those principles.'

And that was the first time I could say:

'I know because that's the reason I don't have any parents.' And the Head said to me, 'See? You haven't got any parents...'

At that point I said to myself,

'No! I refuse to hide my history because I won't put up with them threatening me like this.'

Cool

Just like at secondary school I knew I had to keep quiet about certain things because otherwise I'd be left out, they wouldn't understand and I didn't want to have to explain, well, at university it was the other extreme.

As a daughter of desaparecidos I was one of the 'in group', it was so crazy, it gave me this special status. These things annoyed me – the fact that I was special because I was 'the daughter of', but I was also really proud.

NIETOS (Grandchildren)

When we 'daughters' of disappeared parents have babies, I see that we are all paranoid about the baby. The whole time you're afraid that something's going to happen to him, that he's going to be stolen, taken away (…) I was convinced they were going to take him away from me. It's just there, this fear that you can't understand because it's so strong.

It was very important for me to see if he had a clear grasp of who I was at the same age that I was when my parents were disappeared, at the age I was orphaned. I don't really know why, it was like trying to understand the relationship I could have had with my parents through him.

Now I'm delighted that he's four years old and is still with me and I'm still with him, because you don't realise, but unconsciously you are afraid that the same thing's going to happen. I find it amazing that he's the age he is and he's got me and I've got him. It's like we've survived each other…

I don't want him to be ashamed

'He knows about his grandparents,' María says, looking at little Simón playing in the patio with his train and helicopter.

'What were your grandparents?'

'Mortoreros,' answers Simón without interrupting his game.

The things I had to keep quiet about he already knows.

'They killed my Grandpa and then Granny was disappeared,' Simón interrupts.

For me it's important that he knows these things at the age of four and that he's not ashamed to say it, because I had to find them out when I was much older. If he makes the teachers at the nursery school feel uncomfortable by telling them not to vote for Bussi because he's a murderer, that's fine by me.

18

Dictatorship and propaganda

Like all totalitarian regimes, the dictatorship had a permanently-functioning propaganda apparatus. The following is the prize-winning work from the Competition 'The Day of the Army', which was written (apparently) by a 12 year old, and was distributed to schools in the south of the country.

PROVINCIAL EDUCATION BOARD
Neuquén, 27 June 1980
REF.: Copy prize-winning work Day of the Army Competition

To the Headmaster/mistress of School No. _____

I am writing to you for the purpose of sending you a copy of the work that won first prize in the Competition organised by the command of the Sixth Mountain Infantry Brigade with pupils from Neuquén capital city, on the occasion of the Day of the Army.

Yours faithfully.
CLEMENCIA AURORA CAMPODONICO [signed]
General Director of Primary Education – Provincial Education Board

THE ARGENTINIAN ARMY
'I remember you. Today, Argentinian Army, you are in me. I feel in my heart the desire to shout out your feats of war, both those past and those present, because over time you present yourself – not only here on national soil, but to the whole world – with valour in your struggle against the enemies of peace, the subversives! Why? Why are you in the minds of all the inhabitants of the country? In this way you revive my heart and I am reminded of the exploits of Cabral who, on surrendering up his life, shouted: I die content… we have beaten the enemy! I remember Juan Pascual Pringles, who preferred to throw himself into the sea, off the shores of Chancay, rather than surrender the national flag.

For this reason, Argentinian Army…I am at all times at your disposal to defend what is ours, a zealous guardian of my Fatherland!'
'Before there was war, and not so long ago too, but thanks be to God you were prepared to defend us all equally.

You, who fought in the mountains, seas and skies, against the harmful minds of subversive uncertainty, in order that they might love and respect this free land, and our flag, and so it happened.

They loved you, they love you and they will love you above many other things, since all disheartened minds have been banished to the bottom of a chasm and other new minds are being born, to adore you and to wear on their chests the insignia of our blue and white flag. Thus! Thus will it be for a long time! Because you were born with the Fatherland, you defended it and still defend it, guarding its peace and protecting its sovereignty, even in the farthest corners of the south.

That is why at this moment I feel you are mine, Argentinian Army!'

MARIO CESAR HUARTE, 7th Grade Pupil
Provincial School No. 101

DEBORA VILLANUEVA

Débora was born in Buenos Aires in 1975. She has a younger sister called Verónica. Their parents, Fernando Villanueva and Graciela Valdueza, worked at the Pensions Office in Martínez, in the province of Buenos Aires. Fernando was the staff's union representative. Early on the morning of the coup the military entered their home and abducted Fernando and Graciela. They were both 24 years old.

COMMUNIQUE NO. 13
'In these critical moments for the Republic, the Junta of Commanders in Chief of the Armed Forces calls on the youth of the Fatherland to participate, without reserve and without prejudice, in the process of reorganisation that has been initiated. A process in which the norms of conduct are based on full respect for the ethical and moral values that guide and give purpose to the behaviour of all young Argentinians who deserve to be described as such.'

Junta of Commanders in Chief of the Armed Forces – 24 March 1976

Débora and her sister grew up in Caseros, where they lived for 12 years with their maternal grandmother.

> My grandmother used to tell us that our parents were good people and loved us, but that they were working very hard to make sure we had everything we needed. They used to leave very early for work in the morning, which was why we didn't see them, and they'd also get home very late at night, by which time we were asleep. What a story to tell a three year old! I used to try to stay awake or to wake myself up at night to see them…

Desaparecidos

Their uncle Ricardo, Débora's father's brother, was 17 at the time. Débora remembers him as 'the source of explanations, from periods to the coup…'

> He used to come with my other grandmother to see us at weekends. Sometimes he'd come and get us in the car and take us off. We were sitting, me on the bed and him in a chair. I remember that when he began to talk, I already knew what he was going to say. That was the first time I heard the word desaparecidos.

130

In *Clarín* they published a huge list. I remember it was a sunny morning, my grandmother was crying her eyes out and she wouldn't tell us what was wrong. I knew that there was something in the paper. She hid the paper away, but I watched to see where she put it, I took it out and their two names were marked with a red pen. That's when I felt it was all over.

'The members of the Armed Forces have assumed at this time the commitment to reorganise the Republic's institutions, with the aim of achieving, through freedom, the happiness of its children.'

Major General Roberto E. Viola
La Prensa – 2 May 1976

Lots of bad people

I remember once I had a punch-up with a girl whose father was a policeman. That was when I was 11. The subject came up during a talk at the school: The police are there to look after the citizens, ensure the well-being of the population and their security. The girl came out with the fact that her father was a policeman and he'd had to kill a whole load of bad people. When she said that I realised that he could have killed my parents.

'And why?! Even if they're bad they shouldn't be killed,' I said.

'Besides, maybe my dad killed your dad,' she continued.

At that I grabbed her by the neck.

'You piece of shit!' We were both sent to see the Head, but the one who got the telling off was me, just for a change…

Granny Tona

After finishing primary school, Débora and her sister were taken to live with her paternal grandmother, Granny Tona.

She always used to say that remembering was like twisting the knife in the wound. I used to imagine the knife. One day I got fed up and told her,

'Look, I understand about the knife, but I need to know.'

She sat down calmly and began to cry. First she cried her eyes out and then she began to tell me how my dad didn't like polenta, didn't like to go out dancing…

My parents read a lot of literature. I have the collected works of Edgar Allen Poe and all that stuff. When I was 14 or 15 I was about to start reading a book and when I flicked through it I found the letters that my dad had sent my mum with a poem. It did my head in! I cried so much!

After my dad

In all the photos I have of my dad – both before and after he married – he's with his friend Luis. They used to go backpacking together all over the place. When my sister and I joined HIJOS we put some effort in and tracked him down.

We all went. My grandmother had put her best dress on. First I showed her a couple of photos to see how she'd react. She was so nervous: 'What am I going to say to this person? There are a thousand things I'd like to ask him, but I'm ashamed' and so on.

So we go there, and his wife – a lovely woman – answers the door and invites us in. We were there for hours but it went by in a flash. The thing that affected me most, that touched me to the core and forced me to hold back my tears, was that his oldest son was named after my father.

Birds of a feather…

In October 1995, Débora went to the first national HIJOS camp. It was held in the mountains in the province of Córdoba, in the town of Cabalango.

HIJOS was the explosion. Cabalango did my head in. I remember the scene when I got off the bus and wow! My god! It was a sea of sons and daughters. Could it be? No! There must be others here too. They must have brought their friends! I was in charge of coordinating one of the working committees.

It was while working in that committee that Débora met Martín Vega, known as *el Rata*, a member of the Santa Fe delegation. She swears they did 'no more than exchange glances'. In December that same year, HIJOS participated for the first time as an organisation in the March of Resistance in Buenos Aires. Débora was in charge of sending out information and invitations to the regional groups from the interior of the country and they met again.

Afterwards I called him so that he could explain things to the members from Santa Fe. They had to collect photos for the March of Resistance. When he arrived I'd been working on it for three months.

I hadn't slept for three days. Early that morning we'd stuck all the photos all the way along the avenues. On the day of the march, when we were doing the last leg at six o'clock, before the speeches, I fainted in the middle of the procession. I felt something on my eyes and someone's hand stroking me. I sat up and it was el Rata. I was over the moon…

At present Débora lives in the province of Santa Fe with Martín. They are expecting their first child.

19 ✳✳✳✳

The World Cup 1978

Towards the end of the 1960s Argentina had been selected host country for the 1978 World Cup. It was a golden opportunity for the dictatorship. In the middle of the economic crisis and the accusations of human rights violations, football, the sport that awakens the greatest passions in Argentina, was the perfect vehicle for the dictatorship's propaganda.

Organising the World Cup cost the country approximately 700 million dollars, an exorbitant amount, considering it cost Spain only 150 million dollars in 1982.

'The 1978 World Cup will have two basic objectives beyond the game itself: To show the outside world that the image of Argentina has been deformed by foreign interests and to unite the country's inhabitants around an event that is a heritage shared by everyone, without exclusions.'

Brigadier General Luis Merlo
La Opinión – 16 November 1976

'It will be a great success, not only in strictly sporting terms, but in terms of what it means for the country's image.'

Admiral Emilio Eduardo Massera
Clarín – 1 June 1978

'We Argentinians need to be winners. We have to win in order to unite the country, to develop it, to resolve the problems we have with our neighbours, but always from a position as winners. We are tired of draws.'

Admiral Emilio Eduardo Massera
Clarín – 21 June 1978

THE COURAGE OF OUR PEOPLE
President Videla, together with the members of the Junta and accompanied by Henry Kissinger,* watched the game from the official box. '[The players] demonstrated the courage of the Argentinian people,' said the president, while Kissinger remarked on 'the marvellous way the supporters behaved.'

Clarín – 22 June 1978

ARGENTINA WORLD CHAMPION

Clarín – 26 June 1978

---

* Henry Kissinger, then US Secretary of State, was at the World Cup to celebrate alongside the generals of the military regime.

ALBA CAMARGO

Alba was born in Córdoba in 1963. She's a music producer for rock bands and a devotee of Saint Francis of Assisi. Her father's name was Armando Camargo and her mother's Marta Alicia Bértola. Alba is very lively and has a sharp sense of humour. She has two adolescent daughters, is separated and lives in Buenos Aires with her current partner.

> My dad was the owner of a cleaning company. The cleaning teams used to clean shopping galleries in the centre of town, banks (…) At first our standard of living was very good, but then it started declining as a result of their increasing commitment to their activism – they started to devote much more time to that than to the company. My mum used to work in a medical centre called the Railway Hospital in Córdoba, that has now been privatised. It's opposite Rawson Hospital.

Memories

> My dad was a very special person, he used to laugh and take the piss the whole time. I don't know if you've seen that film, *Life is beautiful*, but anyway, my dad always used to invent a story to make sense of the chaos surrounding us. I had a good life, didn't need to ask about too many things.
>
> He was hopeless with his hands, but very capable with his head. He was funny, used to tell jokes the whole time, my mum would have a fit because he had no sense of decorum. Terrible things would happen and he'd tell jokes. I used to laugh a lot, I found his humour and intelligence fascinating.
>
> I believed in the Three Kings* till I was quite old. Early one morning on the 6th [of January] I was woken by the sound of poles banging together out on the patio – Crash! Bang! I went out and it was my dad putting up a swing. He stopped dead and just looked at me (…) my fantasy was over. So I said to him:

---

* The equivalent of Father Christmas in that children get presents on the Epiphany rather than Christmas day in Argentina.

'Oh no, Daddy, the Three Kings left the swing without putting it up!'

'That's right, sweetheart, that's right...' [imitating her father's serious tone of voice].

The things you do when you don't want to see what you're seeing!

COMMUNIQUE NO. 9
'The population of the Nation is informed that from this moment and until further notice, all administrative and educational activities in establishments of primary, secondary and higher education throughout the territory of the Argentine Nation are suspended.'

Junta of Commanders in Chief of the Armed Forces – 24 March 1976

The coup

I remember the day of the coup. I was living in Córdoba, in a working class neighbourhood called Talleres Sur. I was 13. At half past six these kids who lived around the corner from our house used to come by to fetch me to go to school because it was dark. That day my dad was already awake and told me:

'Go back to bed, sweetheart, go back to bed, there's been a military coup. You're not going to school.'

I was pleased as punch. 'Way hay! Back to sleep!'

From the night before strange things were being reported.

I used to go to school in the morning and afternoon, my brother went to nursery.

I can't remember whether they explained anything to me, the only thing I know is that everything changed in concrete ways. Our whole lives changed completely and very shortly a decision was made to leave the country and live abroad, to go to Mexico. We immediately got passports.

On several occasions I heard my dad and mum having terrible arguments in which my dad used to tell her that she had to go with us, and she'd say that she wasn't going to leave him, that she was going to stay with him no matter what happened.

They used to argue at night, when in theory I was asleep.

July 1976

July 22nd is my brother's birthday. It was a Tuesday, so everything was ready to have the party on Saturday, and also celebrate my dad's birthday that falls on 25 July. They'd bought everything to have the birthday party at my grandmother's house, in the neighbourhood of Juniors. Early in the morning on the 23rd, around 5 am, my grandfather Pedro, my mum's father, arrived. He'd worked on the railways, and had come on a train engine because there was a curfew, there were no buses, no taxis, nothing at night.

At that hour of the morning the train engines shunt around, so he asked one of the workers whom he knew – because he was from the union – to take him to the end of the line because he had to see his daughter. Behind our house were the railway workshops.

He came to our house and woke up my mum and dad. I heard my mum crying, that's what woke me up and I heard that my aunt and uncle had been abducted – my mum's sister and her husband. They were taken away at 1 am, four hours earlier, from her home.

Her in-laws were visiting at the time, and some relatives from the United States, who were also taken away. A wholesale raid.

Hard on our heels

At 7 am they woke me up. My mum came in to say goodbye because she was going off to work. She said:

'I'm going to work. And you two are going to do some things with dad, get up and start getting ready. Albita, pack a bag for Sebastián with enough things for a few days.

We got a couple of bags ready. I already knew what I should pack. At half past eight my dad went to the highway to get a taxi. Later he told me that as he walked along he thought,

'No, I'd better go back, we should all three be together.'

So he came back, picked us up and the three of us left, and at half past nine they broke into our house. There was no one there.

As ever

There weren't any taxis – it was a very poor neighbourhood – so we took the bus. My brother and I were taken to our grandparents'. They were waiting for us, they left us there, and I remember saying goodbye to my dad. My dad spoke to my grandmother and left. So I ran after him and gave him a prescription for a pair of glasses that I had to pick up. It's like you don't realise what is really going on, you're just a kid. I said,

'Please pick up these glasses for me.'

'Okay, I'll get them for you. If I don't bring them to you one of my friends will.'

'Okay, bye-bye.' That was the last time I saw my dad. He was wearing a grey overcoat. As handsome as ever…

That afternoon, at about four o'clock, my brother and I were having a siesta, when they woke us up and my great-aunt said to my grandmother,

'Sara, tell Albita what's happened…'

So my grandmother said,

'They've taken them. Three different people have told us.'

Alba's mother went to work. When she left the hospital she met up with Armando and together they went to get some belongings from their home, but the Army had set up a trap there: a taskforce was waiting for them hidden inside. They didn't only kidnap Alba's parents. A young employee of UnCorCi, the Union of the Blind of Córdoba, was passing just at that moment selling bin bags. He was also abducted and taken to La Perla concentration camp. A month later he was released.

I was left speechless and very afraid. My grandmother took hold of me, began to shake my head, telling me not to stay there lying on my bed, to get up, to go to school…

I started going out again a week later – my grandparents began to take me out – and we went to school to get the outlines of the courses I had to take.

'Ok, come on, let's get moving!'

I was very afraid and kept thinking about my parents, but at the same time you start building up your defences.

Defences

I didn't ask because one afternoon I heard my aunt's testimony and I didn't want to hear any more. I never wanted to hear them talking about any of it ever again. I remember my parents from 23 July backwards, and I'm not interested in recalling what they suffered in the concentration camp because it helps no one. I know what they did to them, and that's enough.

Estela Berastegui, Alba's aunt, was living in the United States of America and was on holiday in Argentina when she was abducted together with her husband. She was detained in La Perla and was then released. Estela saw Alba's parents in that clandestine detention centre.

They stayed on in Argentina and she never stopped, she changed her life. She came to live in Córdoba, started taking all kinds of steps, going to meetings. That's how the human rights organisations working on the cases of the desaparecidos started working, with people like her.

I was at my grandparents'. She was there having *mate*, one Sunday. She was wearing a woollen hat, it was cold I remember, and dressed in a black polo neck. She was talking, and I went over. She began describing what she had seen. My grandmother wasn't there, she was telling my grandfather. I remember that my grandfather was crying and I listened. I don't remember ever crying in public at that time. I used to cry on my own. I remember that I used to go into a wardrobe and cry. I used to open the door and hide inside it because my mum's clothes were in it and I could smell her. To try to feel close to her in some way.

School

Later on I was thrown out of school, because a retired colonel, Coelho, became headmaster. It was Belgrano School, linked to the University of Córdoba. I was called to the office of the vice-chancellor and was told that I was the daughter of subversives and that they didn't want the children of subversives at the school. So I said,

'Fine, what do you want me to do? Give me back my parents and I won't be the daughter of subversives anymore.'

GOVERNOR CHASSEING: I'M NOT A DEMAGOGUE
'For us soldiers, talking to youngsters represents one of the most important commitments we have made for the sake of the Fatherland, I could never like to a young person. When you invited me to talk I was truly moved, I consider that each one of you is at a point in your life where you should pause and take the time to think. (…) Sometimes I wonder, can we remember the Ten Commandments? Could we recite them? That is why we need a moment of silence to review our behaviour. Can we remember the preamble to our Constitution? (…) When young people are given the easy path to follow, when love is not valued, when you do not respect your girlfriend, you cannot build a family. No sir, we want to give you the strength of the first Christians, we ask you to show the strength of the first Christians. We believe in democracy, we believe in the republic, we believe in federalism, we believe in those men who fight on behalf of the rest.'
La Voz del Interior (Córdoba) – 13 November 1976

The place was crawling with soldiers carrying weapons. They'd drawn lines on the ground for us to line up on. Your feet on the lines! There was a dovecote, so they killed all the doves because they dirtied the ground. Can you believe it? Crazy, crazy…

THE 1978 WORLD CUP: ARGENTINA WORLD CHAMPION! THE
IMAGE OF A COUNTRY ON ITS FEET
With this edition claim your plastic Argentinian flag for the same price as the
paper.
   There we all were, in an expression of national unity formed by men and
women, young and old, manual workers and intellectuals, leaders, producers,
the military, politicians, putting aside their class differences and displaying a
profound spirit of fraternity (…) A convergence of profound Argentine
sentiment after a casual event – football, converted into a beautiful excuse –
but whose mechanics of mass appeal and shared feeling have much to do with
what is generally referred to as 'the national spirit'.

Córdoba, Special Edition – 25 June 1978

I'll never forget those orange shirts because people burnt them on the
corner of avenues General Paz and Colón. They burnt them with a
mad fascination, because Argentina had won. I remember I thought
the world cup song was awful. I cried when I saw that, but I also got
excited watching the matches. It's only human.

There are no desaparecidos

In 1980 Alba was studying at the Deán Funes College in Córdoba. The visit of
the Inter-American Human Rights Commission in 1979 had denounced the
atrocities that the dictatorship was committing while the country began to
hear, increasingly often, the word desaparecidos.

I said nothing to my teachers because I didn't trust them. A classmate
once asked:
   'What's all this about the desaparecidos? What are people talking
about?'
   And the teacher replied,
   'What desaparecidos?'
   So I said,
   'My parents are desaparecidos.'
   And she replied,
   'There are no desaparecidos.'
   Ok…there aren't any, fine, you call them what you want…

Malvinas

At the age of 16 I was working and living alone and at 18 I was already
married and had a daughter. I got married to a young man from the
same Malvinas generation and he didn't have to go because I was

pregnant. It all happens to me. I have to go into Batallion 141 of Army Intelligence to show my belly so that he wouldn't have to go to the Malvinas, and I was like,

'I won't have another dead person in my life.'

And plucking up great courage, because the truth is I was terrified, I went in to see an army doctor and show him my belly and say,

'He's married to me and I'm pregnant by him.'

And he was let off.

The inheritance

My grandfather died when I was 19. He called me and gave me the file with all the procedures he had been through since the day my parents disappeared. All the habeas corpus, the interventions by the Red Cross, Europe, everything. Everything he'd done in a file that was five centimetres thick.

I remember it was a glorious sunny day, he called me to his room, and I had no idea what he wanted. I said,

'What do you want, Granddad?' And he answered,

'Look, I haven't got much time left, someone has to carry on with this, it's up to you to continue with it.' He was about to die, he had cancer. He gave me a heavy load to bear, I took it on as best I could, I don't know whether I have fulfilled his expectations. From that moment I got in touch with everyone. From that day on I used to go to the square every Thursday, this was still during the dictatorship. I used to take my daughter with me, come rain or shine, every Thursday… every Thursday…

The man selling bin bags

In 1984 or 1985 with María Elba Martínez [a lawyer from Córdoba] we began to put together a case against Menéndez. In my parents' case they had been in the camp and my aunt had seen them. We did all this and while putting together the facts I tracked down the man who was selling bin bags.

I began to put together the case. I went back to the neighbourhood, to the block where we lived. Among other things that happened, a lot of neighbours shut their doors in my face:

'We saw nothing,' and the door would slam shut, and they'd all seen what happened. I know that they all saw because they parked the cars alongside, where there was a beer warehouse.

I went to UnCorCi to look for the files of people who had worked there in that period selling bin bags, in that area, in that neighbourhood. And the files were there! I came away with a list of about fifty men and began to phone (…) to go to their houses (…)

I did a door-to-door search until I found the one and he didn't want to have anything to do with it. Just imagine, he'd seen hell! I remember his face. I rang the bell, and he answered.

I said, 'My name is Alba Camargo, I'm looking for a person who worked at UnCorCi once…'

'Yes, I worked there.'

'Ah! Did you work in Talleres Sur in 1976 more or less? Do you remember?'

'Yes.'

His face started to change. He was about to take out five guns and riddle me with bullets. He was clearly thinking about that they'd come to get him.

"Look, I'm the daughter of desaparecidos, they were abducted from my house and at the same time a person who used to work for UnCorCi at the time was also abducted."

The guy's face changed completely. What happened was that he must have forgotten and I was bringing it all up again.

'Yes, I worked for UnCorCi, I was arrested…' All this on the doorstep.

'I need you to appear as a witness, you were in La Perla. You haven't filed a complaint? This is your chance.'

'No, no I don't want anything to do with it. Go away, go away!'

I say to him, 'I'm going to leave you my phone number, please call me,' and I left him.

He called me about a month later – I was about to go and see him again – and he asked me what he had to do (…) It's his life too, not just the life of others. He was an innocent bystander. That was what the country was like at that time. He knows he was in La Perla, where he was, and that they did mock executions of my aunts, of him.

The kingdom upside down

Obviously there were thousands of complaints filed against Menéndez, but there were more or less 57 cases that pinned him down. Over time, once the political pardon was issued, we were sent the costs of the prosecuting office and the 57 that proved that Menéndez was guilty had to pay for filing the cases. So they ended up coming to confiscate our possessions because we refused to pay. They came to confiscate things from our homes: a motorbike, a TV, anything. They told my grandmother,

'Ok, we've come to coooonfiscate… the television.'
'And the table, too,' said the secretary.
'And the table, too,' repeated the first one.

In his book *Hacer la Corte* journalist Horacio Verbitsky points out with reference to this case that the Federal Chamber of Córdoba and the Supreme Court not only didn't respond to the charges brought, but also declared that the relatives 'were not interested parties to the case.' 'The Argentinian judiciary's supreme body rejected the appeal against the pardon and demanded that they pay between six hundred and a thousand dollars each,' adds Verbitsky, who goes on to clarify that 'under the law governing legal fees, the plaintiff is only required to pay if the case against the accused is dismissed. None of this had happened in the case of Menéndez, whose trial was abandoned as a result of intervention by the Executive.'

Alba laughs as if she still cannot believe how that happened. Then, more seriously, she remembers the answer her grandmother gave to the people who came to confiscate:

'Take everything if you like. Take everything you can see, why not, since you took my children (…) what do possessions matter to me.'

'I never caused irreparable damage to anyone who was not a Communist.'
General Luciano Benjamín Menéndez – April 1989
Quoted in *Página/12* – November 1999

20 ✳✳✳✳

Sincericide

On 5 February 1975, Executive Decree No. 261 set in motion Operation Independence. With it Tucumán had the sad privilege of witnessing the prelude to the dictatorship. The first stage, which lasted until December 1975, was headed by Brigadier Adel Edgardo Vilas. In 1977 Vilas wrote his memoirs of the operation, explaining that 'When all is said and done my decision to put to paper my memories of my northern sojourn is not taken through a desire for commercial success – which cannot be guaranteed – nor with the aim of justifying what I have done, since I have nothing to justify. What's done is done and I do not regret it.' The text was not published due to a ban from the Army Chief Command, but the manuscript was circulated years later.

Operation Independence was the testing laboratory for state terrorism and in his memoirs Vilas justifies the illegality with which the Army acted. The following are extracts from the manuscript:

'One had to forget for a moment – a moment that lasted ten months – the teachings of the Military Academy and the rules of war, of which honour and ethics are essential components, although many do not believe that it is so.'

My intention, from then onwards, was to supplant, even if it meant using methods forbidden to me, the political authorities in the province of Tucumán (…) If I restricted myself to organising, training and commanding my troops, neglecting those spheres that by law I was not authorised to control – such as the spheres of trade union, commercial, university and social activity – the enemy would continue to have access to the "sanctuaries" available to him up until that time.

Moreover, we came up against another inconvenience that was only resolved over time. While an interrogation carried out by the Provincial Federal Police was legally valid, an interrogation carried out by an army officer was not (…).

From all that I saw and did, I was able to conclude that it made no sense to combat subversion using the Criminal Code (…)

If we tolerated the trade union, religious, educational, economic and political spheres being controlled, not by men, but by ideas that stemmed from the Marxist poison, if (…) we allowed the proliferation of dissident elements –

psychoanalysts, psychiatrists, Freudians, etc. – inciting the consciousness of the people and questioning the roots of the nation and family, we were beaten.

If the struggle we were waging depended on intelligence, the Detainee Holding Centre was the key to the development of the Operation (…) I decided to divide the guerrilla members into three groups in order to ensure that the most dangerous and important never reached prison. In order to avoid unnecessary risks, many from this latter group (…) were held in Famaillá, where they were interrogated until they were of no more use to us. From 10 February until 18 December 1975, 1507 people accused of having close links to the enemy passed through the Centre…'

In December Vilas was replaced by Bussi. On leaving the command of the Operation, all his conclusions pointed to the end of the armed struggle.

'Surrounded by the affection of its inhabitants and the respect of its soldiers, I left Tucumán on 21 December 1975, close to Christmas. While Operation Independence was not over yet, it was a complete success. The armed insurrection had been totally and completely defeated by an army that after a hundred years of peace was demonstrating its combat capacity. My greatest satisfaction was receiving days later, once I was back in the capital, a call from General Bussi, who told me, "Vilas, you have left me with nothing to do".'

Bussi took control of the operation and after the coup was appointed provincial governor. During this period, until he was replaced in 1977, more than 800 people disappeared in Tucumán.

MARIANA EVA TELLO

Mariana was born in 1975. Her mother, Azize Weiss, was a trade union representative, and a Montoneros militant. She only needed to do her thesis to complete her degree in architecture. On 12 July she was shot dead in front of Mariana.

In fact, they came to kill my dad, didn't find him and so they took my mum. They killed her outside the house. One version of what happened says that she ran out and they shot her down with me in her arms. Another version says they took her out to the street, I was right there in the car, they stood her against the wall and shot her dead.

OPERATIONS AGAINST SUBVERSIVE ELEMENTS (R-C-9-1)
4003 i) Apply fighting power with maximum use of violence to annihilate subversive delinquents wherever they happen to be. Military action is always violent and bloody (…) The subversive criminal who takes up arms must be annihilated, given that once the Armed Forces go into combat they should not suspend their operations nor accept the surrender of these elements.

Operations Order 9/77 – June 1977

There was a woman – we never saw her again – who was like a guardian angel to us. She lived above our apartment. She and her daughter saw when they killed my mum and took me. The police took me away and gave me to the family of a policeman, who had me for two or three months. When my dad came home that afternoon, the neighbours started telling him that the place had been crawling with police and that neither my mum nor I were there now. He managed to escape, sent a telegram to my grandparents in Jujuy and they came. My grandmother was detained with my aunt, also my grandfather and my other uncle. One of my uncles ended up in a clandestine centre. My aunt and my grandmother were sent to the women's prison. They were there for three days. In the prison they spoke to the governor and she told them 'I know where the girl is' so they kept up the pressure, 'we know that you have her'. They kept going back for three months until they returned me.

Afterwards they got in touch with a judge who got my mum's body back, but I know that he got into a lot of trouble for what he did. They kicked up an almighty fuss until they handed over the body.

Granny mum

Mariana was recovered by her grandparents and grew up in Jujuy with them. Her father remained in hiding until the return to democracy. Mariana always called her maternal grandmother 'mum'.

They told me that my mum had been killed in a demonstration. It was like a silence of complicity. I did hear some comments, one teacher – the wife of a cop – told my mum that she was the mother of a subversive that it was a good job they'd killed her daughter because she was a Montonera.

There was a large wardrobe with clothes in the house. I used to take them out, I knew they were her clothes. I used to smell them, try them on, look at myself in the mirror. At that time I thought she'd died in an accident. I woke up one morning, at around nine, and said to my mum, 'tell me the truth'.

Malvinas

I remember the Malvinas war. They made us write letters to the soldiers. I wrote to a dead soldier, not to a live one. Boy, was I going to get into trouble for that! I wrote that from heaven they had to be strong because this was a country with bad people who didn't care for human life (…) I told them that they were with my mum, that they were on the same side, that the same people had fucked them over…

The father

I used to cry a lot and wonder, 'why did Dad abandon me? (…) Mum died, but Dad just pissed off.' That really did me in.

I remember one holiday, when I was still a believer. We went through a town in Paraguay where there was a Virgin, so I bought a candle and told her, 'Look, if you make my dad appear, I'll come back.' When we got back from holiday my dad turned up.

During all those years, Carlos, Mariana's father was hidden in safe houses, working as a builder under a false name. At the beginning of 1984 he travelled to Jujuy and gradually rebuilt his relationship with his daughter.

They said,
'Bring your recorder, you're going to meet an uncle of yours.' I had

a good look at him and thought, 'This guy looks a lot like my uncle Mario – one of my dad's brothers. There's something fishy going on here.'

I remember one day in the kitchen, one day that he was cooking for me. He was trying to make things easy for me, he started by saying,

'Do you know how they killed your mother?' And I said,

'Yes, in a demonstration.'

Ever since I've known him, every night he dreams and cries out in his sleep. We sent him to sleep in a bathroom that was being built. You wake him up and he says, 'What's the matter?'. He dreams he's being persecuted the whole time. He cries…'

When my dad turned up I was attending Pedro Eugenio Aramburu* School, I was nine. Every year the military used to go and hold an event in his honour. My grandmother was a teacher there, it was her turn to make a speech and she told the headmaster,

'If you want, I'll give the speech, but don't ask me to say anything positive.'

They gave us a preparatory lesson (…) that 'Aramburu was a soldier of the Nation', that he 'died a hero's death', that 'no one knows who killed him', and so on…

And I, as always ready to speak up, was like this [raising her hand impatiently].

'I know! I know! The Montoneros killed him, they kidnapped him. They kidnapped him and killed him. Do you know why they killed him?'

And the teacher said, 'No! No! That's enough!'

Secondary school

Going to secondary school in Jujuy was like an ideological persecution for me. I always felt different inside the school and my fellow students always treated me as if I were different. At one point the confrontation between us turned nasty. I used to talk in class, voiced political opinions, liked painting, so the other kids saw me first as a 'hippy', 'a dirty hippy'. Then I joined the students' union and I became 'a fucking lefty'. They used to pass me notes…'John Lennon and Che Guevara were drug addicts and faggots.' Crap like that.

---

* General who helped overthrow Perón's government in 1955; he was de facto president between 1955 and 1958.

Holy Week and the idol

My dad had just come to Jujuy to see me, he got his passport and told me,

'Get ready because any day now we're going to have to leave. Otherwise we're not getting out of here alive, thing's are turning nasty here…'

He told me that some officers had rebelled, that they were planning another coup, that we were going back to the old days, and what struck me most was that I was going to have to be apart from my dad again. I remember thinking, 'I'm not going to live in a country with those people again.' I was really upset.

I wrote on a sheet of paper, 'We children defend democracy' and stuck it in the window of our house. I wrote a letter to Alfonsín too, because he was my idol. I told him he had to defend our democracy, that a lot of people in the country had suffered, that my family had been persecuted, that we were all happy now. I sent it to him and he never replied.

'Before the crowds gathered in the Plaza de Mayo [President Alfonsín] announced that he was setting out for Campo de Mayo to invite the rebels to surrender. There he had a meeting with the leader of the uprising and once back in the capital he told reporters that the rebels had abandoned their stance and would be tried.'

Clarín – 20 April 1987

'We have achieved our objective,' said [Lieutenant Colonel Aldo] Rico.

Clarín – 20 April 1987

The pardon

By that time I had a clearer idea of who they were. I went to the marches and took my little cousin with me. She was three and asked me:

'Mari… Is this a procession?'

'Yes, yes, this is a procession.' She was only three – what could I say?

'And the soldiers. Where are they?'

'Inside! That's precisely why we've come to march, so they don't come out again!'

'(…) Menem referred to the marches in repudiation of the pardon that took place yesterday in Buenos Aires and the rest of the country: "They can go on all the marches that they like. We are living in a democracy. Never before was there so much freedom in Argentina as there is now".'

Clarín – 31 December 1990

Mariana lives in Córdoba where she is studying for a degree in psychology. She is currently preparing her dissertation in which she is analysing the effects of socialisation on poverty. She is doing her fieldwork in a shantytown near Córdoba and is an assistant lecturer on the course 'Strategies for community intervention'. She lives with her boyfriend and when her studies allow her, she devotes time to her second vocation, drawing and painting.

21

Old friends

THE PROVINCIAL GOVERNMENT HELD A DINNER IN HONOUR OF THE PRESIDENTS OF THE CHAMBER OF COMMERCE

'The government and military are duty bound to thank all those active in Tucumán society who have made our administration possible. However, I wish to make special mention of some actors who deserve our recognition for their often silent support which has made our job easier. Among others, the chambers of commerce have played a role that is well-known for its stance of unity with this process we have taken on, the provincial governor [Domingo A. Bussi] stated at the end of the dinner given in the Nineteenth Infantry Regiment in honour of the Tucumán chamber of commerce to mark the end of the year.'

La Gaceta – 15 December 1976

RECOGNITION FOR GENERAL BUSSI

'The provincial governor, General Antonio Domingo Bussi, examines the medal presented to him by the president of the Sociedad Rural de Tucumán (Tucumán Rural Association), Dermidio Martínez Zavalía, who visited him together with the rural leader Rufino Paz Posse.'

La Gaceta – 4 December 1977

Please don't go

The Sociedad Rural Argentina is one of the country's most conservative organisations. From this organisation came the dictatorship's Minister of the Economy – José Alfredo Martínez de Hoz, one of those principally responsible for the country's indebtedness with international banks.

Just like the majority of Argentina's business groups, the Sociedad Rural not only was a great supporter of the regime, but when the dictatorship began to totter, and there was talk of possibly calling elections, the Sociedad Rural sent a letter to the de facto government requesting that the military regime remain in power.

THE SOCIEDAD RURAL ASKS FOR THE POLITICAL TRANSITION NOT TO BE HURRIED.

Headed by its president, Dr Juan Pirán, leaders of the Sociedad Rural requested an interview with Harguindeguy and gave him a letter in which they express their opinion on different aspects of the current situation facing the country.

Clarín – 5 September 1980

EDUARDO NACHMAN

Eduardo was born in 1956 and has three younger brothers. His mother is called Alicia and his father was called Gregorio Nachman.

> He was a theatre director and also worked in an estate agents' office run by my grandfather. He was well known in Mar del Plata and a great promoter of the theatre in the city. He used to organise concerts, famous singers and actors like Charly García and Nito Mestre used to stay at home with us; Pedro y Pablo – Miguel Cantilo and Jorge Durietz – Pappo, China Zorrilla, Nacha Guevara (…) I remember the last show we did with Closas, which I was also in. The theatre was in the centre of Mar del Plata.

'The theatre, cinema and music became a terrifying weapon used by the subversive enemy. Songs of protest, for example, played an important part in the creation of the climate of subversion that was being promoted: the songs denounced situations of social injustice, some real, others invented or manipulated.'

Lieutenant General Roberto Viola
La Prensa – 26 December 1979

> He used to boast that he was the only supporter of Argentinos Juniors in Mar del Plata and of course he was the only one who'd go out and celebrate on the rare occasions that Argentinos won. Alone.
>
> A lot of times they used to throw gas into the theatre, or simply close it down. Teams of inspectors would come round and close the theatre because the fire extinguisher was at an angle, or its hose was black when it should have been red or other crap like that. We used to do street theatre. He was convinced that if the people couldn't go to the theatre, the theatre should go to the people. He used to do plays in prisons, during the Cordobazo, or in occupied factories (…) He was a committed activist.

'Father'

> Once they came to raid the theatre. I was working there. When I wasn't acting I used to work as a usher or in the bar. The police came looking for my dad and we said,

'No, he's not coming in today, he's in Buenos Aires.' The police gleefully searched the building. I remember that my mum was beside the coffee machine. My uncle who was also disappeared was there, Elías Seman, a leader of the Communist Vanguard.

At one point my dad and my uncle come out disguised as priests. The cops see them, my dad blesses us and says,

'Good afternoon, brothers' and I say,

'Good afternoon, father…'

My mum almost died because she thought I'd said 'dad'. And that time they managed to escape.

March 24 1976

I remember that it was a grey day and the military were out on the streets. All the army, all the Naval Command (…) half the streets in Mar del Plata were cordoned off and there was no public transport. We were hiding books and pictures, amongst others a 'Che' by Carpani, and another portrait that was like Alonso's 'Che'.

When the coup happened, my dad was forced to give up the theatre building because of the pressure and threats he was subjected to, but he carried on doing theatre. What's more, in May 1976 we represented Argentina in the international theatre festival in São Paulo. We did two very politically committed plays. One was 'A run-of-the-mill sacking', a play by Julio Mauricio, which was about something that was still a rarity at that point – the abduction of a worker. The worker was Lachovsky, the union representative at the Peugeot factory, who died under torture. At that time it was almost unthinkable…

June 19 1976

It was the Saturday before Father's Day. My dad was organising a season of French films at the Alliance Française. That day they were showing his favourite film, *The beauty of dialogue*, featuring his favourite actor. I had a motorbike and a small car too. I had to go and fetch the film reels and I don't know why, I called home. My younger sister, who was eleven at the time, answered and said,

'Everything's fine, don't come…'

I realised that something terrible was happening, so I stayed the night in a hotel near the bus terminal and I went home the next day, by day. That's when I found out that there was a group of armed men in our house.

Eduardo's father had gone to the building where the estate agent was. He went to get some blankets for some relatives who were staying with him. As he was leaving the office a group of policeman turned up asking him to accompany them to clear up 'a problem with a warranty'. Nachman, without putting up any resistance, got into the Investigations Department's Peugeot and that was the last that anyone knew of him.

'In order to achieve their objectives, the subversives have used and try to use all imaginable media: the press, songs of protest, comics, cinema, folklore, literature, university classes, religion and basically, they have tried, unsuccessfully, to use panic.'

Vice-Admiral Armando Labruschini, Naval Chief of Staff
Clarín – 4 December 1976

We lived on the seventh floor. There were three lifts and I saw that one was on the sixth floor, one on the seventh and one on the eighth. I got out on the eighth floor and went down the stairs. There was an armed man on the stairs. I entered my home and my mum was crying, trying to get in touch with my brother, who was studying medicine in La Plata, to tell him not to come home.

Trying to see him

The president of the International Red Cross was in Mar del Plata. I went and told him that my dad was detained. I told him that I was going to go to Battalion 601 to look for him and that if I didn't come back he should go looking for me. I went to look for him and was beaten up. They were surprised, I went in and said,

'I'm looking for my dad, the police haven't got him, so he has to be here.'

That's when the show started (…) I wasn't to look them in the eye, they started getting all cocky with me, pushing me around, 'just wait here'(…) I had a rough time in there, they stripped me, beat me up (…) I went there early in the morning and at 6 pm they came looking for me. What I wanted was to try to see him and for them to legalise his status as a prisoner.

'After spending last night in the bosom of my family as all the inhabitants of the province of Buenos Aires surely did too, this Christmas, this 25 December 1976, I am sending out a message of peace and hope that after this Christmas is over and on the eve of a new year in the life of the Nation, the Argentinian people manage to find the broad consensus that will allow us to follow the path of peace and progress to which we all aspire.'

Brigadier General Albano Eduardo Harguindeguy
Province of Buenos Aires Radio
Quoted in *La Gaceta* – 26 December 1976

Nothing is going on

We received constant warnings to keep quiet, we were told that if we didn't make what had happened public, there was a chance he would reappear. We couldn't talk to anyone. It lasted a couple of months, during which time we looked for him all over, it was horrible, trying to lead a normal life, lying to all my friends that my dad had been contracted to work in Mendoza. Whatever. Until things got really sticky and I hid out in the countryside between Mar del Plata and Balcarce, a bad situation. I didn't want to leave Mar del Plata in case my dad turned up.

Fleeing

I told my mum to get my clothes ready and buy me a ticket to Buenos Aires for November 6, my birthday. I cut my hair, bought a suit and a briefcase. The father of a friend of mine, a former policeman who had been kicked off the force because he was a Peronist, tailed the bus for almost a hundred kilometres along highway 2 in an old Chevrolet.

In 1978 I won a scholarship to a drama school, using my mother's surname. I couldn't be Nachman. I used to live in different places, in a garage in Caballito, then with a great aunt. My family moved to Buenos Aires after 1978. We spoke little, out of fear, distress (…) we tried to avoid the subject and carry on living our lives.

The buses

I used to ride the buses looking at people, to see if I could spot him, maybe he was mad, maybe he'd lost his memory; I sat there imagining how he would have changed physically so that I would still recognise him. I was constantly searching. I always used to look out of the window, not inside the bus, or first I'd look at my fellow passengers, as if I were checking and registering them all and then I'd look out of the window.

I couldn't go back to Mar del Plata for four years. That distressed me enormously. My adolescence had been cut short, overnight my daily routine, my youth had been interrupted. I had a partner who couldn't take the sudden change, so that was the end of a very close relationship. I was studying for a degree in history at Mar del Plata

University and getting really good grades. Everything came to an abrupt end…

Eduardo trained to be a teacher. He has two children called Alejo and Paula; he's separated and currently lives alone. He teaches in a primary school and gets home at 5 pm. Twice a week he organises recreational activities in a social project.

One day during a march, his son Alejo asked him why he didn't join HIJOS; the explanation Eduardo gave was that he was much older than most of the members of the group. But Alejo persisted, saying that even so he was 'a son' and that he should be involved…

Despite describing himself as a 'sonosaur' and claiming that on account of his age he should really 'be part of the Council of Elders of HIJOS', Eduardo approached the group and is involved presenting a radio programme called *La lucha que nos parió* (The struggle that bore us).

Gregorio Nachman Hall

It was in 1995. Some time before we heard that they were going to name a theatre after him in Mar del Plata. A few days before the inauguration our tickets arrived, the official invitation and off we went, feeling very nervous. We all went. The director of the theatre spoke and revealed a plaque. I was very moved to find myself there in the theatre with so many friends that I hadn't expected to see: friends of my dad's, students, fellow actors who my dad had directed. That was very moving – to realise that my dad isn't just important to me or to his immediate family. And I found myself crying for him for the first time, moved to tears by something that had to do with my dad.

The great forgiver

'When the men responsible for this Proceso, whether civilians or military, are investigated, the prisons in this country will not be enough to hold them, and, figuratively speaking, an entire province will have to be fenced in to shut them away.'

Dr Carlos Saul Menem
Tiempo Argentino – 18 June 1983

It happened three years ago. I was standing at the door of a primary school where I was head, at about a quarter to eight. Just an ordinary day in the heart of the Belgrano district, opening the school doors for the arrival of the pupils, when a burgundy Peugeot 505 goes past with

Jorge Rafael Videla inside. It goes past slowly because the lights are red and it was slowing down. He was driving, his wife beside him and behind them came their bodyguards' car. Although I am a reasonably controlled person in general, I was overcome by a feeling of vertigo, of anger, by a desire to hurl something at him. The first thing I did was to look behind me down the corridor that led into the school where a fire extinguisher was usually kept. Luckily it wasn't there. A week earlier it had been moved. I moved closer, made sure it was Videla and began to shout. There were some people walking past, but I stood there in front of his car and started banging the bonnet and shouting at him. Straight away, the butcher from opposite the school, who was unloading some trays with tripe, brains, giblets and that kind of thing, said:

'What's the matter with you?'

'It's Videla!'

'Really?!'

He came over, saw that it really was Videla and began to fill his windscreen with bits of offal, brains, tripe (...) The first thing Videla did was to switch on the windscreen wipers. His wife was looking at the car behind, but the guards didn't get out because it was a narrow street, with cars parked on both sides. I could see how Videla in desperation was pressing the windscreen wipers switch, but all he achieved was to flick all that stuff from side to side as if it were waving, making it absolutely impossible for him to see anything through the film of grease mixed with water.

Then the bodyguards got out of the car and we left. I went back to the school, feeling very nervous, very worked up. I drank a glass of water and went back to the door to wait for my pupils...

'When I pardoned the military, I consulted with the Holy Father and the Church leaders. The Pope said he considered it to be a measure that would contribute to bringing peace to Argentina.'

Declarations by President Carlos Menem in Rome
Página/12 – 22 November 1999

22

Metamorphosis

The media in general were submissive to the dictatorship. In many cases they gave explicit surpport to the regime. And with the return to democracy, a number of figures linked to the dictatorship underwent a great metamorphosis.

Mariano Grondona, one of the most influential journalists in Argentina, was a fervent sympathiser of the dictatorship and wrote the Military Junta's first speech. He also presented (together with Bernardo Neudstad) the only political programme that was allowed to be transmitted during the military regime (in which, obviously, the dictatorship was never criticised).

Today, however, Grondona works as a political columnist for the newspaper *La Nación* and presents the television programme *Hora Clave*. The following are some of the opinions he expressed during the military dictatorship.

'What would be left of Argentina without the sword and the cross? Who would want to go down in History as the one who denied her either of them? Argentina is Catholic and military. There is no greater responsibility than to preserve that.'

Leader from *Carta Política* monthly magazine,
Mariano Grondona – August 1976

'Both the COHA [Council of Hemispheric Affairs] and Amnesty International are well known to be extreme left-wing organisations, that specialise in attacking and constantly denouncing those regimes capable of resisting the onslaught of subversive terrorism…'

Nobel Prize: For or Against Argentina?
Mariano Grondona – *El Cronista Comercial*, 15 October 1980

'To use one image, in 1976 the country was like a heart failure patient in a very serious condition, with his coronary arteries blocked. What was carried out between 1976 and 1981 was a delicate and basically successful by-pass operation…'

The Scalpel Theory
Mariano Grondona – *El Cronista Comercial*, 1 April 1981

JOSEFINA GIGLIO

Josefina is a journalist, she was born in 1970 and has a younger brother. She is the daughter of Carlos Alberto Giglio, an architect, and Virginia Cazalás, a psychologist. On 19 May 1976, when Josefina was five years old, her father was abducted. The following year, on 7 December 1977, her mother was kidnapped.

A classic

We were living in La Plata when they went underground. There are several houses in La Plata designed by him. We came to live here in Buenos Aires. The only memory I have of my dad is when we moved from La Plata to Buenos Aires. We were in the living room, there was a sofa bed, I came running from the kitchen, threw myself on top of him and kneed him in the balls. That was a classic, I was always hitting him there. I remember my dad laughing and crying at the same time.

I remember how my mum cried when they took my dad away. They woke us up in the middle of the night in another apartment. Someone came in a Citröen to fetch us.

I remember that I was sitting in front and thinking,

'How strange, my mum in her nightie.' My mum was crying, with me on her lap. She was pregnant at that point; my brother was born in July and this was in May. We were heading somewhere and I thought, 'Mmmm, something's up…' I think she told me 'They've got your dad.'

Because I miss him

I had a false name at that time: María José Roldán. I remember that it was crazy, because I still went to the same school. What changed were the houses we lived in. I remember one time going to the wardrobe, taking down a brown leather jacket of my father's and my mum saying to me in a psychoanalytical tone:

'Why did you do that?'

'Because I miss him.'

But I never spoke to her about that. I don't think so…

Part II

My brother was born in July. I had measles or mumps, the baby was crying and I couldn't pick him up. No one knew where we were. When my dad was captured, they took my grandmother from La Plata, my grandfather from Tres Arroyos, my uncles in Moné Cazón (…) All to make my mum give herself up.

It was about 11 pm, a warm night. In a flat on Ramón Freire Street. I remember that they banged on the door like they do in films. They said,

'Open up or we'll break it down', or something like that. I was in bed, wearing pink knickers. We used to sleep in the living room and in the bedroom were a couple. I remember watching the door. There were a whole lot of them, with long guns and in plain clothes. There were a load of men outside in the passage. They took everyone away. I always wonder whether my mum said anything to me, but I can't remember her saying anything. The image I have is of the lift going down with my mum (…) Her face descending…

They knocked on a neighbour's door to leave us. I remember clearly the neighbour saying,

'What am I supposed to do with these children?' And my brother crying a lot.

We went to the police station and they start asking me about my relatives. I had a clear idea about my grandparents who lived in Tres Arroyos. So when they ask about my grandparents I say 'Polo Cazalás'.

'Polo isn't a name,' the solider told me.

And I just said,

'My grandfather's called Polo.' They called the Tres Arroyos police station and they came to get us.

Tres Arroyos

I started living a kind of normal life. Tres Arroyos is a town in the province of Buenos Aires, in the south-east, in the bump, before Bahía Blanca. I went to the same school my mum went to as a child. My grandfather is a well-known business man. The people knew and there was like a tacit agreement. Once a kid came, who wasn't even a friend of mine, and said the typical, 'My mum told me your dad's a terrorist.'

To tell the truth, I have the feeling that my life beforehand had been so chaotic that when I arrived in Tres Arroyos I felt, 'Ahhh! How nice! These people have been living in the same house for forty years.' I remember once saying to my grandfather:

'And you always lived here?'

'Yes,' he replied, 'I was born here.'

'That can't be possible,' I thought. In the space of two years I had known millions of houses, had had another name…

Simple but moving

My grandfather Cazalás – Polo – is a man who tells the truth. I once asked and he told me:

'Your parents were against the government and that's why they took them away.'

He always spoke so rationally about it. For example, he'd say,

'Your parents were old enough to know what they were getting into, I warned them, this was inevitable.' It was very frustrating because I was going crazy (…) At one point I had a very strong fantasy that my mum was exiled in Spain and that she was going to come and rescue me.

There's a photo of my mum with my brother on her lap and on the back of the photo I wrote 'Disappeared on 12/7, reappeared on…' and the second date always remained a blank. I thought that they were going to turn up again. I was seven or eight. I was in the bedroom I shared with my brother that looked out over the street.

It was summer, I was feeling optimistic…

The grown-ups

One thing that happened during the dictatorship, which I can't place in time, but that was a trigger. My grandfather had a fizzy drinks factory and was a representative of Quilmes beer. One day he got a letter in German and we started imagining all kinds of wonderful things. I thought it was from my dad. We sent the letter to be translated, I remember that it cost a great deal, we couldn't find a German translator, we had to send it to La Plata (…) and it turned out to be a letter advertising tops for beer bottles…

At that time it was unimaginable that a letter advertising something would arrive at your home. And that was when I realised that the grown-ups were also vulnerable – they were also hoping…

For you

Not my grandfather, but my grandmother was a woman who used to say the whole time, 'when you parents return, when they get back, when they get back...' At one point I told her, 'They're not coming back.' I was very upset by the contradiction. Do you remember the silly women's magazine *Para Ti*? They issued some postcards saying 'We Argentinians are right and human'? They were postcards to send abroad – photos of Argentina at peace – and I remember sending a couple.

'And if using the gangs the accused placed a hood over each of the victims of the kidnappings, they also placed a great hood over the whole of society through their psychological campaign.

They organised mass publicity campaigns, gagged the national press, which was not allowed to publish news about the desaparecidos since they could not avoid the truth from travelling beyond borders and having repercussions abroad, they claimed that the international denunciations were the fruit of an anti-Argentine campaign organised by subversive elements. (...) And with this whole lie about the anti-Argentine campaign, they not only denied the facts, but transformed those who made or repeated the denunciations into sub-versives.'

> Extracts from the case for the prosecution
> State Attorney Julio Strassera – Juicio a las Juntas

The dictatorship intoxicated the population with propaganda. Popular magazines like *Gente, Somos,* or *Para Ti* practically functioned as spokespersons for the official discourse; a media bombardment apparently inspired by Joseph Goebbels' theory, to 'lie and lie till some of it sticks'. In 1979, after the denunciations made by the Inter-American Human Rights Commission at the end of its visit to our country, the magazine *Para Ti* included postcards for its readers to send abroad, which denied the existence of state terrorism.

To: _____   Address: _____
'Argentina – the whole truth' Popular celebrations during the World Cup.
The war is over in Argentina. These banners are the symbol of the peace that we have won. The Football World Cup was a test that we had to take and we passed. You, who live far away, dared to judge us. You listened to subversive criminals and gave them a stage to speak from. You didn't hesitate to condemn a country that, at a very great cost, managed to overcome an enemy that sought to destroy us. If it were necessary, we have already sent out our message of peace. Now it is you who should decide whether it is necessary to continue passing a negative judgment on a country that chose to bet on the future.

> Postcards to be sent abroad – *Para Ti* magazine
> Editorial Atlántida – August 1979

Malvinas

I remember a schoolteacher I had who was the only one to refuse to pay homage. At that time all the libraries and squares began to be called Malvinas Islands and The Patriotic Gesture (…) A language teacher who was fantastic – she was called Marta – said,

'I don't agree with it, I think it's a mistake.' She said it in the classroom. But anyway, she was the 'divorcée' among the staff, the 'separated' teacher. Do you see what I mean? Everyone knew…

'In order to subvert people, through the stages previously indicated, Marxism avails itself of the following procedures: (…) The destruction of the traditional concept of the family (through divorce, cohabitation, etc), replacing that concept with another that serves the political needs of the party.'

Subversion in the education system (Getting to know our enemy),
Ministry of Culture and Education – Buenos Aires 1977

From Tres Arroyos to La Plata

When she finished secondary school, Josefina went to live in La Plata with her paternal grandmother. There she started studying journalism.

When I went to live with my grandmother in La Plata, I couldn't stand that Italian thing with grief. I think it was very unfair of me. My grandmother went into mourning the day they took my dad away, everything was much more closed and painful, typical Italian. In Tres Arroyos there was no discussion to be had.

My grandmother in La Plata though, was one of the first to walk around the square, the first to present a writ of habeas corpus. She appears to be very strong, but behind doors it was unending grief.

I opened a file and there were all the writs of habeas corpus, the letters to Monsignor Plaza (…) because they wrote to God and the Holy Mary. The replies stated 'we know nothing', 'we have no information…'

'…Argentina is one of the most peaceful countries and where human rights are most respected. I cannot see that at this moment in time in Argentina people are being imprisoned or killed, or that human rights are being violated…'

Monsignor Octavio N. Derisi, Bishop of La Plata and Vice-chancellor of the Catholic
University of Argentina, Declarations – 11 September 1979

The letter to Videla must be there. What struck me was that before that one all the letters had been written on an old typewriter of my grandfather's and the one from my grandmother was written by hand.

'Your Excellency, Mr President, Don Jorge Rafael Videla (…) I am writing to you to inquire about the whereabouts of my daughter who was with her two small children when she was taken away (…) and until today her little girl asks after her and I don't know what to say…"

I was deeply touched and felt hugely impotent, she didn't know whom she was appealing for help from…

'It is the revenge of the subversives and a load of rubbish. This is like Nuremberg turned on its head, with the criminals judging those who overcame terrorism…'

Monsignor Plaza, Thoughts on the trial of the ex-Commanders – 21 May 1985

A kid from La Plata disappears after the return to democracy, 1993

I was a fellow student of Miguel Bru's, a kid from La Plata who was disappeared. Miguel was a friend of ours, he was a great person. He was the most hippy, the most working class, he lived in a squat.

I had two or three groups of friends at university: the activists, the posh group and the working class group, which was how I met Miguel. We studied first and second year together. At one point he stopped going to class and I no longer saw him at the university, but I still used to see him in those groups.

'Enanito's (Shorty) having a barbecue!', the word would go round and we'd all go and there'd be Miguel. One day Silvina comes and tells me:

'You know that Miguel's disappeared?'

'Oh, don't be stupid,' I told her, 'he's probably shacked up with some girl.'

'No one's seen him for a week.'

Miguel Bru was seen for the last time on 17 August 1993. Three months previously he had filed a complaint against the police of the station number nine in La Plata for illegally raiding his home. He was kidnapped by members of that police station and died as a result of torture. He was 23 years old.

ORAL JUDGEMENT FOR THE CRIME OF THE STUDENT MIGUEL BRU
Police station number nine in La Plata. It is suspected that Bru was tortured to death.
'Another witness said that he'd seen the youngster after he disappeared (…)

Relatives of prisoners held at that police station in La Plata say that prisoners are systematically tortured there and that their shouts of pain can be heard outside the building.'

Clarín – 3 May 1999

He was just another kid. He was a dreamer, a lovely person, a hippy, he spent the whole time with his dogs. He used to come to classes and the dogs would wait for him outside the department.

We learnt that Miguel had lodged a complaint because they had raided the house where he was living. The neighbours used to complain because he'd play the drums 'all hours of the night'.

Miguel went to house-sit for some friends in Bavio, on the outskirts of La Plata. They followed him there and picked him up. They took him to the police station, tortured him – there are people who saw him – and he died on them. Miguel was like this [holding up her little finger]. They say they buried him in a cement block. I found out about this and it was really crazy because I realised it was something that didn't stop happening. Something that could happen to us again…

JUDGMENT IN THE BRU CASE: HISTORICAL JUDGEMENT PASSED BY A COURT IN LA PLATA

Two policemen are given life for torturing and killing a student.

Miguel Bru was 23 years old in 1993, when he was tortured in a police station in La Plata. He was subsequently disappeared and his body was never found. Another two policemen were found guilty of negligence and covering up the crime (…) For many this was an emblematic judgement. Simply because those who have now been found guilty had managed to transform Bru into a ghost, into someone who had apparently been swallowed up by the earth. Only through the persistence of his mother, Rosa Schonfeld, did this story have a different ending. There was no evidence to show that the youngster had ever been in the police station. Nor were there the marks of torture on a mutilated body.

Clarín – 18 May 1999

Josefina lives in the capital. She rents a flat in San Telmo and works as a journalist for the daily paper *La Nación*.

23

Downhill

At the beginning of the 1980s the cracks in the dictatorship start becoming more evident. Sources of international credit are few and far between and the economic situation becomes chaotic. Denunciations of crimes of state terrorism are being heard more and more frequently. The architect Adolfo Pérez Esquivel, a human rights activist, wins the Nobel Peace Prize. The government declares that this award is part of an 'anti-Argentinian campaign'.

'In Argentina we are living well and we still have enough to eat seven days a week. Only a few countries can boast of this – of having food to eat seven days a week. The country's problems are not as critical as people claim. Many of the problems are magnified, even the economic problems.'

Brigadier Omar Rubens Graffigna
Somos magazine – 14 August 1981

UNEASE WITHOUT LIMITS
Massera believes men and procedures must be changed
Retired Admiral Emilio E. Massera expressed the opinion that 'there needs to be a changeover in the men currently in power in the national government, in the face of the failure of the current military process, initiated in March 1976. As a former co-protagonist of the process, my own unease knows no limits when I see that, more than five years after the beginning of what was going to be an important era in the country's history, we have achieved none of our objectives, except the armed victory over terrorism.'

He also added that 'a very high price has been paid by the women and men of this land for us to now settle for saying that it was an experiment, and that the experiment failed. (…) You have to travel up and down the republic, as I do, to see that, from one end of the country to the other, the citizenry is convinced that it failed.'

La Prensa – 3 October 1981

PRIMATESTA CALLS FOR FAITH IN THE FACE OF THE ECONOMIC SITUATION

The archbishop of Córdoba and president of the Argentinian Episcopal Conference, Cardinal Raúl Primatesta, urged the population to 'have faith' in the face of the current economic situation and pronouced in a homily that 'this is not the time to give up. (…) If God has put us on this earth to work, why should we give up now, he wondered. Have we perchance lacked enough food, or perhaps we have lacked the confidence, strength and faith to work? Finally, he urged the crowd who had arrived in a procession from different points in Greater Mendoza, to 'raise their hands and ask for forgiveness'. As long as we do not know how to ask for forgiveness our lands will not bear fruit, he affirmed.

La Prensa – 14 October 1981

NAZARENO BRAVO

Nazareno is the son of Juan Humberto Rubén Bravo and María Carrera. He was born in Mendoza in February 1976. Eight months later, on 21 October, his father was kidnapped.

My dad was an actor, he used to do radio dramas and was active in the Argentinian Actors' Association. As soon as he left secondary school he started acting. He was 26 when he was arrested. My mum is still alive and still works as an actress today.

We were living in a boarding house, because we couldn't afford anything else. After they took my dad away we lived in La Plata for a year because we'd been told that he was there. But it was all lies, things that never turned out to be true. When we returned to Mendoza we started living with my maternal grandparents.

That little world

I was always aware of the fact that my dad was missing and I had an idea that he wasn't coming back. Those are the first memories I have, which came from the way people talked at home. It wasn't only my dad who was disappeared in my family, there was also an aunt and uncle –my mother's sister and her husband.

I clearly remember the meetings at my grandmother's house, and going to church (…) A lot of the women who later formed Madres de Mendoza used to get together to make *empanadas* and go out to sell them, to pay for the adverts asking where their relatives where.

Nor can we fail to mention the brutal treatment and constant persecution suffered by the Madres de Plaza de Mayo, including all kinds of threats, aggression and even the disappearance of some of the organisation's members, all for committing no crime other than asking for the reappearance of their children alive, thus becoming – at the blackest moments in the dictatorship – the spokespersons for the civic conscience of the Nation.

Nunca Más, CONADEP Report (1984) Chapter III

I remember quite a lot about all these things. You could say that I grew up in that whole little world of bureaucratic procedures and of meetings held by the Madres, Familiares…

JOSÉ LUIS D'ANDREA MOHR
'In May 1985, also in Río Negro, I signed a letter in which I described the Juntas and leaders of the Process as criminals and cowards and the Madres de Plaza de Mayo as heroes. That signalled the end of my military career. I had to appear before the Honour Tribunal, presided over by the same man ten years later. This time I was accused of:
• Acting disloyally towards my comrades or the institutions of the armed forces, and
• Publishing for reasons unknown opinions that affect the military hierarchy or leadership.'

Memoria Debida – Ediciones Colihue, 1999

And your dad?

As far as she could, my mum always told me the truth. I used to say quite confused things. In the explanations I came up with I invented ten thousand different ways for him to have died, like in an accident, illness, etc. They were all quite tragic things.

In fact, I think I was more paranoid than necessary, given the degree of interest anyone showed. I can't remember being that interested in the lives of my friends' parents. That was none of your business. Later on, my grandfather was a useful presence in a lot of tricky situations, because a lot of kids thought that he was my dad. That let me off the hook…

My dad the astronaut

I remember once talking to some friends outside my house; we were all little, must have been around five years old. We were telling stories and, like all children, each was trying to outdo the others. They happened to be talking about the fact that the father of one had got into a fight, the other said, 'well, my dad had an accident. And he didn't hurt himself!', and trying to outdo them all, I said,

'My dad was killed by the police.'

There was a long silence and my mother called me in. Clearly they'd been listening to our conversation. She called me inside and explained that it wasn't such a good idea, it wasn't very sensible to go round saying that. To me it seemed so normal…

Hope

When my mum told me that she was going to live with the man who is now her partner it did my head in. My first reaction was to say, 'And what if dad comes back?'

In fact never before then had I ever really believed that he would. It was more a defensive reaction to the news, and more because I'd had my mum to myself for nine years. By then I was ten years old and she told me that no, he wouldn't be coming back…

The first time I remember thinking a lot about my dad was when we won the elections to the students' union. I was up for president. When we won I felt very close to my dad, maybe because of his union activism. It was a moment in which I thought about him a lot, thought he'd be very proud of me…

That night

I reconstructed what had happened through my paternal grand-mother, who for family reasons I only saw again when I was 20. What she told me was that they were there in the boarding house. She's one of those superstitious old ladies, always consulting the cards and that kind of thing. A real character. That day she'd spent the whole day with the feeling that something bad was on the way. My grandmother didn't know that they were PRT activists. She told me that my dad had me in his arms for a long time, that she was cooking and that they came in through the windows, broke down the doors and everything. It was a group of about eight men, who weren't wearing masks or anything like that. They said they were from the joint security forces and later on we found out that several were from the police. They tied my mum and my grandmother to the bed, I was in my cradle, they left me there and took my dad away.

And they stole everything they could lay their hands on, as they always used to, they walked through the patio and took the clothes that were hanging on the line. At that time people used cloth nappies, and they even took my nappies.

There was a whole lot of information that could never be checked, but there were several clues as to what happened to him. On the same day that they abducted him an ex-prisoner saw him at the Godoy Cruz Seventh Police Station, which was one of the clandestine centres. After that there were a couple more bits of information, but they were few and far between.

'On 15 October 1976 members of the provincial police arrested me at the bus station in Mendoza. Without blindfolding or handcuffing me, they took me to Godoy Cruz Seventh Police Station, where they put me in a cell. There I was interrogated while being tortured with an electric cattle prod for three consecutive days. On 21 October they transferred me to another part of the police station, where they showed me Juan Humberto Rubén Bravo (who is currently disappeared) who was in the custody of two guards. Five days later I was transferred to Mendoza Prison, where I was legalised.'

Pablo Rafael Seydell – File No. 6918, Conadep

The La Plata clue

We were given the information by a policeman because that same taskforce, during a subsequent action – another kidnapping – started fighting over a gold watch belonging to the victim. They start bickering among themselves, the argument got more and more heated and one shot another. A policeman called Cirella. The policeman is arrested, and in the papers it was reported as a brawl. Obviously nothing was said about it being an abduction. Then Cirella, from the prison where he's being held, asks to speak to my paternal grandmother. When my grandmother goes to see him he tells her that they'd arrested my dad by mistake, that he was a good boy, that he [Cirella] wanted to help her, that he felt so bad about having shot a fellow policeman, that what he wanted to do was to confess everything and die.

He gave her information, but what happened is that afterwards, knowing the criminal mind of the military, it wouldn't be at all strange to think that it was just a dirty trick. Our attention was diverted to La Plata for a whole year. We even offered a reward.

Time passes

It was like I had a lot of things in front of my nose and I couldn't see them. Different processes take place in each person's head and they are framed by the context in which one grew up.

Nazareno rents a flat where he lives alone. He has six subjects to complete to finish his degree in sociology and he is preparing his dissertation. He is a Gimnasia supporter 'in good times and bad' and also participates in HIJOS. In the morning he works doing surveys, has a siesta after lunch, in the afternoon he gets down to studying, and at night visits his girlfriend.

If I had any choice, I'd not be in HIJOS, I'd rather be with my dad. It's not something that I love doing, being in HIJOS. There are times when we're all together having a beer, or at a birthday party, having a laugh, and I find it very strange to think that we all went through something and that we met because our parents were activists, and because of state terrorism and all that. These are things that I can't get my head round the whole time. There are times when it all makes me feel very depressed.

I am very proud, I think it's fundamental, but the ideal would be for justice to be done. For there to be no need for HIJOS, nor Abuelas, nor Madres...nor Nietos (Grandchildren), as I am sure will one day exist. That's where you feel the impunity...

24 ✳✳✳✳

Iceberg ahead

The history of the Argentinian-British conflict over the Malvinas/Falkand Islands dates back to the year 1833, when a British expedition invaded and occupied the islands that at the time were inhabited by a few Argentinian cattle farmers. Prior to this, France had taken possession of the islands in 1764 in the name of Louis XV, giving them the name Malouines. Spanish sovereignty was subsequently recognised by the French and the islands were handed back in 1767.

In 1811, after the declaration of independence, a group of Argentinians took possession of the archipelago. In 1829, the government of Buenos Aires created the Political and Military Command Headquarters, located on Soledad Island, and Luis Vernet was named governor. On 2 January 1833 the British warship Clio anchored off Puerto Soledad and the British invaded the islands. That marked the beginning of 149 years of diplomatic claims by Argentina.

In 1982 the dictatorship found itself in a cul-de-sac. Unable to find an adequate response to the economic and social problems it had unleashed, it decided to take drastic action and so it was that early in the morning of 2 April the Argentinian people were surprised to learn that the army had occupied the islands. Twenty days later, Argentina was at war with one of the greatest military powers in the world. It was an absurd war that cost hundreds of lives, and which was motivated by the crazed desire of the military to cling on to power.

WE ARE HERE TO STAY
Saturday, 10 am in the Malvinas Islands. Personal interview for *Somos* with the governor, General Mario Benjamín Menéndez.

'What is the population saying?'

'Our relations with the islanders improves daily. Many of them already understand the situation and are beginning to collaborate. The rest will come round to our point of view over the course of the coming days.'

'What did you say to the islanders?'

'That we have not come to invade the islands, but to reclaim them.'

'Are you expecting the English fleet?'

'We are preparing for any eventuality. We have come to the Malvinas and we are here to stay.'

Somos magazine – 16 April 1982

GLORIOUS SATURDAY
Plaza de Mayo. 150,000 voices shout 'Argentina'. A gathering without political overtones.
'While the crowd unfurled banners (some sober and others more audacious) Ministers Saint-Jean and Aguado viewed the spectacle. Galtieri on the balcony remarked: "If they want to come, let them come. We shall do battle with them".'

Somos magazine – 16 April 1982

'In time of war social tensions diminish since the whole nation is focused on the goal of winning the war.'

Alvaro Alsogaray
Somos magazine – 23 April 1982

SERIOUS LOSSES CAUSED TO THE ENGLISH INVADERS
La Prensa – 10 June 1982
(The same day that the surrender was signed).

MIGUEL CEBALLOS

Miguel was born in Córdoba in 1967. He lived in Trelew, then in San Juan and finally returned to his native Córdoba to study law.

I'm the eldest of three siblings, after me comes Ramón and then my sister Amalia, the youngest. My dad's name was Miguel Angel Ceballos and my mum's called Frida Angélica. My dad was an economics student and president of the Córdoba Federation of University Students.

We used to live in Villa Marta (Córdoba), in a rented house. I lived there till I was about three and a half, when things started getting tricky and my mum decided to go and live in the south. We went to Trelew, in the province of Chubut.

My dad stayed here and it was a kind of ad hoc separation. My mum had been threatened here in Córdoba, walking along the street on her own, they told her they were going to kill her. She talked to my dad and my dad decided that he was going to stay.

Shortly after Miguel moved to Trelew his father was arrested and transferred to Rawson prison. When they released him, before returning to Córdoba, he went to see his family.

I remember my dad from when he got out under the 1973 amnesty, during the Cámpora government. I remember that he came to stay for about four days. I have a few memories of the visit. He looked a lot like me, but shorter. We were sent outside. I remember that we were out the back making a go-kart with roller bearings and my dad had a long talk with my mum. Then he appeared again and put the rivets on.

I had no idea that my dad had been in prison and had come out. What I do remember is how excited my mum was during those days that my dad was there. They used to laugh like crazy, then cry and hug each other…

It was decided that we were going to be together again. Then he was arrested in 1974 and placed at the disposal of the National Executive.

San Juan

Miguel's father, an ERP militant, was detained in Penitentiary Unit I in Córdoba. Miguel and his family moved to the province of San Juan, which was where 'Negrita', his mother, was from originally. There they lived with their maternal grandparents, Wilda and Juan.

My parents' story was very intense. My mum married in 1967, already pregnant with me and between then and February 1970, when my sister was born, they had three children. My mum's family had a very close relationship with my dad, they loved him very much. I remember that I went to primary school in the morning. Every day I'd wake up, I'd sit on my bed and my grandfather would help me get dressed. So one day there I was and he said to me:

'No, kid, go back to bed, you're not going to school today.'

And I asked, 'Why not, Granddad?'

'Because there's been a coup.'

I didn't know what a coup was. What I did realise was that he was very, very worried.

That same day, when I got up, I saw that my grandfather was digging a hole with a spade, putting books in a bag and burying them.

By that time my mum had restarted her degree in medicine in Mendoza. She used to go from Monday to Friday and come home at weekends. At school everything was the same. San Juan was a very peaceful town, I can't remember seeing anything strange. We used to say that he was in prison and leave it at that. I now realise that we were carefully protected by the teacher and headmistress. At home great changes took place.

Banned visits

My grandmother was getting us ready to go to Córdoba to visit my dad:

'You're going to see your dad in prison, which is a horrible place, you're going to see lots of iron bars (…) your dad may not be very well (…) you mustn't get upset…'

We were in the kitchen, which was the heart of the house. My grandmother always used to talk to us there.

Afterwards we realised that the story of the visits was all a lie to torture my dad more. It was just the military messing us about.

Once I came to Córdoba on my own with my mum. We were staying at my paternal grandparents'. My grandfather came in and said:

'Right, let's go! Come on, I'll take Miguel!'

My grandfather was manager of the Banco Nación, clearly he'd got a message. My dad knew we were there, through those strange post systems that were used in the prisons. A lot of information got out via the common prisoners. We parked on Torrado Juárez Street, and left the car, a Renoleta, there. It seems he had coordinated with my dad that he would look out of the window to see us. My grandfather had told me so and I remember that he picked me up so that my dad could see me out of the window. I remember looking, but I couldn't see him.

The telegram, October 1976

We were in San Juan, it was midday. My maternal grandfather had died by then. We were at home having lunch. My grandfather Miguel Angel sent a telegram from Córdoba telling my mum that they had killed my dad. My mum was really upset...

She screamed and cried, fell to the floor and we couldn't pick her up. It was the only time, never again did I see her in such a desperate state. My mum is a very calm person, very rational, a woman who never loses control.

Afterwards she shut herself away in a room with my grandmother and we could hear her crying hysterically. I felt very bad for her. We wanted to go into the room, we cried and banged on the door. My aunt tried to hold us back, but she couldn't control us. My mum came out, told us to come in, so we all three went in and she told us that they'd killed him. I had never seen her like that.

I feel that one of the things that they deprived me of, besides my dad and all the rest, was the ability to feel that loss. I was so shocked to see my mum like that that all I could say was 'Oh, mum'.

I remember that afterwards, during the days that followed, my mum would start crying every now and again. The telegram said, 'Dear Negrita, they've killed Niky.' That's what they called him.

Penitentiary Unit I in Córdoba was practically taken over by the Army from April to December 1976. A number of prisoners were shot during that period. The same as in the case of Miguel's father, the Army claimed that they died in 'escape attempts'. Other communiqués, like the one referring to the execution of Raúl A. Bauducco, revealed an even greater degree of hypocrisy: 'I was in the same cell as Gustavo De Breuil and Jorge Oscar García. As is known, both were killed by the military, who claimed in the information released to the press that they had died in an "escape attempt". Their murder was witnessed by Jorge De Breuil, since they forced him to watch the execution of the group that included his brother, telling him to tell us afterwards what had happened, since the same fate awaited all of us. Similarly, the prisoner Bauducco was killed in front of all of us, on 5 July 1976. An NCO hit him on the head and when he couldn't get up threatened to kill him. He took out a gun, loaded it and shot him in the head. On 14 July that year I could see out of the window when the prisoner René Moukarzel was tied to a stake out in the patio, had cold water thrown over him and was beaten up. He died early that morning. Lieutenant Alsina played an active part in his death. Until December 1976, twenty-eight political prisoners were killed in different circumstances, as a result of the regime applied in that prison.'

José María Niztschman (former prisoner in UP No. 1 – Córdoba)
File No. 7597 – Conadep

IN A PRISON ESTABLISHMENT
The second clash happened at 10.20 hours in Block VI of Penitentiary Unit I, while a routine check was being carried out of persons detained for subversive activities. On that occasion, one of the criminals, Raúl Augusto Bauducco, leapt on the leader of the military security patrol in an attempt to wrest his weapon away from him. The soldier's reaction was immediate and automatic, shooting dead the subversive criminal.

La Prensa – 8 July 1976

My mum came to Córdoba on her own. She stayed with my grandfather and grandmother. My grandfather told her all that they'd done to get hold of the body. My dad's now buried in Frías, in Santiago del Estero, because that's where he was born.

Taking control

We were in a bad state. My mum was widowed, my grandmother was widowed. In the summer of 1977 my grandmother spoke to my mum and told her she had to finish her degree, that she would take care of us, that somehow we'd get through …

I remember that all five of us took the decision; they got us three little ones all together, and told us that we had to make a go of it.

'We're a family, Negrita has to finish her degree, she has to graduate as a doctor, for your grandfather's sake, for your dad's. You have to go to school and carry on, you have to be strong and we mustn't let ourselves be defeated by this.'

All this in the kitchen…

My mum was distraught and my grandmother Wilda took control of the situation. My maternal grandmother was the daughter of Germans and had very little schooling, just primary school, but she had a huge library! (…) I think that was what created such an affinity between that old couple and my dad – a fascination with reading. My grandmother always used to tell me how they'd discuss the books that they'd both read.

My mum went to Mendoza to study, we stayed on at school and my grandmother…the things she did!

That separation was difficult, I used to miss my mum horribly. I remember that there was a housecoat of my mum's hanging on a coat hanger which she used to wear to do the housework when she came home. I remember that it was white and pink. When she wasn't there I used to go into her room, take it down and smell her smell because I missed her so much.

On Friday nights we used to write her letters. We would each write a letter to my mum – my grandmother included – so happily…

The graduation ceremony

I didn't understand what death was, I couldn't understand the concept, I didn't know what it meant to kill another person, I couldn't get my head round the idea, I was very little. I didn't understand the concept until 1980, and in 1980 it became very clear to me. My mum was about to graduate. In the end she graduated from La Plata, because in Mendoza she had to do a residency, whereas in La Plata she could graduate directly. When she graduated we all went along. For us it was a momentous event. When the graduation ceremony was over we went out to supper, to celebrate, and when we got back I remember my mum sat on the bed, she closed the door and said:

'Today I graduated as a doctor, and from today on we're going to be together, we're going to be a little family again and we're going to get through. We're going to be okay, we're going to be together and we're going to be able to say to those bastards that we're alive.'

She let slip 'those bastards'. The way she stressed the word made an impression on me.

When we asked she said:

'Those bastards are the ones running the country. The president and everyone else are murderers who killed your dad and a whole lot of other people…'

That's when that thing began of saying 'murderer' whenever we saw someone in uniform. It wasn't just that my mum had graduated, it meant a lot more: it was a reply, a way of saying, 'we're here and standing'. That was the turning point.

Secondary school

We returned to San Juan. My mum was given a job in the countryside, in a town 250 kilometres from the capital, in the province of San Juan. The 'family on the move', we called ourselves. It was a town with 5,000 inhabitants on the border with Chile.

There were some great people at the secondary school, in my class there were 22 of us. I remember that I talked about things there and no one understood anything, it was a very different way of life. But the teacher understood and knew what I was talking about. Carlos Fuentes, the math teacher at Cornelia Saavedra Agro-technical school. A great guy.

I was really angry at that time, because I felt very alone. I entered my adolescence without a father and resented him for that. I hated him because I felt that he'd chosen something else and hadn't chosen us. I didn't understand anything, didn't understand anything about revolutions, nothing, the only thing I knew was that I didn't have my dad and I needed him.

I remember that I used to talk to that teacher about these things. I remember that I trusted him a lot, I told him that I was really mad with my dad and he spoke to me about ideals, glory, about what it meant to participate in a movement and be really committed to something. I remember him telling me,

'You'll understand your dad when you really commit yourself to an idea, when you really believe in something, you'll understand him. You can't understand him now.'

To the letter

In 1984 my grandmother died and we stayed on in San Juan. My mum by then was director of the hospital. I switched to a regular secondary school and finished in 1985. In 1986 I was doing my military service. Afterwards I was very sorry…

I once met someone – I was walking down a street in San Juan with my mum – before the draft. He was an elderly man who'd been a friend of my grandfather Juan and he gave me a talk: that he had never known anyone as upright as my grandfather, so honest, and so on…

Miguel puts on the voice of a political speech maker, raises his finger and remembers the speech:

'Your grandfather always said that one should never take advantage of one's prerogatives, that one could be in a better social situation than others, but that one always had to empathise with the one at the bottom, with the most unfortunate. You, with your education, are not the same as a kid your age living in Sierra Chávez'. Sierra Chávez is a very inhospitable and arid town in the middle of a desert in San Juan.

His words remained engraved on my memory. When the military service papers came through, my mum said:

'I'm going to put together a file for you, I know the president of the Civil Medical Junta...'

My mum was more upset than me when I said:

'No, I won't take advantage of any special prerogative, I want to be treated the same as anyone coming from Sierra Chávez. Because you're a doctor, you've got contacts and can put together a medical history that will let me off the hook, and what about the kid from Sierra Chávez...?'

End result: my number came up, number 928, and I was drafted.

At the service of the military

I didn't have such a bad time of it during my military service because I managed to get posted to a section where I didn't have to do anything. I worked in the Quartermaster's Office, the part with all the clothes and blankets. All I did was guard duty, but I wasted a year and a half there.

One day the Quartermaster and the company chief came and asked me straight out about my dad.

'Come here, soldier,' and they shut me up in an office, the Quartermaster sat down in front of me and the company chief stood behind me and they asked me who my father was.

'Where's your father?' (...) What my father had done, they said they knew who my father was, that as soon as things got difficult I'd be the first to split and that I wouldn't ever make a Dragoon (...) That was the title given to the best four soldiers in the company; there was a ranking of merit and I was second at the time.

I came out of military service dazed and bewildered, it did my head in, really affected me (...) I spent months eating holding on tight to my piece of bread, clicking my heels, waking up at night. I was in a permanent state of anxiety. I think that unconsciously it all meant a lot more than I was aware of at that point. It was like a challenge to me. I had to do it and seize the chance to find out what those people were like.

Those people…

It allowed me to have an informed opinion about the Argentinian Army and the military personnel who make up the army. I have seen the misery and I have also seen that almost all the members of the Army are psychopaths: extremely cruel, violent, ill-educated, resentful (…) I saw how they used to crap on each other, how the NCOs tried to get each other into trouble; how the officers used to torment them as if they were a higher caste; how they used to make them feel – as they used to say, literally – like 'shitty niggers', as though they were great gentlemen themselves.

I made a study of them not based on hearsay. All based on what I saw over 18 months. I was very struck once when we were eating, an NCO came over and began to take all the meat out of our lunch pan. One of the rookies got mad and said:

'Hey! What are we going to eat? Water?'

And the NCO shouted, 'Shut up!' He was acting like a thief, an example of human wretchedness. That kind of person, those sort of people are the ones who committed genocide. They were the ones responsible for carrying out the acts of genocide. They don't think, they obey and if they have to kick someone's head in they do it. But at the same time they are cowards, I have seen cowardice, the cowardice of not assuming responsibility for one's actions.

Once a bayonet sabre was lost and an NCO had stolen it. We were punished for two months. They treated us like shit…! We were violently woken at five in the morning, and went to bed at ten o'clock at night. You can't imagine the state we were in by the time we went to bed, full of aches, shouting with pain…'Brisk movement', they called it. My kneecaps are completely fucked as a result…

In the end it was proven that it was an NCO and nothing further happened. We never heard that anything had happened to him, but we had a bad time of it.

On 6 March 1994 (three days after starting his military service in an Army barracks in Zapala, Neuquén), the soldier Omar Carrasco disappeared. The Army claimed that he had deserted, until a month later, his body was discovered inside the regiment. The crime shook the country, and as a result on 29 August 1994, former President Menem, with a populist gesture, put an end to military service. The decree contended that by abolishing military service the aim was 'to continue with the reorganisation and modernisation of the Armed Forces' and that 'the incorporation of voluntary conscripts would improve the operational capacity of the Forces.' An explanation as elegant as it was false.

Law in Córdoba

Miguel returned to Córdoba where he started a degree in law. He also began working in human rights organisations.

In Córdoba I went to an exhibition organised by Amnesty International and was really struck by it. I became the coordinator of a national AI group, *el Abrojo*, based here in Córdoba. I was also campaigns' coordinator on the national executive committee. I started working with human rights at a universal level, and in an international organisation.

I had a vision of human rights throughout the world. Sometimes it's easier to see things from the outside in order to understand what happened here. From when I began to understand what a prisoner of conscience is, what it means to be imprisoned for having different ideas and all that, I began to feel closer to my dad. That's when I began to understand him. That's when I understood what Carlos Fuentes had said to me.

My father's friends

I didn't want to meet any of them because my first experience with someone who had known him was really bad, because I look so much like my dad. I went to see him, I knew that he'd been a good friend of my dad's, that they'd been in prison together (…) and I thought, 'this doesn't help me and it doesn't help anyone'. Besides everyone used to tell me that my dad was a great bloke, an excellent person, a leader and I wanted to get to know the man, wanted to see him as an ordinary person.

Later on I got in touch with another organisation, of ex-prisoners. There I met all the people who had been with my dad in prison. They told me how he'd died, what he last days were like, everything…

My dad was given the job of talking to the prison authorities: they all came to an agreement and then he'd take their requests along to the authorities. They told me that one day [Colonel] Sasiain came in and told them, 'We're going to kill all of you, no one will be saved, you're all condemned to die.' That's when they invented the slogan 'another day, another victory' and started leaning on each other so as not to give up…

'The Commander of the IV Airborne Infantry Brigade, Colonel Juan Bautista Sasiain yesterday praised the defence of mankind and its values in his farewell speech to the unit's subordinate personnel who have recently retired. "The army values each man for what he is, because it is a Christian institution," said Colonel Sasiain.'

Clarín – 10 April 1976

It was nighttime, they came into the cell, grabbed my dad and took him away. My dad turned around and said goodbye to his companions. He didn't say anything, just looked at them, raised his fist and left (…) He was fully aware that they were going to kill him. The prisoners heard the shots. He was 36 years old.

Penitentiary Unit Number I – Córdoba

At one time on Sundays I used to take the number 52 bus and go there. I needed to be in that huge place where my dad had been, walk around or look at the things my dad had seen. I used to go alone, it was a purely emotional thing, very personal, no one knew.

On 13 December 1998 the ex-prisoners organised a tribute and invited me to participate.

On that day they got me to speak. And I felt…! Only then did I feel that I had really come to terms with my dad's death, that act was what brought things to a close for me emotionally. My family was there, my siblings, my mum. I applied for permission to put the plaque in place. The survivors located all the prisoners' relatives. It was a huge event, very emotional. We spent the whole time holding each other, like all the other families. My mum was terribly moved.

Today

My brother has two children. When they were born I wished my dad had been there, to see his grandchildren. I would have liked to share these experiences with him.

I feel like I was robbed of my parents, the pain of my dad's death, not knowing him, trying to remember what his voice sounded like, what his touch felt like, or how he told me off. They robbed us of all that and I also feel that they robbed my nephews of their grandfather and that my children won't have a grandfather. They shat on me, they're shitting on my nephews and they're going to shit on my children.

I went twice to his grave in Santiago. I'm about to go and bring my dad's remains to San Juan, in December I should finish with all the paperwork. I'm going to go and fetch my dad and bring him here, where my two grandfathers are. Besides, my mum told me that when she dies she wants to be with my dad, that she wants to be buried together with him. She was a young woman when my dad died and she never had another partner.

To top it all

Miguel works in a law firm. He starts work at 7 am, breaks for lunch and continues till nine at night. He's finished his law course and has to pass four more exams to graduate.

He loves music, blues and rock, and describes himself as a great fan of his nephews, Martín and Facundo, so whenever he can he goes to San Juan to visit his family.

I remember that once I went to have an ice-cream in the Plaza España. I was sitting there, I ate the ice-cream, left and bumped into an acquaintance. We chatted about something or other. Two or three days later I bumped into him again and he said,

'Hey, you know what, the same day I saw you a little while later Menéndez was here also having an ice-cream.'

In the same ice-cream parlour, but not at the same time. I left and he arrived. I find that so incredible, that's Argentina for you. That's what our country is like…

25

The Rattenbach Report

At the end of the Malvinas/Falklands war, the third Military Junta was relieved of its command and replaced by the fourth and final president of the dictatorship. In addition, an investigation was ordered, the purpose of which was to establish who was responsible for the defeat. The report was published in full in the book *Memoria Debida*, by former captain José Luis D'Andrea Mohr.

On 2 December 1982 the Junta ordered the creation of the 'Commission to evaluate the Southern Atlantic Conflict'. The members of the Commission were: retired Lieutenant General Benjamín Rattenbach, retired Major General Tomás Armando Sánchez de Bustamante, retired Admiral Alberto Pedro Vago, retired Vice Admiral Jorge Alberto Boffi, retired Brigadier Carlos Alberto Rey, and retired Major General Francisco Cabrera. On 16 September 1983 the Commission completed its task and presented to the Military Junta the 291 pages that comprised the main body of its report, together with scores of appendices.

274. (…) In short, the decision [to occupy], which had remained latent, was influenced by specific political developments, such as, for example, the need to produce a significant occurrence that would revitalise the *Proceso de Reorganización Nacional* (…)

783. In the first place, it must be noted that the general feeling in the country, at the time when the decision to occupy the Malvinas/Falklands Islands was taken, was not the most suitable for confronting an international political incident of this nature.

784. Contributing factors included:

(…) The prevailing socio-economic crisis, with the country struggling under the weight of such problems. (…)

785. If the international climate had been favourable towards the national objective of recovering the southern archipelagos, it would have been an ideal opportunity to pursue that objective. But this was not the case since:

The national authorities were coming under harsh attack for the problem of human rights, which meant that their position internationally was seriously undermined.

The Argentine Republic was at the time subject to US sanctions, with embargoes on weapon imports, which limited its freedom to equip itself and adequately modernise its military supplies. (…)

Conclusion

788. The moment freely chosen by the Military Junta for the recovery of the archipelagos in the Southern Atlantic fundamentally benefited the enemy.

The human cost of the military adventure ordered by the Third Military Junta amounted to 641 dead and 1208 wounded and disabled, plus the hundreds of cases of suicide among ex-combatants [since the end of the conflict].

'The Rattenbach Report called for the death penalty for the three members of the Military Junta, who were found equally responsible, since the Junta was a collegiate body. During 1983 the fourth Junta passed its 'self-amnesty' law and in November of that year ordered that all documentary material relating to the struggle against subversion be burnt.'

D'Andrea Mohr, *Memoria Debida*, Colihue, 1999.

The Armed Forces justified the crimes committed during the dictatorship by claiming that the country was at war. Point 874 of the Rattenbach Report (ordered by the very same dictatorship) clearly states that the Malvinas/Falklands war 'has been the only war waged by the Nation so far this century…'

Failure and stampede…

THE MINISTER OF THE INTERIOR YESTERDAY MET WITH LEADERS OF POLITICAL PARTIES

La Prensa – 17 June 1982

THE ARMY NAMES AS PRESIDENT GENERAL REINALDO B. BIGNONE
'Since no agreement was reached in the Military Junta, the Navy and the Air Force decided to withdraw from the Proceso de Reorganización Nacional. The country's 'irrevocable' return to institutional politics will take place at the beginning of 1984.'

La Prensa – 23 June 1982

BIGNONE HOLDS INTERVIEWS WITH LEADERS OF SEVERAL PARTIES
'The multiparty alliance [an agreement between the two main political parties, the Peronists and the Radicals] will attend, and has requested that the regime open without delay the way forward to national reconciliation around the Constitution.'

La Prensa – 24 June 1982

'The military governor of the Malvinas/Falklands, General Mario Benjamín Menéndez, yesterday avoided commenting on the recent statements by Lieutenant General Leopoldo Galtieri, and insisted on referring to the war for the Malvinas/Falklands as that which "we did not lose for lack of courage".'

La Voz del Interior (Córdoba) – 5 April 1983

CAROLINA GHIGLIAZZA

Carolina was born in 1974, in the Military Hospital in Campo de Mayo, where her paternal grandfather was a doctor. Her parents, Ricardo Mario Ghigliazza and Irma Noemí Tardivo met in the Peronist Youth movement. Then Ricardo joined the PRT and travelled to Tucumán where he was disappeared on 19 September 1975, when he was 26 years old. Irma worked as a teacher in a school in Moreno, in the province of Buenos Aires. She was abducted on 8 July 1976 when she was 25 years old. Carolina and her younger sister grew up in General Rodríguez, with their maternal grandmother.

The fantasies

At that time I think I still thought they were away on a trip. The harder you try to remember, the more you invent stories. I remember the images I had, the thoughts…I could see my dad falling out of an aeroplane and coming home with a leg and an arm in plaster a long time afterwards; they wouldn't let him leave the hospital because he was still hurt. My mum had lost her memory or had gone so far away that she couldn't remember how to get home. I used to see women in the street – this happened on various occasions – but straight away I'd say, 'No, it's not her…'

I remember that my grandmother told me that they cared a lot about the poor, about poor children, she spoke to me about them as if they were superheroes, angels, prophets, saviours. I believed it all, but it also made me wonder: if they were so great, why weren't they around for us? If they cared so much about children, shouldn't my sister and I come first?

I sensed that something wasn't right. Well, anyway…we were 'well looked after', there were others who were more in need.

The memory is going to fade

My sister is a year younger than me. The earliest memory I have is from my fourth birthday. I remember I was at home and I said, 'Okay, I'm turning four and if I don't remember now what happened to my parents, I'm never going to remember because as time goes by the memory will fade.' And no, I couldn't remember anything.

I always got on badly with my grandmother, extremely badly. Her way of telling me off was to say that I was a lot like my parents, that I spoke like them, that I was making the same mistakes they'd made...

I didn't agree with the things she said to me, with the limits she imposed on me, with her banning me from going out. The rest of the family took the line that 'she's elderly, you have to understand; or, she suffered a lot, you have to be understanding; she's your grandmother, you have to make allowances...'

Until the day she gave me the keys to the house, when I was 15, my grandmother not only locked the door: tables, chairs were wedged against the door (...)We were afraid that people might come in, whether police or robbers.

The search

There were always two of my mother's diaries in the house. One from when she was a kid, which was fairly illegible and full of unimportant anecdotes. The other had pages ripped out by the military and tales about my dad, basically my mum relating her relationship with my dad; that she'd met a boy, who was a leader of the Peronist Youth, who was very intelligent and very polite, extremely friendly, that she thought he also felt something for her. And then she starts writing how they got to know each other, fell in love, started going out, what a wonderful man he is...

I can't remember when I discovered it, we always knew it was there. Once we'd learnt to read we would chance taking it out. My grandmother had it carefully hidden away in a drawer, but we knew where it was, and it wasn't locked. If she knew we had it out my grandmother would have said that we shouldn't think about those things, that it was done, that it made her very upset to remember my mum. She would have started crying, really awful scenes, so we wouldn't get it out in front of her.

Somehow, at some point we got it out at siesta time for the first time. And read it. The first few times we read it together, I guess in the hall. It was an old house, huge, so my grandmother was in her room asleep and we had the rest of it to ourselves. The last paragraph – which we could never finish reading – had a very moving part which said 'I wish they had killed me, I can't live without him.' The last part was addressed to us: 'I haven't the strength to go on...'

There are pages missing from it, I don't know how many times the military came to the house and took away papers and other things belonging to my mother, but at least twice.

Armed teenagers

I remember the Malvinas. I knitted half a scarf, sent chewing gum and cigarettes. I saved up the money I was given for snacks and bought things for the soldiers. I remember the fear at school. Fear of the war, fear of hell. Fear of the soldiers, fear of the weapons. In fact, I didn't understand anything about the outcome of the war, I understood nothing about political results or gains or losses. I had images of teenagers buried, hiding (…) Boys the age of my cousins who were in hell, in trenches and with the bullets raining down on them. It was all that I could understand about what was happening. I didn't understand why they were fighting. I didn't know what the Malvinas were, the only thing I knew was that there was a war going on, that we were in it and that armed teenagers were going through hell.

1983

I was eight years old. I remember Luder and Alfonsín. People joked about Herminio Iglesias, stupid things, Freudian slips. I remember that everyone was going to vote for Alfonsín, especially the women, I don't know why [she laughs].

I think I still hoped…I can't remember exactly until when… perhaps not much longer. It was a fantasy hope, from when I was very little…

Them

I think they were together for a year, then they got married, I was born and a year later my dad was killed. When they killed my dad my mum was pregnant. He was an electrical engineer and I don't think he completed his degree in social work. My mum was a schoolteacher and was studying for an arts degree. In general the answers to my questions about my dad took the form of family anecdotes, questions about what kind of person he was.

My mum was abducted from a school in Moreno, a town 15 kilometres from General Rodríguez. She was living in Rodríguez with my grandmother, my sister and me and worked in Moreno. I found this out a couple of years ago; among the mass of papers I found a document that is the complaint filed by my grandmother on the day my mum was kidnapped, 8 July 1976. My mum was working at the school and they came to the house, where my grandmother was with my sister and me, with an aunt of mine who was pregnant and had a baby. The soldiers came in, beat them up, turned the house upside down – this wasn't the first time it had happened – and grabbed hold of my grandmother. They told her to tell them where my mum was because otherwise they are going to kill them and take the three babies. So my grandmother tells them that my mum is in Moreno working at the school, teaching.

A few days after I found this out, I mentioned it to my aunt, my mum's sister. My aunt tells me that that's what happened and gives me my mum's handbag with her wallet, pencils, cigarette case and lighter, all that was left in it.

Even less at school

When I was older, my schoolmates from primary and secondary school – because I always went to the same school – found out that there had been some kind of Proceso or something or other in Argentina because it had happened to me; because they had a classmate who was the daughter of desaparecidos, otherwise their parents would never have spoken to them about it. One of my best friends is the son of my nursery school teacher and the nephew of a friend of my mum's. He's told me several times that if he knows anything about the Proceso, if he ever took an interest or studied or read anything about what had happened or had wanted to find out more, it's because he met me, otherwise at home his family never talked about it, in spite of the fact that he had an aunt who had been persecuted by the military, had been tortured and had been saved. What's more, these things just aren't talked about at home…And even less at school.

Holy Week

I'm at home with my aunt, my cousin, my sister and my grandmother. The door's locked, utter panic, the military are coming back. They've taken power. Completely terrified. Hanging on to the TV's every word. My sister and I like this [opens her eyes wide].

'What will we do if the military come back? I don't know…Let's carry on doing what we want.'

'The house is in order.' Who is that man? That man's just been with the military. Which house is in order? Whose house?!

The military should come back

I've often heard people talking about some crime or about the economy, or during the period of hyperinflation, and they say things like 'when the military were in charge these things didn't happen'. They killed you for speaking out! You didn't die of hunger because they killed you before you died of hunger (…) When the military were in power you couldn't complain that you were hungry, so what are you going on about? 'The military should come back' or 'my dad says that we have to get the military back'. What military? Why do you want the military to come back?

'No, no, no. If you toed the line nothing happened to you.'

Among neighbours, old women, older kids from school – an incredible culture of death among them.

'We must only abandon the Process when it has spawned offspring.'

Declarations by Videla
Clarín — 29 May 1977

The theatre

I started doing drama when I was 12 years old. They decided to have art workshops, including drama. I put myself down for drama straight away, because I was fascinated by it. I had never seen any theatre, they didn't take me to the theatre, but I was fascinated anyway. And besides, everyone encouraged me, saying I had an innate talent for it.

A cable TV channel opened in General Rodríguez, they hold an opening party and Esteban Mellino comes to it. At that time there weren't any drama classes at the Cultural Centre in Rodríguez or anywhere else. He'd come to do a show.

'This guy can put me in touch with someone who could teach me drama,' I thought, so I said to him:

'I'm an actress.'

'Oh really, that's great…'

'Yes, but wait a minute, I want to study drama. Where can I go?'

'I've got a school,' he tells me and gives me the address. So I tell them at home that I'm going to study drama with Esteban in the capital. No! They practically chain me to the house. No one wants to take me there, far less to study drama. 'Not the theatre!' My grand-mother tells me that she doesn't want a 'floozy' for a granddaughter. My paternal grandfather gives me a lecture, he always used to give me these long lectures, lay down the moral line. He told me:

'If you get involved in the theatre world, it's like going down a muddy river in a canoe. Sooner or later you're going to get dirty.' Like the theatre world was a pile of shit and if I got involved I'd end up a piece of that same shit. That was the message…

A drama course began at Rodríguez Town Hall, and since they wouldn't let me go to the capital I started studying there. I finished secondary school and signed up for the National Conservatory of Dramatic Arts, here in Buenos Aires. By that time they were completely resigned. I used to travel in every bloody day, I'd get up at five in the morning to get to the Conservatory by eight.

Life's ups and downs

Three years ago I came to live in Buenos Aires with a fellow student from the Conservatory, who is also the daughter of desaparecidos. There were plays dealing with our stuff; I had already been to see Memoria (Memory), which was the play before Cinco Puertas (Five doors), but the idea that I could make it here seemed so impossible (…) So anyway, one day I turn up, I talk to Omar Pacheco who runs the company, and he says,

'Look I make my living from this, but I'm not going to stop someone who wants to learn drama from doing it just because they don't have the money to pay.'

I thought, 'This man's unreal…' I started doing workshops and around three months later Omar asks me if I feel ready to play the role of Argentina in Cinco Puertas. Everything comes round.

Acting to live, living to tell the tale

It was a very special day. We were rehearsing, the play was practically ready. We were doing a run-through. I read the texts in the play and at that point they weren't recorded yet. In the scene where I play with the doll, which is when I recite most of the text, I felt the magic of the theatre, of being Argentina. A different kind of energy, a different physical sensation, a different voice reciting the words and a general feeling of emotion in the whole theatre. And when I finished that scene, a feeling of peace, of freshness…

For a long time I couldn't find a convincing explanation. I felt that they'd done something really important, there aren't a lot of people who would give their lives for an idea. I think that such a powerful idea is greater than any individual and I believe in that idea, the idea that the world can be a better place, that everyone has the right to be happy, I find it incredible that children are dying of hunger. I have the chance, I thought. 'What do I do best out of the things I can do and like doing?' 'What I do best is act.' Okay, starting from there, starting with what I most like doing I'm going to struggle to fulfil that idea, to make it a reality. Give in to my desire to shout out that this is what happened to me.

At the end of the play I get to go up to a place from where I can see the faces of all the people in the audience, and I see fear, pain, shame…

Absence and the encounter

Working on creating the scenes was very moving. The best thing you can do is to give yourself over body and soul to your character, to the role. That's when it becomes magical. I think the role, I live the role. When it's the scene where I say 'Absence, the encounter with one part of the truth…' I often see the paper from the Register of Births, Marriages and Deaths, where it says my mum is an unidentified body, that she died of brain damage from a blow to the head and that they found her body on a road in Tigre. That's what I see…

PROVINCIAL REGISTER OF BIRTHS, MARRIAGES AND DEATHS – PROVINCE OF BUENOS AIRES, TIGRE REGIONAL OFFICE RECORD No. 663, In Tigre Administrative area: ibid. Province of Buenos Aires, on 7 August 1976 (…) Declares that on the 7th day of the month of August of the year nineteen hundred and seventy six, at two o'clock. Place: public highway Route 27 Villa La Ñata, Tigre THERE DIED: an unidentified person from a traumatic brain haemorrhage due to violent shock to the head (…) The deceased woman was 1.65 cm tall, weighed 50 kilos, brown eyes, white skin, short black hair, wearing a pair of trousers, a red jumper and black moccasin shoes.

The dictatorship threw the body of a woman down on a road in Tigre; the young woman had bled to death from a blow to the head. The discovery of the body obliged the legal bureaucracy to carry out the procedures that applied in the case and got rid of the body without trying to identify it.

Recently, through an investigation carried out by teams of forensic anthropologists, it was established – through the comparison of fingerprints – that the body described in Record 663 was the corpse of Irma Noemí Tardivo, Carolina's mother. However, her remains have still not been located.

Today Carolina is 25 years old, the same age her mother – that white skinned, brown eyed woman – was when she was kidnapped, while teaching at a school in Moreno. Carolina lives in Buenos Aires where she is still studying and acting.

26

Amnesty or amnesia or both...

QUARRACINO DEFENDS LAW OF OBLIVION. DESAPARECIDOS.
The president of CELAM (Latin American Episcopal Conference) explained that it was 'a kind of legal instrument that recognises the drama that the country has been through, and also the guilt of those responsible for it – but without naming names – and that points to ways of going beyond what happened.'

The bishop also warned that any attempt to resolve the problem by resorting to the law would lead to 'a poisoning of human relations' in the country. (...) 'I understand that it is preferable to talk of a law of oblivion rather than an amnesty law, because "amnesty" is a cold legal term, while "oblivion" has a deeper, more human, more profound meaning.' (...) He clarified that 'I am not proposing that the justice system should not take action when it should take action, but that there should be rules or limits – although I cannot say what they might be – to avoid that poisoning.' (...) He then recalled the words of Jesus when he said 'let he who is without guilt cast the first stone...' (...) 'I am also reminded of the parable of the prodigal son: when the young man returns home, the father does not call a lawyer.'

La Voz del Interior (Córdoba) – 3 April 1983

'...in Argentina there are no mass graves and each corpse is in its respective coffin. Everything was entered in the proper registers, following normal procedures...' "Desaparecidos?" You mustn't confuse the issue. You know that there are desaparecidos living peacefully in Europe...'

Monsignor Juan Carlos Aramburu (Archbishop of Buenos Aires – Cardinal)
Statements made to *Il Messagero* (Rome) – 19 November 1982

'(The amnesty law) is inspired by the traditional magnanimity of the Argentinian people and is the basis for a united front working jointly on behalf of the Fatherland (...) it is in line with the spirit and letter of the Holy Gospel. Jesus asks us to forget offences and if it is our brother who insults or wounds us, we should forgive him seventy times seven, that is unconditionally.'

Monsignor Antonio Plaza (Archbishop of La Plata)
Declarations – 25 September 1983

'...the Madres de Plaza de Mayo and the human rights groups that belong to international organisations must be eradicated, just as the exhumation of unidentified bodies must stop, since it is a disgrace for society…'

Monsignor Carlos Mariano Pérez (Salta)
Declarations – 23 January 1984

'...if they told me that Camps had tortured some unknown nigger, I'd let it pass, but how can they say that he tortured Jacobo Timermann, a journalist who was the focus of a sustained and decisive world campaign... if it hadn't been for that!…'

Father Christian Von Wernich (Chaplain of the Buenos Aires Police)
Siete Días magazine, 30 July 1984

'…The Church does not need to examine its conscience, far less ask forgiveness from Argentinian society…'

Monsignor Edgardo Storni (Santa Fe)
Declarations – 2 May 1995

DIEGO REYNAGA

Diego is the youngest of three siblings. He was born in Tucumán in 1973. His father, his brother and his sister are doctors. His mother, Ana María Sosa, had trained as an Education and Social Psychology teacher at the Pichon Rivière school. She was teaching at Juan Bautista Alberdi Primary School and at a school in Simoca, a small town to the south of Tucumán.

MESSAGE FROM GENERAL BUSSI ON THE OCCASION OF HIS
ASSUMING THE POST OF GOVERNOR
The provincial governor, General Antonio Domingo Bussi, last night sent out a message of greeting to the people of Tucumán on the occasion of him assuming the governorship of the province. The letter issued by the military leader reads as follows: 'On the occasion of my assuming the post of governor of the province of Tucumán, I wish to extend to the people of Tucumán my most cordial greetings. We express once again our faith in God, Our Father, whom we beg to enlighten us with wisdom, to find the right path towards the goal that we have set; to give us the strength to not stray from the path; to instil in us a sense of justice in order that we may exercise impartially the authority invested in us.'

La Gaceta – 24 April 1976

Ana María was an activist of the Revolutionary Communist Party (PCR, Partido Comunista Revolucionario). On 8 August 1976 she went to celebrate Children's Day at Colonia II at the Concepción Sugar Refinery. There she was kidnapped and currently remains disappeared. Diego was three years old.

Silence

The reaction in our house was to protect us from aggression. Protect in quotation marks (…) that protection included, throughout the whole period, trying to pretend that nothing had happened. Everyone got annoyed if you talked about her, or mentioned her name, except us, who wanted to know. My grandmother also lived with us (…) I think that after a time we began to adapt to that role of not asking that they had imposed on us.

NOW WE MUST WIN THE PEACE, SAID GENERAL BUSSI

'(…) Neither the ERP nor the Montoneros can call themselves a guerrilla army because neither one of them is. I have seen true guerrilla fighters in Vietnam, naked and with dynamite strapped to their chests, hurling themselves at the enemy's cannons. In contrast these people are the worst type of human beings: they are cowards, they flee from battles, use betrayal to attack, kill defenceless people. There is nothing national about them, they have no flag, they are estranged from God. That is why they are not guerrilla fighters. That is why they only deserve to die.'

La Gaceta – 17 October 1976

We were away on a trip, a holiday in Buenos Aires in 1978; I was five years old. I remember that we were in the hotel and it seems that since we wouldn't stop asking for mum, my dad said to us: 'Stop asking about her because she's not coming back…'

Now that time has passed, I put myself in his shoes and realise that it must be painful to have to give an explanation – a pseudo explanation, because even he didn't know the truth – to something inexplicable.

Filling in the gaps

I remember that when I started at nursery school, I didn't have an explanation. I can't remember them asking me, it wasn't mentioned.

I have felt abandoned, and had a feeling of forced absence because of her. She 'who had abandoned me'. I had to fill the gap, if your mum's not there and no one explains why to you (…) and so, 'she's a bitch, she just fucked off!'

Yes, she's alive

I was in the first year of Gymnasium Prep School, I was ten years old, and they asked us to draw a family tree with all the information about our relatives.

I remember that I did it on an Olivetti typewriter that I have at home, and I had to redo it several times, because the first time I wrote: 'Is your mother alive? Yes.' And when my brother read it – obviously he had a clearer idea than I did at that time – he tore up the paper and said,

'No she's not.'

'What do you mean she's not alive? Yes she is, she's alive…'

And I did it all over again (…) Until in the end my father drew my family tree. By that time it was assumed that she had died. My dad had re-married.

'With respect to the desaparecidos, this situation as such is a mystery. If the person turned up they would be treated in a certain way. But if the disappearance becomes a certainty, their death receives a different treatment. While the person is disappeared they cannot be treated in any particular way, because they have no identity, they are neither dead nor alive.'

Declarations by Videla, *Clarín* – 14 December 1979

Before that another similar thing happened to me when I went to get my identity card in 1981. My uncle went with me, my dad's brother. At one point the secretary, or whoever was attending us, began to ask for my details:

'Is your mother alive?'

'Yes.'

When my uncle heard that, he made me get out of the chair. He said,

'You stand here, I'll sit down and sort this out for you.' And he told the woman,

'Look, his mum is disappeared…' I'm not sure how they sorted it out, I think it's something that still hasn't been sorted out…

The word 'Bussi'

I remember that in 1981 I heard that word: I must have been eight years old. I used to go everywhere with my grandmother, so I went to the hairdresser's with her to get her hair cut. Like any good hairdresser, this one liked to talk, so she began to talk about how bad things were in the province, that if General Bussi were to come back everything would get better. I remember that my grandmother was absolutely furious and said,

'You have no idea who he is, he's a murderer!' She was completely beside herself with anger.

That's the first memory I have of Bussi, while we were still under the dictatorship.

'The prisoners were taken to the Escuelita [a clandestine detention centre in Tucumán] in ordinary cars, either in the trunk, or on the back seat, or on the floor. They were taken out using the same method and from what little was known, when that happened most of them were taken to be killed. If any of the prisoners died, they waited till nightfall and then wrapped him or her in an Army blanket and put them in one of the private cars which then left for an unknown destination.'

Testimony of former prison guard Antonio Cruz – File No. 4636, Conadep

The humming

When I was little I used to say 'kidnapped' more. Those are the contradictions that exist, because on the one hand, we had adopted a practically passive attitude towards the subject, but on the other, we recognised it as a kidnapping, which is something that you cannot assimilate. I think it's important that I called it a kidnapping, we had an idea, something bad had happened to her. And not because she wanted it to happen. I think that you recreate the sense of abandonment so long as you lack the elements necessary to construct a story. At that point I needed to have something to fill the void.

We used to fantasise about her returning, what happened was that at that time we weren't getting on very well with the woman who is my dad's wife today. Obviously not (...) no one had explained anything to us, we couldn't understand what was happening. Because of the way he was, he couldn't talk, not only couldn't he talk about my mum but about any of what was happening. But over time, as things shifted, he realised that he had to change the way he was treating the subject and I think he really made an effort...

What I'm remembering now is spending hours in front of my grandfather's bookcase. It was a generous bookcase, although not particularly large, but there was something there. I used to sit down and look for it, although I'm not sure exactly what I was looking for. A mystery to solve. But anyway, I ended up reading several things from that bookcase. It was a place – and still is – that made me want to consume it all.

1983

Well, I thought my mum was going to return, that it was possible. They didn't tell me off for saying so. My siblings said nothing, but I think that they also hoped so, felt a bit optimistic. My sister is five years older than me and my brother two. I remember poring over the papers for a long time, hoping to read my mum's name there. I now remember that previously they said my mum was an unidentified body, that's what they called it before. At that point the papers were reporting on the mass graves, and a whole set of information that wasn't...promising.

'The military process will not accept any person or institution putting it in the dock for having saved the Fatherland, even if there exist or appear to exist some pseudo desaparecidos or pseudo unidentified bodies.'

General Antonio Luis Merlo, Governor of Tucumán, *Clarín* – 6 November 1982

A lot of time went by before we could speak out at home. They couldn't speak. When he was little my brother was the most disobedient in this respect, and then later when we were older I was the one who used to speak out. It was one of those steps that someone takes, it doesn't matter who's the first to do so, what's important is that the steps are headed the right way.

The search

I remember this well because it was in 1989, I hadn't started at university yet. My brother was the one who began to ask questions, who wanted to know. I remember that he went to see a psychologist and that triggered off a series of actions that were designed to find out what had happened to his mother. One Monday, at 8 am, my aunt – my mum's sister – dropped by; it was an unusual time for my aunt to come by, who besides wasn't speaking to my father at the time. She sat down and told my brother:

'Look, your mum did these things and this is what happened to her.'

I wasn't there, he told me she'd come to talk to him 'because I wanted to know', but he didn't tell me the details of what she'd said. I don't know how my aunt found out that he was wanting someone to give him some information. My dad found out that my aunt had been there and so he went and spoke to her. I wasn't there that time either, but afterwards I think he felt obliged to come and tell me.

Life

He took me to a bar, sat me down and said: this is what happened. I said something to him, I think maybe I was too hard on him, but it was how I felt at the time. I told him that he was recounting an anecdote and I wanted the whole history.

Histories are told as part of life and there isn't one special day to tell them, rather they come naturally. In evoking histories one mixes up the present and the past with elements that appear absurd. For example, I remember my grandmother singing lullabies, I don't know why. And that memory transmits to the listener the feeling that it is an experience being relived with tenderness. My dad was giving me a mess of information and I wanted him to tell me what happened in a different way, a way that was more alive. Over time I have come to see that this was a big step for him, to come out into and say 'okay, I'm going to stop pissing about and I'm going to talk'. To talk even if it's just to give information. After a time I realised that he still felt a void.

Beginning to talk

I wasn't ready to face the truth…besides, I think it would have destroyed me at that time. I had strong outer defences, but inside I was all broken up. Finally it became unbearable, towards the end of secondary school. I had a breakdown and at that point did finally talk to a friend about it.

We hadn't been allowed into a party so we had to have the chat in a car belonging to another friend who had been allowed in. We were good friends, we talked a bit about everything and he asked me what had happened.

I must have been very drunk. Anyway, I told him that she'd been abducted (…) I remember that my friend reacted very violently and said 'The sons of bitches!' and got upset. I was upset, but quiet.

The clue

The tribute they organised to my mother at the teacher training college in 1996 was very emotional. There was a feeling of great human warmth, because each person spoke of how they had met her, about everyday memories of her. My dad was present at the tribute and I saw that he was broken up, holding back the tears…and that wasn't very common for him. At the homage organised by the Communist Party they read a poem dedicated to my mum by a woman who had been in prison with her. At the time I didn't grasp the full significance of that fact.

GARZON TO INVESTIGATE MILITARY JUNTAS FOR THE GENOCIDE OF SPANIARDS
'The actions taken by the Spanish legal system to clarify the disappearance of 266 Spanish citizens during the dictatorship in Argentina have already provoked the first official responses. While the National Criminal Court is bringing specific charges of genocide, the Menem government declares that it will not extradite members of the military.'

La Vanguardia (Spain) – 4 July 1996

When I presented the papers in Spain the lawyer told me that they needed items of proof. That's when it dawned on me and I went to talk to that woman who was living in Jujuy. I phoned her and then went there. It was pretty shocking. There's a point at which you think that there is nothing more that can shock you, but when you have a person-to-person contact that point is passed. She told me that she'd been beaten, tortured (…) Everything you already know, but when it comes from the horse's mouth, it's different, it feels different…

'I can't say exactly whether on the 9th or 10th of August, I heard them bringing in a man and a woman, whom they were beating up, and I heard that they were called Angel Manfredi and Ana María Sosa de Reynaga (…) The next day I got to talk to her, as she was put in the cell opposite me. She told me that they had been detained in Colonia II at the Concepción Sugar Refinery in Tucumán, celebrating Children's Day on 8 August with the families that lived there. A van from the Refinery had arrived loaded with army personnel and they had been abducted. The guards caught us talking and hit us to make us be quiet.'

Declaration by Diana E. Fabio before the Spanish Consulate
Córdoba – 13 October 1999

When Diana was legalised, she told my mum that they were going to release her and asked what she could do for her outside. My mum was very happy and said,

'Look after my children.' When she told me that I was stunned, but afterwards I felt happy to know that practically her last words were meant for us. It wasn't just all horror. I always remember what Beatriz says to Virgilio in The Divine Comedy: 'I am driven by love.' That's in our blood, my mum had something of that in her.

The day of shame: 'Bussi for Governor'

I feel better about it now, not because Bussi's in power, but because I now know what I'm dealing with. Before, I used to say 'What a son of a bitch!' – and I still say it – but I now know that you can't count on the people of Tucumán for a lot of things. The day he assumed the governorship [in 1995] there was an act in the Plaza Irigoyen and from there we marched to the Plaza Independencia. There were pregnant women, kids, elderly people…everyone responded. Quite a lot of people went, but fewer than I'd expected. I was hoping things would explode that day.

Vocation

I was undecided, but knew that I was going to do something in humanities. Now my ideas are more developed. At this moment in time I'm planning on trying to revive a tradition in psychology that existed in the 1960s and 1970s, that was repressed by the dictatorship and afterwards, with the return to democracy it's like it never existed. It relates to social psychology, has a lot to do with important figures from this country and internationally, like Pichon Rivière, José Bleger, Ulloa (…) What I'm trying to do is see what can be recovered from all that, not do exactly the same thing, because a lot of things have changed. People have changed a lot, there are new symptoms…

The fruits of impunity

I saw him once at the airport, in 1993. I couldn't say anything to him…My dad was arriving by plane and I went to meet him with my brother. People were getting off the plane and Bussi got off too. He was alone, my dad was behind him. I was up there, my eyes full of anger, but I couldn't shout 'Look it's that son of a bitch!' We saw him there. We were both completely stunned. I felt a huge sense of hatred, of impotence. We had to swallow our anger.

'I once saw how a naked prisoner was buried alive, with only his head left above ground; they wet the earth all around him and packed it down tight; he was left there for 48 hours. This caused very painful cramps and skin infections. I twice witnessed executions at this camp; the first shot was fired by General Antonio Bussi. Afterwards he would make all the high-ranking officers take part in the firing squad. The execution ground was located about 3-400 metres away from the Arsenal, in the woods. A security cordon was put in place at 20 metres and another at 100 metres. Pistols of 9mm or 11.25mm were used, and the executions always took place between 23:00 and 23:30 hours. Every two weeks between 15 and 20 people were murdered.'

Testimony of former prison guard Omar Eduardo Torres – File No. 6667, Conadep

I had another encounter with Bussi at the university. There was a meeting the day before in the MEDH, where they told us that Bussi was going to go to the vice-chancellor's office, so we went there at 8 am. He had been declared persona non grata, but that was in 1984 or 1985. We were at the entrance to the university, but there were only a few of us, the same as ever. He came in with Germanó…Alone!…And we were all afraid. There we were standing in front of the man with this sign saying, Truth and something or other. He passed us and said, 'look at that lot' and carried on walking. But he's a scary figure, really scary (…) Someone at the back said, 'Aren't we going to shout at him?' and so that started off and he just ran away. When he came out again we were also waiting for him, but this time we were feeling bolder.

Raúl Topa

Bussi was governor from 1995 to 1999. At his behest, a lot of ex-employees and friends of the dictatorship returned to the administration, among them Raúl Topa, who occupied the post of vice-governor.

One day I went to the commemoration of the AMIA attack,* in 1997, I think it was the third anniversary. I went from time to time, and besides my girlfriend is Jewish. The thing is, I arrived at the square where the event is taking place and I see that bastard and think 'No! They're not going to let him speak?!' And the people who had organised the tribute, the leaders of the Jewish community in Tucumán, had invited him to speak. And so Topa began speaking. About the right to know the truth…about justice…And I couldn't take it any more. I felt that if I didn't speak out it was like letting shit happen and turning a blind eye. I shouted he was a murderer, that's what I said:

'You're a Nazi,' and 'You murdered my mother.'

He was a *capucha*, up to his neck in the repression.

THREE YEARS AFTER THE AMIA ATTACK. MASS COMMEMORATION
Hundreds of people remembered the tragedy that ended the lives of 86 Argentinians. Insults to the vice-governor. A young man interrupted Raúl Topa's speech saying 'You killed my mother' and changed the climate of the commemoration.

The act, which takes place the third Monday of each month, began at 1pm and since last Friday was the third anniversary of the tragedy vice-governor Raúl Topa was present, and received a barrage of insults while giving his speech. 'Murderer, get out of here, you killed my mother,' shouted a young professional who came within a few metres of the president of the chamber.

La Gaceta – 22 Julio 1997

He shut up – I shut him up – and everyone was silent. I carried on shouting at him, this woman came and took me away. Told me,

'No, no…this is about something else,' and,

'Don't say that,' [in a calming voice].

He carried on speaking. I thought it was awful because I was the one thrown out.

---

* Refers to a terrorist attack in 1994 on the main Jewish community building in Buenos Aires.

AN ISSUE OF A POLITICAL NATURE. TOPA'S REPLY

The vice-governor gave his opinion of the insults directed at him during the AMIA commemoration. 'False and incredible accusations.' (…) Topa later explained that 'for me this is simply an issue of a political nature, the origin of which I don't know, and which I don't understand, but neither do I reject it, quite the contrary.' The vice-governor said that 'as always we have come to accompany the whole Jewish community and its main representatives, who have welcomed us and we have been mutually involved since the very first time that an event was organised to demand justice in the AMIA case and in the case of any other terrorist act.'

La Gaceta – 22 Julio 1997

I didn't know what to do. I thought, 'I've got myself in trouble now.' I had really exposed myself and those bastards are the mafia, they're organised crime. That day I was all alone. People there didn't back me up, not a single one of them. I was afraid that something would happen to me, to my father, to someone…

On 13 April 1998, national daily *Página/12* published a blackmail letter that Eduardo Rodolfo 'Pochi' Constanzo had sent to the then vice-governor Raúl Topa. Constanzo had taken part in the repression in Tucumán until 1977, when he was transferred to the Second Army Corps Operations outpost. In June 1999, Topa was elected mayor of Tucumán.

STAINED WITH BLOOD

'I deeply regret having to communicate via this medium with someone whom I regard as a true "friend", since the countless telephone calls that I have made to you (all unsuccessful) are going to bring me a phone bill that I am in no financial condition to pay.

I hope that by the time you receive this letter, you will have shared a good Christmas feast in the company of your family, something that I will not be able to enjoy for obvious reasons, with which you are already fully acquainted.

I take this opportunity to remind you that the two of us are stained with blood, for the sake of a cause which we both upheld with a profound and patriotic conviction. I would not wish for you to forget the long-standing union between the Topa and Constanzo families, as a result of which your grandfather (Nelo) was my godfather. I believe that if your deceased father were alive today, your answer to my humble request for (temporary) help would have been different. I do not wish you in the future to think me disloyal, if in some mass media mention is made of episodes in which you, as much as I, took part in the years 1975 and 1976. As you must appreciate, I wish to preserve the traditions of our families, our memories and customs and our friendship, over and above the sad circumstances in which I currently find myself, in coming up against the "forgetfulness" of a friend who promised to give me what I asked for. Today you are the vice-governor of our province, tomorrow you will be just another citizen, as I am now. I ask you to reflect on my thoughts and you will see that I am not mistaken. I send my love to your wife and child, I hope that 1998 will be much better for both of us.'

Your true (not casual) friend, Pochi Constanzo.

Página/12 – 13 April 1998

27

The plague

'…For all the reasons given above, the Military Junta declares: (…)That the Armed Forces acted to fulfil a mandate issued by the National Government, and shall do so again whenever it may prove necessary, and making full use of the experience accumulated during this painful episode in national life.'

The Military Junta's 'Final Document'
(Resolutions) – 28 April 1983

'Indeed, as he listened to the cries of joy that rose above the town, Rieux recalled that this joy was always under threat. He knew that this happy crowd was unaware of something that one can read in books, which is that the plague bacillus never dies or vanishes entirely, that it can remain dormant for dozens of years in furniture or clothing, that it waits patiently in bedrooms, cellars, trunks, handkerchiefs and old papers, and that perhaps the day will come when, for the instruction or misfortune of mankind, the plague will rouse up its rats and send them to die in some well-contented city.'

Albert Camus, *The Plague*, 1947

VICTORIA OLIVENCIA

Victoria was born in San Juan in 1975, but she grew up in Mendoza. She's the daughter of Daniel Horacio Olivencia and Ana María Montenegro. On 23 October 1976 her father was kidnapped and some time later Ana María, her mother, remarried.

> Before he became a Montonero, my dad was an anarchist. He was a member of a group called *Los Libertarios* (The Libertarians). My father was president of the students' union in the department of Psychology. He graduated as a psychologist and then he was disappeared. My mum was the secretary of the students' union. She graduated, but not until the return to democracy.

Malvinas/Falklands

> They made us do drawings at school and say the Lord's Prayer. It was a state school and I wouldn't pray because I'm not a believer. So the teacher called my mum and told her that if her daughter was Jewish she should keep me away. I wasn't Jewish, I was from Mendoza, just from the provinces…

'Today the Fatherland is threatened from within and without. For that reason our work must be total: it must be directed at both the body and soul (…) We are comforted by the sight today of the captains of the Armed Forces demonstrating their faith in the protection of the Mother of God, a faith that dates back many years, to when San Martín first gave an example of it.'

Monsignor Olimpo Santiago Maresma, Bishop of Mendoza
La Nación – 9 September 1976

The trial

> Another very strong memory I have is of the day of the trial of the juntas, when they passed sentence on those bastards, because my mum was shouting and crying, she was really happy. I didn't really understand what was going on, it was more a sharing of emotions. Although I didn't know why, I could see that my mum was happy. Something important was happening.

'The elimination of trials was a true subversion of the law: lawsuits were replaced by denunciations, interrogation by torture and reasoned sentencing by a Nero-style thumbs down. (…) For this reason, the accused are responsible both for the situation of those officials who had done such terrible things that they could not bring themselves to kiss their own children, and of that power-crazed colonel who styled himself "the master over life and death" (…) But there is something worse still: not only did they give orders for actions to be taken that were unworthy of the Armed Forces, but when they ought to have faced up to the responsibility for their commands, they denied that they had given such orders, denied any knowledge of the actions taken by their subordinates, denied knowing about the abductions, torture and deaths…'

Public prosecutor Julio Strassera
– Extracts from the case for the prosecution, Juicio a las Juntas

They didn't talk about it much. It was like everyone knew, so it didn't get discussed. So I would bug them about it. I remember when I was about ten years old we went to see Margarita, who is one of the Madres de Plaza de Mayo in Mendoza. I imagine we went about some paperwork and my mum was talking to Margarita about some rather strange things to do with my dad, and that's when I thought, 'What's the story here? I have to find out, I have to investigate.'

As soon as we left Margarita's, my mum told me that my dad was disappeared, that he was a Montonero militant…We were in the car. I didn't even have time to investigate.

Once bitten…

I was in Mendoza, I remember that all hell broke loose at home. The uprising freaked my mum out. It was a huge to do. Chaos everywhere. I was with my younger brother, the next one down, and they took us to my grandmother Lidia's house because my mum was going to leave the country. I remember the feeling of anger. The radio always on at the centre of these awful situations. They've crapped on us again…

FELLOW CITIZENS: HAPPY EASTER!
'The mutineers have abandoned their stance…

As is right and proper they will be arrested and tried.

A group of men are involved, some of them heroes from the Malvinas/Falklands war (…)

I ask the people who have entered Campo de Mayo to leave. You must do so, and I ask all of you to go home to your children, to celebrate Easter in peace in Argentina.'

[President] Raúl Alfonsín in response to Holy Week military uprising,
Clarín – 20 April 1987

Prejudice?

We were in the first or second year of secondary school and one of my best friends suddenly said that he was going to join the army when he was older:

'Oh well, great,' I say,

'That way I'll know the face of my torturer.'

And he just stared at me as if to say, What on earth is the matter with her? That's when I told him that I was the daughter of a desaparecido.

Every time I spoke about my dad I always used to cry. It was something I couldn't explain, I didn't know what to do about it, didn't know what to call it. I began to deal with my history shortly before joining HIJOS.

I knew that my dad was dead, that I had another grandmother who lived in Buenos Aires and I grew up with a 'substitute' paternal family, if you like. I only saw photos of my dad three years ago.

HIJOS

I started studying sociology and in the first year I sat near Facundo Guerra and Nazareno Bravo. On 24 March I went to the march organised by the Madres de Plaza de Mayo in Mendoza and a friend tells me that sons and daughters of desaparecidos are meeting in the MEDH. I thought: 'What are they going to do?' I don't know, I imagined a dark place, a group of people crying...[she laughs loudly].

And I was told,

'Do you know who else is going? Facundo Guerra.' So I phone him with my "poor daughter of a desaparecido" line [again she laughs] and tell him,

'I'm also a member of the gang.' We got together, chatted and he took me along to the meeting. That was in April 1995.

Historical reconstruction

I called some of my dad's friends and they gave me a series of phone numbers. So I ring one of them and tell him I'm the daughter of Daniel, that I'd like to talk to him and he says 'okay, we can meet on such-and-such a day'. I didn't have the nerve to go alone, so I asked

Nazareno to come with me. We arrive, knock on the door, and this girl comes out. We ask her,

'Is your dad in? And she says,

'Yes, I'll go get him.'

So she goes to a neighbour's and comes back with an old man. I thought he looked rather old to be a friend of my dad's, but I go up and say,

'Hello! I'm Daniel's daughter!'

I greet him with a kiss, Nazareno kisses him and the old man looks at me and says, 'Who are you looking for?'

I tell him, 'So-and-so.'

'Aaah! He lives opposite.'

Can you imagine!

My father

I was at the university. Facundo asked me to get his father's file, so I did him the favour. There's an enrolment book, with the student number, our fathers' names, their identity card number, the degree they were doing and their grades, so you can go and ask to see their file, the file with all their documentation, because they were students at the university.

I started looking through those big old books from 1974 or 1972, I can't remember what period it would have been, and I come across 'Daniel Olivencia'. And I think, 'This is MY father!' The man looking after the students' section just happened to be someone I knew from my neighbourhood. And I completely forgot about getting the file for Facundo…

'Look, could you get me Daniel Olivencia's file?'

'Yes,' he said, 'I'll get you it straight away, Victoria.'

I didn't know what I was going to find in it. He lets me in, gives me the file and as soon as I open it I see two passport sized photos! And he says to me:

'Your dad can continue studying if he wants to.'

I look at him and say,

'No, he can't, my dad's disappeared.'

'Oh…take whatever you want.'

And obviously what I chose to take was the photo. It was incredible. And he was registered for a different course, for Political Science.

Historical reconstruction Part II

There were eight or ten of us. We started to think about possible activities and we decided to hold a concert. We organised a gig with a bunch of musicians, it started out as a way of raising money and ended up being the launch of HIJOS in Mendoza. It was amazing.

In October 1995 Victoria travelled with the Mendoza delegation to the first HIJOS national camp in Córdoba province.

We went on the bus. When we arrived at Cabalango it was great. You couldn't believe it, so many sons and daughters [of victims of the dictatorship], there together. At night we all sat in a circle together. In fact, we were scattered all over and then a circle started forming. There were a couple of people singing and one particular thing I remember is this: a skinny boy from La Plata stood up and introduced himself. He said he was a magician, he called on a friend to be his assistant and began to do magic tricks. He made handkerchiefs appear, made things out of paper, and then someone shouted out:

'Hey, great, but if you're such a fantastic magician, why don't you make our parents appear?'

I didn't find it hurtful, I loved it. I needed to start seeing the desaparecidos in another light. Maybe we can't see our parents, but they're present in a load of things.

Searching

Before it was just a name. That's all it was: I was the daughter of Daniel Olivencia and my brothers' surname was Salatti. In fact it was when I started to put together my whole history that I felt the need to find out, to fill in that name. The feeling of needing his presence, there to give me a hug, and I'm not talking about when I was a teenager, I'm talking about two months ago maybe.

I don't find it at all easy, this process of reconstructing my history bit by bit, and as a result, the neediness I just talked about. So I ignore it all for a while, but suddenly I find the thread again and start tugging at it a bit more. I have to do it, it has to be possible.

28

Who, me?

With the return to democracy in 1983 the new government passed Decree 158/83, ruling that the Armed Forces' Supreme Court should conduct a pre-trial hearing against the members of the first three Military Juntas. The Armed Forces' Supreme Court did not comply with the legal deadlines, it also endorsed the actions of the Armed Forces. For this reason, in April 1985 the Federal Appeal Court began hearing what would become known as the 'Trial of the Juntas'. The trial aroused great international interest since for the first time in Latin America an illegal regime was being tried in the very country where it had been in power.

'The Junta had no responsibility for the struggle against subversion.'

Lieutenant General Jorge Rafael Videla
Juicio a las Juntas

'I knew of only five disappearances or deaths.'

General Roberto Viola
Juicio a las Juntas

'Occasionally a person may have been detained for some period of time or for the duration of an investigation. But they were always referred to the relevant authorities, whether the police, the courts or a court-martial.'

Admiral Eduardo Massera
Juicio a las Juntas

'It may happen that I have moments when my mind goes blank, as if I had lost consciousness, on account of a circulation problem.'

Brigadier Orlando Ramón Agosti
Juicio a las Juntas

MARIANA EVA PEREZ

Mariana was born in Buenos Aires in 1977. Her parents, Patricia Julia Roisinblit and José Manuel Pérez Rojo, Montonero militants, were kidnapped on 6 October 1978. Patricia, who was eight months pregnant, was detained in the Navy School of Mechanics. Numerous testimonies of survivors indicate that on 5 November 1978 she had a son, whom she named Rodolfo Fernando.

We were living in Palermo, we hadn't been living in the neighbourhood long, we were always moving from one house to another. My dad had a shop that sold books, toys and party novelties in Martínez, in the province of Buenos Aires. Apparently the gang first went to the shop and abducted my dad and a kid who worked with him. Then they came by the house, where my mum and I were. They then went to my grandparents', who weren't at home, so they left me with a sister of my grandfather's.

The age of why

Until I was four or five I had made up a story about my parents, I don't know where I got it from. I used to fantasise that my parents were in an aeroplane that never landed, and that's why they couldn't come and get me, or call me, or write to me. One winter's day I got it into my head that I wanted to put on a summer dress and, since my grandmother wouldn't let me, I started shouting that I wanted to go with my mummy. That's when my grandmother told me. She told me that my parents were disappeared, that we didn't know where they were, that the military had taken them away…

My grandmother used to stand me on the loo to brush my hair. I have an image of me standing there and my grandmother telling me. That same day, or the next, we were walking through a square, the memory's crystal clear, a square in Belgrano in front of a church and I was asking, 'But…why did they take them away?'

'I wish to make clear that the citizens of Argentina are not the targets of the repression. The repression is directed at a minority of people whom we do not consider to be Argentinians.'

Videla, *La Prensa* – 18 December 1977

I accepted what they told me quite naturally, so the word 'desaparecidos' didn't seem at all strange to me. I could accept that level of uncertainty. That was it, they weren't there, and no one knew if they were coming back or not.

Demands at school

At school, everyone, both teachers and classmates, knew my history. I never lied. When I started in the first year, one day I stood up in class and told the teacher that I wanted her to explain to my classmates why my grandparents brought me and picked me up from school, and to explain what the desaparecidos were.

It was a state school, and when I started we were still under the dictatorship. The memory that makes it quite clear to me that it was still during the dictatorship was that under their smocks the boys had to wear a shirt and tie. In the second year this was no longer the case. That for me marks the difference...

1983

During the election campaign I was a diehard follower of Alfonsín and at first I used to watch every speech he made on national TV. My grandfather was a lifelong supporter of the Radical Party, but I had also placed other expectations on Alfonsín. Shortly after he took office I told my maternal grandmother that Alfonsín had let me down, because I thought that when he was president they'd open up the prisons and all the desaparecidos would come back.

I have to tell you something

It was night time, I remember the street and everything – Pampa Street, in Belgrano...I was seven or eight years old. My granny Argentina had come to fetch me from my English class and was explaining to me that the next day we had to go and have some blood taken. I wasn't at all happy about it, I'd never had blood taken; just once Granny Rosa had given me an injection and it was as if someone had stuck a sword in me. It was awful, I hate needles. I said,

'But why? Why?' She didn't dare tell me.

'Look Mariana,' she said, 'I have something to tell you, but I don't want you to cry, okay?' She said it very kindly.

'Okay, what is it?'

'When they took your mummy away, she was eight months pregnant. So you have a brother who we are looking for.'

I was very pleased, the first thing I thought was, I won't have to play on my own any more. I was delighted with the idea of having a brother – it was a drag being an only child, I didn't like it. Besides I have no cousins or anything, so I was my grandparents' only grandchild. Both my dad and my mum were only children.

It was a connection to my parents, but what I didn't see at the time was the sinister side of the appropriation of my brother. There was a boy that they thought might be him, but in the end it turned out not to be.

I remember that in Durán Hospital they told me that I wouldn't feel it, that it was like a mosquito biting you…

Letters

When I was nine, we were given a writing exercise. The task was to write a letter to a relative, so I wrote a letter to my brother. I finished it and went to show the teacher. Showing her the letter was like telling her. Poor thing! She was stunned. She knew about my parents, but didn't know about my brother.

Abuelas

I used to go to Abuelas but didn't understand what they were doing. When I began to understand what it was about, looking for the kids who had been born in captivity, I used to think, 'He's not this one, but he'll be the next one.' It was like that, something imminent. It was the joy of knowing I had a brother and the greater joy of knowing that we were going to find him. Besides at that time, in the 1980s, they were being discovered one after another.

My grandmother is very sensitive, which is why sometimes I hold back, I know that if I say anything she'll start crying. So the thing with my brother was a very personal process, I began to look at myself in the mirror in a different way…to wonder what he looked like.

You look at yourself in the mirror and think 'What will we have in common? Will he have the same nose as me? Will he have my mouth?'

Someday…

Since she was very little Mariana had enjoyed writing. In 1990 the Abuelas de Plaza de Mayo published a collection of poems and prose writings by her and

Yamila Grandi. The book, titled *Algún día* (Someday), includes texts that Mariana wrote between the ages of eight and 12.

Buenos Aires, 7 December 1988

Dear Rodolfito,

Did you get the letter I sent you in 1986? It was the first (and only letter) I've sent you, but I hope that you've received all the messages that I send you every day in my head. (…)

Sometimes I wonder, when we meet, What will I say to you? And I reply: we will surely look at each other, and I (the weak one, all moved) may start crying; then, after looking at each other as if we cannot believe it, I might give you a hug and say, 'My dream's come true.'

I am waiting for that moment. While we wait, talk to me often, because I need you a lot. When you want to see me, look for me in your deepest dreams, as I do. See you soon!

Mariana Pérez, *Algún día*…Abuelas de Plaza de Mayo, 1990

Full stop to justice

When they were discussing the Ley de Punto Final, I was very intrigued by a law with such a strange name. One Saturday I was spending the weekend at my maternal grandmother's and she had left something behind at Abuelas, so we went to their offices. On the way she told me about the Ley de Punto Final and when we arrived, while my grandmother was looking for what she'd left there, I sat on the floor with a piece of paper and a marker pen. I wrote straight off a kind of poem-letter to Alfonsín in which I asked him to put himself in the shoes of a girl who couldn't accept the Punto Final because she couldn't stop hoping for her disappeared parents.

PUNTO FINAL (EXCERPT)

…And all of this, for what?
And the 'full stop', why?
I just want you to think, President
Of kids who, like me
Without my brother/Born in captivity
Without my parents taken up to heaven,
Every time the doorbell rings
Hope that it's their
Family at the door,
'Happy and smiling'.

Mariana Pérez, *Algún día*…Abuelas de Plaza de Mayo, 1990

It's strange because a few years ago I re-read that text and was surprised to find that at the end it says I was waiting for my parents to return, and it was dated December 1986. I thought, 'Was I really still expecting them to come back then?' I can't remember having hoped they would return for so long.

The thing is, I can't really say when I stopped hoping they'd come back. I'm not sure when I stopped waiting for them, when I began to...not 'resign myself', that's not the right word...

With my brother it's totally different, it's another story, it's the anguish of knowing that he's alive somewhere and I don't know where.

The next one

I had an economics teacher when I was 15 who was a real fascist, everyone knew it. The day he started he made us say our names and surnames one by one down each row, and the names and surnames of our parents, and the professions of each one. So it went, each in turn until it came to me. I felt the eyes of all my classmates on the back of my neck. I felt that everyone was waiting to see what I'd say. And so...

He said:

'Name and surname...'

'Mariana Eva Pérez. My dad's name is José Manuel Pérez Rojo...'

'What does he do?'

'Nothing.'

'And your mother?'

'Patricia Julia Roisinblit.'

'What does she do?'

'Nothing.'

'What?'

'No...They are disappeared.'

'How? Some kind of accident?'

'No, they are desaparecidos. Desaparecidos from the dictatorship,' I say.

'Okay, next...'

That was the most upsetting thing that ever happened to me. Of course! 'Some kind of accident?' 'Yes, the sinking of the Titanic! An earthquake!' If you say desaparecido, what can it possibly refer to? Clearly...

Activism

I know that by 1996 I was very involved. When I was 19 there came a point at which I realised that if I didn't find out about their activism, I would understand nothing about them. If I didn't get to know them as activists I wouldn't ever know them properly, it was something that had been an extremely important part of their lives.

In the beginning I used to get really disheartened: 'No, no I'm not going to find anyone, they're all disappeared', and then I began to find people and they tracked down others and in the end I got in touch with quite a few. For example, there's a woman called Miriam Lewin who's a journalist. I knew that she'd been in the ESMA with my mum, that she'd seen my brother and that she knew my mum from before.

'…I had seen her once at a picnic in Luján. We'd chatted, she was pregnant at the time with her first child, Mariana, I found out later she called her. And later we met again in the ESMA. (…) She told me that she'd been kidnapped by the Air Force, and that they were holding them in a kind of farm in the west of Greater Buenos Aires and that they'd brought her to the School of Mechanics to have her baby. I spoke with her on several occasions, always thanks to the kindness of the guards. Finally, one day, I came out of the *pecera*, where an officer registered inmates, and I see that they're taking her out of a kind of cell and taking her to the basement and she tells me, 'it's time'. She was wearing a mask, what they called a *tabique*. So they called Mrs Osatinsky, another prisoner, and she accompanied her downstairs, to the basement, where she was going to give birth in the sick bay, with some guards. Hours later, concerned to know the outcome of the birth, I asked the guards to take me down to the basement and I waited there. The other prisoners tell me that she had a long labour, and then at one point, the doctor, Mañasco or Magnasco, comes out of the sick bay and tells me to go in. There I find another prisoner, whose surname is Larralde, I can't remember whether her name's Amalia or Amelia, who had assisted at the birth, since she had studied to be a nurse. Patricia was on the bed with her feet up, they were putting in stitches and Mrs Osatinsky was holding the baby and washing it. Patricia's face had a kind of eczema on it from the effort and she was very pleased to have had her baby in spite of the circumstances. It really was a terrible scene.'

Testimony of Miriam Lewin de García – Juicio a las Juntas

Time

'For a long time I have been waiting for you with open arms. For many years, too many. Years of searching for your face in the mirror, of inventing your features by looking at mine. Years of thinking that if I saw you on the street I wouldn't recognise you. Or would I?

I wait for you anxiously, full of doubt and fear. Every morning I love you more, with a profound and unalterable affection.

I have a place ready for you in my life and in my house. A whole lot of things that I have not yet said to you, kisses, hugs, laughter to share. And a handful of stars, which, when you return, I'm going to give to you.

But you are far away; and I am here, crying out the injustice of fate on this white page.'

22 May 1990
Mariana Pérez, *Algún día*…Abuelas de Plaza de Mayo, 1990

This year my brother will be 21, in November. When I walk down the street it's an automatic reflex, any boy of roughly my age who I pass, I immediately look at him. I've got a thing with the nose, I'm not sure why. I have quite a particular nose – which is like my dad's – and I have this idea that my brother might have my mother's nose. My mother had a turned up nose. Up until now I haven't followed anyone, but I'm afraid that the day might come when I've become so crazy that I begin following some young man.

It always takes over on the bus, because one's going along not thinking about anything. When I see little kids or teenagers, I get upset because I remember myself looking for my brother at that age, and now time has passed and it's never coming back. It makes me sad, he's no longer a teenager, you know, I won't ever see him with spots. I won't ever be able to take the piss out of his pock-marked face…

Until the last

It's something that we don't talk about, but everyone knows. My grandmother – the one who works with the Abuelas – tells me she's at peace because she knows that I'm going to carry on. That the only thing she wants is for us to find my brother and for him to know that she searched for him right up until the last moment of her life. Gradually getting me used to the idea that she may never know him. My grandmother Rosa is 80 years old…

'Someone is trying out a brilliant scam, which is completly unfounded, such as a judicial resolution based on the fact that these children existed, when they may not exist or may be hidden with their relatives,' the repressor Jorge 'Tigre' Acosta said to the court, without batting an eyelid.'

Página12 – 17 September 1999

The other day I saw her in a film that's being made about the Abuelas and I was really moved. They showed about ten or 15 minutes. It moved me to see her say that the message she'd like to give my brother is 'for you to know that I looked for you from before you were born.' It's true, because as soon as they took away my parents she began moving heaven and earth in her search.

A western

It was a short time ago. There's another girl who also has a disappeared sibling, she's called Clara. She's got a kid, studies and works. We met over the phone, and a long time went by before we met in person. Her sister was born in the Pozo de Banfield. When we got to know each other she told me that once they'd done the blood test on a girl who could have been her sister, and that it turned out not to be her.

She had always been bugged by the question of who that girl was and if she might be someone else's daughter. Until one day she suddenly says, 'I went to see María de las Mercedes. I went and knocked on her door, we chatted and she's going to have blood taken again.' It turns out that the girl knows why she'd been tested ten years before and that she hadn't matched with the family that they thought was hers. There was information missing in the blood bank. I almost fall over backwards, I wanted to throttle her – poor thing – but I said,

'You're crazy, how did you dare do that? What if the girl wanted to know nothing?'

We start talking and she tells me that María de las Mercedes's birth certificate is signed by Bergés and that she was born on 27 December 1977. That she was going to be tested again and that she was going to accompany her to the Right to Identity Commission for them to order the analysis to be done, because she, too, had been left wondering whether she was or wasn't the daughter of desaparecidos. That she wanted to know and to find her family.

They had got her from Bergés' clinic by knowing one of the nurses and they had adopted her as their own child. When they went to fetch her, they were asked what birth date they wanted to register her with, and they asked what was her real birth date, and at the clinic they told them '27 December'. So they decided to keep the date...

That's what María de las Mercedes told Clara, and Clara told me.

Clara told me this over the phone and I lay down on my bed with the Librito Rosa out of curiosity. Let's have a look, who could it be? And I realise that there was a case of a baby girl born in the Pozo de

Banfield on 27 December 1977. And I say,
'Blow me, it can't be!'
I consulted the genetics people and the family still hadn't been analysed. I tell them, 'Let's get a move on, this girl is going to see whether it is her family or not.' And it turned out it was.

DAUGHTER OF A DISAPPEARED URUGUAYAN COUPLE IS IDENTIFIED
She's 21 years old. The daughter of parents kidnapped in Argentina. It is suspected that the military sold her to the family of an engineer. This is case number 63 to be identified by the Abuelas.

The Abuelas de Plaza de Mayo are celebrating the 63rd identification of a child of desaparecidos, announced officially yesterday (…) in the context of a very special case. The girl, who is 21, found out her true history a few days ago and is a victim of the Condor Plan, organised in the 1970s by the Southern Cone dictatorships, to provide mutual collaboration between the military in actions of illegal repression. Her parents were Uruguayans and were kidnapped in Argentina, where they had fled from the military regime in their own country. (…) The young woman, whose name is María de las Mercedes, and whose surname is being kept secret for the moment, spoke for the first time on Friday with one of her blood relatives, who live in Montevideo.

(…) María de las Mercedes's true mother, Aída Sanz Fernández, was kidnapped at her home in San Antonio de Padua on 23 December 1977. She had been living in Argentina for more than a year (…) Aida was on the point of giving birth and her mother was in Argentina, having travelled from Montevideo to be with her at the birth. In the same operation her mother was also abducted, and remains disappeared. María de las Mercedes's father, Eduardo Gallo, was also abducted at the same time (…) The false birth certificate, which names another woman as her biological mother, is signed by the police doctor and repressor Jorge Bergés. María de las Mercedes will now meet two uncles, three half-sisters (daughters of her father) and her only surviving grandfather: her family, who are waiting for her in Montevideo.

Clarín – 23 June 1999

She met her whole family, who are from Uruguay and for us it was just amazing. For me it felt like I'd found her with Clara, who'd dared to go see her, and with Demián, who works in genetics. What is so incredible is that we're the new generation, we did it ourselves, three kids up late one night. The lunatic going to knock at her door, me lying on my bed and Demián rushing to see these people in Uruguay.
The girl was sure they were going to tell her that there was no match. She had asked Clara to go with her to the Commission and at

the last moment she said,

'No, don't come, they're just going to say no anyway.' But they said yes, and that same day she spoke to her uncle on the phone and soon afterwards travelled to Uruguay.

Mariana lives in a small flat with her boyfriend and a cat named Jacinta. She is studying Political Science at the University of Buenos Aires and works with the Abuelas de Plaza de Mayo. In April 2000, a few months after this interview, Mariana received a phone call giving information about the existence of a young man who had been appropriated by members of the Air Force. And so Mariana found her brother.

Historical Notes on the Dictatorship of 1976–1983

Alejandro Andreassi Cieri
Sant Cugat del Vallès (Barcelona),
January 2004

The testimonies collected in this book reveal to the reader the disappearance of any vestige of a normative and civilised society in Argentina between 1976 and 1983. The establishment of the most brutal military dictatorship that the country has suffered gave rise to a totalitarian regime that practiced State terrorism as a systematic political tool. The origins of this catastrophe must be sought in factors internal to Argentinian society, related as much to its recent as more distant history, which combined with the international context of the era resulted in the coup of 24 March 1976. The dictatorship was the result of a military coup that overthrew the constitutional government presided by María Estela Martínez de Perón and replaced it with a military *junta* made up of the commanders in chief of the three armed forces: Videla for the army, Massera for the navy and Agosti for the air force. But the leading role of the military must not obscure the profoundly classist nature of the dictatorship, and as such the active participation of civilians in the general direction of the genocidal project, as well as in the economic and social benefits that they aimed to obtain.

The coup signified, once more, the type of political intervention of the most concentrated and elitist sector of the Argentinian bourgeoisie, that since the 1930s had failed to gain access to government through democratic means. It was the culmination of a long series of violent interruptions in the working of democratic institutions initiated with the coup of 6 September 1930, when General Uriburu overthrew the civilian government of Hipólito Irigoyen. The figure of a 'military party' was progressively consolidated as a political tool of that dominant elite that could not impose its government or projects by democratic means, and resorted instead to the systematic imposition of authoritarian governments each time that constitutional governments took decisions that affected their interests or were insufficiently diligent in the control or repression of trade unions, leftist parties or the working class. The image of the 'military party' reached its full maturity with the coup of 1955 that ended the government of Juan D. Perón.

The real nature of the 1976 dictatorship is better defined by a coalition of those seeking to overthrow the government, where civilians and the military divided the work between them. The first, as representatives of the most concentrated business and economic power, formulated and implemented social and economic programmes, and the latter controlled political power directly. This combination of military leadership and haute bourgeoisie was materialised in the organigram of state power: at the head of the Economy Ministry, setting out the political aims of the dictatorship, was José Martínez de Hoz, a businessman member of an exclusive circle of large landowners and financiers, with excellent connections to international and particularly North American banking. The design of the extremely liberal economic programme of the dictatorship was down to Martínez de Hoz, as head of a group of important figures and conspirators of financial markets and the extreme right. Their economic interests were compounded by a rabid anti-Peronism and anti-Communism and they were part of a group of owners or executive board members of large companies that had worked extensively in the cabinets of the previous military dictatorship (1966–1972).

Many of the them held high office in the all-powerful Economy Ministry under the direction of José Martínez de Hoz. In the run up to the coup, he had orchestrated, from his position as an important businessman and using his connections with the military, a concerted effort from industrial business interests, large landowners and agribusiness exporters in one organisation, APEGE (Permanent Assembly of Professional Business Entities). APEGE was used to put pressure on the government of Isabel Perón in favour of their interests, clearly against those of the majority of the population and to destabilise the government to obtain a favourable change in the leadership of political power. The project, in the planning since 1974, included the internationalisation of the Argentinian economy, favouring agricultural exports to the detriment of industrial development, with an unrestricted opening to foreign trade, a drastic concentration of wealth, the reduction of credit to small and medium enterprises, all sustained by external debt. The economic and social structure of the country was to be turned around in ten years, to impose the freeing of trade, the deregulation of social welfare and the protection of increasing financial markets. The stability of ten years was not planned on the basis of the ballot box or consensus, but on a political and social paralysis that depended on repression, of a systematic nature without historic precedent in the country.*

The government presided by Isabel Perón, increasingly besieged from the right, had given the first steps towards the economic and social aims the dictatorship would impose, with an adjustment decree formulated in 1975 by her Economy Minister Celestino Rodrigo. The measure was deemed insufficient, by those planning the coup, to guarantee social order and the subjection of workers and their trade union organisations to their ultraliberal plans. For that reason power was to be taken by the 'military party' that continued the praetorian practice that it has been intermittently repeating since 1930: once they took political power they imposed through a terrorist dictatorship the aims designed by civilian elites.

The national context in which the coup took place was characterised by a combination of factors that interacted together. In May 1973 a democratic government had

---

* María Seoane, Vicente Muleiro, *El Dictador*. Buenos Aires, Sudamericana, 2001, pp. 25 and 42

come to power that tried to respond to the population's demands arising from the resistance to the previous miliary dictatorship. In that government, where in the first phase the left of Peronism would predominate, tried to renew and bring up to date the social pact that had been established in the first Peronist governments from 1946 and which had been systematically attacked by dominant social groups and those responsible for the coup of 1955 that overthrew Perón. The social pact of 1946-1955 had been accepted as the lesser of two evils by the elite and the middle classes, as long as it did not interfere with their mechanisms of accumulation and profits. In terms of political culture, these affluent classes held that the 'golden age' of Argentina was the exporting nation that predominated between 1880 and 1930. The landowning elite, known as the oligarchy in political parlance, had designed the country towards the end of the nineteenth century, with Argentina as the bread basket of the world, out of a European heritage and with the promise of becoming a Latin American power until the crisis of 1930 – thanks to these myths it had retained its political and cultural hegemony over the majority of the Argentinian middle class.*

In 1973 those same circles of economic power showed their rejection of contributing to the recovery of a social pact that had allowed the development of a welfare state during the 1940s and 1950s and that had been maintained, albeit with increasing difficulty, after the fall of Perón. The dominant class and an important part of the middle class never accepted the redistributive capitalism and populist proposals of Peronism, as they required the support for industrialisation and the development of a large internal market, which implied an increase in the participation of salaried workers in GDP and the decrease in social and income inequalities, and therefore the transference of resources from agricultural exports towards urban industrial development which went against the interests of the landed bourgeoisie. They simply lived with it until circumstances and the renewal of the 'military party' allowed them to get rid of that social pact.

The democratic political phase begun in 1973 continued and reinforced the existing social mobilisation and one of its main manifestations was the organisational capacity of trade unions, which went beyond traditional unionism and the political groupings of the left, both inside Peronism and outside. It reinforced patterns of resistance and the questioning of the established order in large sectors of the population, among which young people from the working and middle classes were predominant due to their activity and dynamism. For that reason the imposition of the interests of the dominant classes and the accumulation of capital depended increasingly on a diminishing role for the state in the economy and society, as well as the disciplining of labour and the subjection of lower classes.

These internal developments must be articulated with the international context to complete the picture of the possibilities for a coup and a genocidal dictatorship.

---

* For a definition of hegemony, see Raymond Williams, *Keywords. A vocabulary of culture and society*, London, Fontana Press, 1985, pp.144–146

From early in the 1970s there was a great accumulation of excess capital looking for profitable investments, created by the rise in oil prices and the profits obstained by North American transnational companies. A combination of recession and the high costs of labour in developed countries meant there was a 'supply crisis'[*] that meant business was not ready to continue producing in the context of the postwar social pact that implied an improved capacity for negotiation for labour and therefore costs to capital, reducing profit margins. All of which led to the questioning of the welfare state by dominant classes.

There was a convergence of mutually favourable interests between capital in Argentina and externally, that points to the coup of 1976 as a political offensive on the part of financial and business elites, an attack on labour by capital and not at all a defense against a hypothetical revolutionary threat as held by the propaganda orchestrated by the military dictatorship to justify the destruction of democracy and its policies of state terrorism.

What were the characteristics of the military dictatorship of 1976? In the first instance its class content, something that would not be so different from past dictatorships in Argentina in the twentieth century. The main difference was the establishment of a system of control and domination that did not brook any contestation on part of the lower classes to capitalist interests. For the first time in Argentinian history a military regime tried to suppress any vestige of union organising, not even tolerating compliant or unrepresentative unions that could be controlled, as had happened in the past.

The political and social mediation with power that had been exercised, even under authoritarian regimes, by organisations controlled by those in power was replaced by a policy based on terror, carried out by a repressive state apparatus. It was not a decision taken only by psychopaths drunk on power, but it fitted with the aims set out by the coalition of those planning the coup referred to above. Their economic project implied the privatisation of services and state companies, the recovery of the old emphasis on agricultural exports, financial activities, trade in imports, key enclaves of technological production dependent on transnational companies and military expenditure. Meanwhile national industrial production and small and medium companies would disappear.[†]

The result was the inverse of what had been Argentinian development in the previous 40 years: deindustrialisation to be made up by imports.[§] Carrying through these aims meant a reduction in labour power needed and the increase in a 'superfluous' population that could only be contained through repression and abandon-

---

[*] David Anisi, *Creadores de escasez. Del bienestar al miedo*, Madrid, Alianza Editorial, 1995

[†] Some industrialists were favoured by the measures taken, relating mostly to insider contracts and tax evasion. See Jozami, Angel Argentina. *La destrucción de una nación*, Barcelona, Mondadori, 2003, p. 298 for examples.

[§] Jorge Fonseca, 'La dictadura militar instaurada en 1976 provocó una desindustrialización restitutiva de importaciones', *El País*, Madrid, 08/02/2002.

ment to economic and social regression. The plans of Martínez de Hoz only required half of the population the country had at the time of the coup, so that the destruction of union organising was a major objective, as even docile organisations might provide the kernel for future resistance movements.

The point was to build a 'new' Argentina, in which the industrial working class did not have a role, or at least the importance and weight it had acquired in the previous forty years. In that situation there was no need for a redistributive state that provided essential public services. Videla was clear in his first speech, when he said that the aim of the dictatorship was the 'end of one historical cycle and the beginning of another', adding that the intention was to create a 'new order' through 'national renewal'.*

The other paradigmatic aspect of this dictatorship was the use of Terror as an instrument to fulfil its domination. State terror was the 'political' means applied to further economic and social projects favourable to society's elite. It was required by the nature of the violence being done to the bulk of the population, to ensure no collective resistance was possible. But terror also had a performative function, to shape a new type of inhabitant, closer to a subject than to a citizen, submissive and at the same time expressing the policies decided by the regime, to be seen as the only ones possible, without alternative. The military and their civilian accomplices sought to create not only a 'new' Argentina but also a 'new' type of person who would conceive of domination as the 'natural' way to organise society. The result was the subordination of the population through the institution of a permanent state of emergency (state terror), which brought about support or at least passivity through fear. It may be paradoxical that fear might lead to support, but we must remember the mechanisms of compensation and displacement that arise in a society that has been reduced by its masters to a powerless state.

As Bruno Bettelheim commented in relation to his Nazi guards in the concentration camp where he was detained, being subjected to arbitrary power leads to a feeling of dependence.† The terror unleashed by the dictatorship reaffirmed the sensation that there was no limit to the will of the dominant power that assumed its own permanence and used the ambiguity of the public nature of repression – kidnappings took place in daylight, often with large security operations where arms were brandished ostentatiously so that all those in the environs of the victims could witness the display of power. At the same time, secrecy surrounded the fate of those kidnapped and detained, and the uncertainty over their whereabouts was transformed into uncertainty over everyone's future and a consensus arose of the necessity to please, to appease the inscrutable intentions of the dictatorial power. These conditions led to self-repression, where each kept watch over him or herself, convinced that those in power, the 'guards' were aware of all their actions.

---

* Jozami, op. cit., p. 273.
† Bruno Bettelheim, *Sobrevivir. El holocausto una generación después*, Barcelona, Crítica, 1983

229

To ensure its aims, the dictatorship dehumanised its victims, portraying them as beasts, separating them from the rest of society to avoid any possible solidarity from those who might help them, an effective means of eliminating them without death, in such a way that genocide becomes a murder without murderers, and also without victims, as they die because of what they are, not for what they've done and that's why they don't deserve to live. Turning the victims into 'things' allows for the absolution of the executioners, transforming the first into a logistical bureaucratic problem to be solved and the latter to the one who solves a problem. If any phrase pronounced by any of the spokespersons of the dictatorship best reflects this totalitarian approach based on crime and terror, it was that spoken by General Ibérico Saint Jean, governor of the province of Buenos Aires, in an interview with the *International Herald Tribune*: 'First we will eliminate the subversives,* then their accomplices, then their sympathizers and finally the indifferent and the undecided.' The aim was the elitist and restricted 'reconstruction' of Argentinian society, where labour rights were abolished, real wages dropped steadily and collective bargaining was not allowed, atomizing the labour movement already attacked by repression and almost disintegrated through deindustrialisation. Basic liberties were suppressed while basic health and education services were eliminated or made more expensive, making the least able to pay take the brunt of transformations. At the same time a strict ideological control was imposed in the arenas of culture and education which used spying and encouraged denunciation. A distinctive trait of the regime is that state terror destroyed the moral fabric of civic culture in Argentina, establishing a reign of impunity for the crimes committed by the military and for those responsible for the economic and social policies supported by their violence; an impunity that survived the dictatorship and was maintained by the constitutional governments that succeeded it.

The results of totalitarianism soon became visible, showing how the aims of the coup were fulfilled. Real wages fell by 40 per cent in relation to the average over the previous five years; the proportion of wages to GDP that was 49.8 per cent in 1974 was reduced to 28.9 per cent by 1980, a drastic transference of income from waged workers to capital that meant an extraordinary increase in the rate of business profit.[†] At the same time there was a reduction in public expenditure and the beginning of the privatisation of state enterprises, while state-run services raised their rates, all leading to a notable deterioration in the standard of living of workers and poorer sectors of the population in general. Taxes on traditional agricultural exports were abolished, as well as any subsidies to non-traditional production, reinforcing the extreme dependency of Argentina on a few exports, holding the country ransom to the landowning class. The measures were rounded off by the reform of the financial sector that decentralised the banking system and created a free monetary market, while it sustained high interest rates and an overvalued currency to attract foreign

---

* 'Subversive' was the term used by the dictatorship to label all opposition and resistance to their policies.

[†] Jozami *op. cit.*, pp. 275–76.

capital, giving rise to a speculative spiral and the massive transfer of rent from industry to finance. This in turn initiated the indebtedness that continues to this day as a perverse mechanism standing in the way of economic recovery.

These economic policies completed the destruction of social cohesion initiated through repression. The weakening of the working class through economic recession reinforced and complemented the offensive against political dissidence, suffocating the possibility of resistance or contestation. The reciprocal effects of repression and economic policy consolidated the military and the economic elites in power.

Moreover, there were direct links between repression and companies that collaborated closely to inform of militant workers or lent their buildings for the detention and torture of prisoners, such as happened in the case of Mercedes-Benz, Ford and Ingenio Ledesma.*

In spite of the dictatorship ending when Raúl Alfonsín became constitutional president in December 1983, its effects and consequences extend into the present in all areas and at all levels of society in Argentina. It marked a profound moral break and the deterioration of civic values, as well as undermining the confidence of citizens in the political system, specially due to the impunity many of the crimes of the dictatorship have enjoyed.

The current Argentinian crisis has its roots in the bloody military dictatorship of 1976. The quarter of a century that has passed has continued the concentration of income and the increasing polarisation and social inequality and the consequent destruction of social protection for the most vulnerable. It has meant the definitive destruction of the social pact that had been in place since the 1940s and the application of neo-liberal policies that today are called 'globalisation'.

The responsibility of the subsequent Radical and Peronist governments lies in having continued, with tiny variations, the policies initiated by the powerful Economy Minister Martínez de Hoz in 1976, a continuity that is closely linked with the refusal to bring those responsible for crimes against humanity to justice. For that reason the struggle for the full observance of human rights and the punishment of those responsible for the crimes committed between 1976 and 1983 is not only a necessary condition for the moral reconstitution of Argentina, but also a step needed to build an alternative vision of social development that repairs the devastation wreaked by neoliberal policies. To attain not only a more prosperous society, but one that is fundamentally freer, fairer and where solidarity thrives.

---

* Adolfo Pérez Esquivel, 'La complicidad del poder económico con la dictadura: el caso Mercedes Benz', http://www.derechos.org/nizkor/arg/doc/benz1.htm. Regarding repression in the Ingenio Ledesma (Jujuy) see 'Luis Ramón Arédez desaparecido el 13 de Mayo de 1977', http://www.desaparecidos.org/arg/victimas/a/ aredezl/. On the collaboration of the management at Ford in the repression see Nunca Más, 1984 (see Bibliography)

Glossary

Abuelas de Plaza de Mayo
Grandmothers of the Plaza de Mayo is a civic association of women that aims to locate and return to their rightful families all those children kidnapped by the dictatorship.

Alfonsín, Raúl
President of Argentina (1983–1989). Came to power on a banner of human rights. Among his first actions were the derogation of the amnesty law passed by the military before leaving power and the creation of Conadep (see below). He is remembered for having given in to the pressure from the military to curtail the trials against them by passing the laws of Full Stop and Due Obedience (see below).

Conadep
Comisión Nacional sobre la Desaparición de Personas, created in 1983 to investigate the violations of human rights during the dictatorship. The results of their work were published in a book, Nunca Más, which was a bestseller in Argentina.

Familiares
Familiares de detenidos desaparecidos por razones politicas
An important human rights group made up of relatives, including men, of those disappeared and also political prisoners in normal prisons.

HIJOS
Hijos por la Identidad y la Justicia contra el Olvido y el Silencio, an association created in 1995 bringing together the children of the victims of state terrorism.

Menem, Carlos
President of Argentina (1989–1999). He signed a blanket amnesty that benefited all those military leaders not covered by the laws of Full Stop or Due Obedience. The amnesty also covered all those who had taken part in uprisings against the government since the return to democracy.

Juicio a las Juntas
Trial of the Juntas, took place in 1985 when a civilian court secured the right to judge the military that had made up the leading juntas during the dictatorship. The court found them guilty and imposed sentences of varying severity.

Juventud Peronista, PJ
Peronist (Workers') Youth was officially created on 1 May 1973 to bring together grassroots union work involving young Peronists.

La Noche de los Lápices
The Night of the Pencils took place in the early hours of 16 September 1976, when Buenos Aires police kidnapped seven secondary school students. They were between 14 and 18 years old and were members of Union of Secondary Students. They were taken from their homes in the night. The testimony of the only survivor, Pablo Díaz, included the account of the torture and murder of his companions.

Ley de Obediencia Debida
Due Obedience Law was passed by the government of Raúl Alfonsín (1983-1989), absolving middle and low ranking officials in the military of any responsibility for human rights violations. See Semana Santa 1987.

Ley de Punto Final
Full Stop Law, passed on 23 December 1986 to put a limit to the number of cases the justice system might deal with against the military.

Madres de Plaza de Mayo
Mothers of Plaza de Mayo, one of the best known human rights organisations in Argentina, formed in 1977 when a group of mothers first walked in silence around the Plaza de Mayo.

Movimiento Ecuménico por los Derechos Humanos (MEDH)
Ecumenical Movement for Human Rights, created in 1976 just before the coup.

Montoneros
Eventually the largest of the guerrilla movements in Argentina in the 1970s, with its roots in Peronism and an urban focus. A number of other leftist Peronist organisations fused with them in 1973 and members also joined from legal Peronist organisations such as Peronist Youth.

Partido Revolucionario de los Trabajadores/Ejercito Revolucionario del Pueblo (PRT/ERP)
The main non-Peronist leftist guerrilla organisation, with its roots in Cuban *foquista* theory and Marxist-Leninism.

Semana Santa 1987
Holy Week uprising, which took place in April 1987. Sectors of the military protested against the trials against them. A demonstration of unprecedented proportions took place in the Plaza de Mayo to support the democratic government and reject military pressure. President Alfonsín negotiates with the rebels and agrees to the law of Due Obedience.

Triple A
Anticommunist Alliance of Argentina, far right paramilitary death squad active from 1974; from 1976 it became part of the repressive apparatus of the dictatorship.

Bibliography

Almirón, Fernando, *Campo Santo*. Buenos Aires, Editorial Siglo XXI, 1998

Barco, Susana Leda, *Los corredores de la memoria*. (Unpublished)

Barón, Ana, Mario del Carril, y Albino Gómez, *Por qué se fueron. Testimonios de argentinos en el exterior*. Buenos Aires, Emecé Editores, 1995

Blaustein, Eduardo y Martín Zubieta, *Decíamos Ayer. La prensa argentina bajo el Proceso*. Buenos Aires, Colihue, 1998

Camarasa, Jorge, Rubén Felice y Daniel González, *El Juicio, Proceso al horror*. Buenos Aires, Sudamericana-Planeta, 1985

Caraballo, Liliana, Noemí Charlier y Liliana Garulli, *La Dictadura (1976-1983)*. Buenos Aires, Eudeba, 1999

CONADEP, *Nunca Más*. Informe de la Comisión Nacional sobre la Desaparición de Personas, Buenos Aires, Eudeba, 1991

D'Andrea Mohr, José Luis, *Memoria Debida*. Buenos Aires, Colihue, 1999

Di Vito, Pablo, *Historias de alguna vez*. Rosario, P. Gráfica, 1997

Frontalini, Daniel y María Cristina Caiati, *El Mito de la Guerra Sucia*. Buenos Aires, CELS 1984

Galeano, Eduardo, *Las Venas Abiertas de América Latina*. Buenos Aires, Siglo XXI Editores, 1974

'Informe de la Comisión Bicameral Investigadora de las Violaciones de los Derechos Humanos en la Provincia de Tucumán', España, IEPALA, 1991

'Juicio a las Juntas', in D'Andrea Mohr, José Luis, *Memoria Debida*. Buenos Aires, Colihue, 1999

Kaufmann, Carolina y Delfina Doval, *Paternalismos Pedagógicos*. Rosario, Laborde Editor, 1999

Kaufmann, Carolina y Delfina Doval, *Una pedagogía de la renuncia. El perennialismo en Argentina (1976–1983)*. Universidad Nacional de Entre Ríos, 1997

López, Ernesto, *El Ultimo Levantamiento*. Buenos Aires, Nueva Información, 1988

Paoletti, Alipio E., *Como los nazis, como en Vietnam*. Buenos Aires, Edición Cañon Oxidado,1987

Pérez, Mariana Eva y Yamila Grandi, '*Algún día...*' Poemas y prosas. Buenos Aires, Ediciones Paz, 1990

Rosenberg, Tina, *Astiz – La Estirpe de Caín*. Buenos Aires, Documentos *Página/12*, 1998

Verbitsky, Horacio, *El Vuelo*. Buenos Aires, Planeta, 1995

Verbitsky, Horacio, *Hacer la Corte*. Buenos Aires, Planeta, 1993